The forb

Utrecht Studies in Language and Communication

16

Series Editors

Paul van den Hoven
Wolfgang Herrlitz

The forbid/ allow asymmetry

On the cognitive mechanisms underlying wording effects in surveys

Bregje Holleman

Amsterdam - Atlanta, GA 2000

The paper on which this book is printed meets the requirements of "ISO 9706:1994, Information and documentation - Paper for documents - Requirements for permanence".

ISBN: 90-420-1341-9
©Editions Rodopi B.V., Amsterdam - Atlanta, GA 2000
Printed in The Netherlands

Elk antwoord dat je vindt is een nieuwe vraag

'Each answer you find is a new question'
Hans Riemens, from: "He ja, mmm fijn", Mike Boddé

PREFACE

This book marks the completion of a six year research project. It all started in 1993, with the analysis of a communication audit. If respondents answer a survey question by saying they are 'not satisfied' by the communication processes in their organisation, is it valid to conclude that the communication processes within that organisation should be changed? While studying and evaluating this standardized questionnaire, I became intrigued by the communication process between researcher and respondents: what do respondents do when answering survey questions? By addressing survey interaction, a direct link can be made between the field of communication studies, the quality of survey data and the conclusions based on these data.

Elaboration of this idea resulted in a research proposal that focused on question wording effects in surveys. By looking into the cognitive mechanisms underlying wording effects we can shed more light onto processes of text interpretation and question-answering as a whole. In September 1994 I started working on this project as a research trainee at the Centre for Language and Communication (later part of the UiL OTS).

In the early days of this research project, I decided to focus on the 'forbid/allow asymmetry'. The original plan was to move on to other wording effects once I had achieved a grasp of the causes of the forbid/allow asymmetry. This book shows that it took longer to unravel the mechanisms underlying the asymmetry than I originally thought. More importantly, it demonstrates that a lot can be learned and said about general question-answering processes by focusing solely on the use of 'forbid' and 'allow'.

Many people have contributed to the realization of this book. Here I like to mention some of them. I could not have written this book without Huub van den Bergh. He helped me with the statistics and the experimental designs, but more importantly, his enthusiasm inspired me during the whole project. I hope to have the privilege and joy of working together with him in future projects. Next, I would like to thank Paul van den Hoven. He was a critical reader of my work. Further, I thank Joost Schilperoord, who read this book in its pre-final stage and gave elaborate and valuable comments.

I am very much indebted to the students who took part in the research group 'Formuleringseffecten' in the course three months in 1997. I enjoyed working with them on the ten experiments that are reported in the two final chapters of this book. I also thank my former colleagues at Utrecht University and the present colleagues at the Free University Amsterdam: with many of them I had inspiring talks about forbidding or allowing, linguistics, methodology, surveys, cognitive processes and related subjects.

Finally, I would like to express my gratitude to the scholars outside of my own institute who were willing to read preliminary versions of my chapters and share their knowledge with me: Jaak Billiet, Herbert Clark, Nico Molenaar, Willem Saris, Harry Vorst and Deirdre Wilson provided me with valuable and constructive remarks. Footnotes in several chapters show that parts of this book were published elsewhere in a slightly adjusted version. Last but not least, I thank the anonymous reviewers who commented on these articles.

CONTENTS

Chapter 4

ATTITUDE RETRIEVAL VERSUS MAPPING AN ANSWER

Chapter 5

THE COMMUNICATIVE SETTING AS AN INFLUENCING FACTOR

Chapter 6

COMMUNICATIVE RESTRICTIONS AND THE ANSWERING SCALES

OVERVIEW OF TABLES (T), BOXES (B) AND FIGURES (F)

Chapter 1

A COGNITIVE PERSPECTIVE ON
THE FORBID/ALLOW ASYMMETRY

1.0 INTRODUCTION

QUESTIONNAIRE BY FRANKA, ABOUT THE WAR

1. heeft u spullen uit de oorlog?
   [have you got stuff from the war?]
2. heeft u gezien of er iemant dood is gevallen?
   [did you see anybody drop dead?]
3. zijn er ook huizen gevallen tijdens de oorlog?
   [did any houses fall over during the war as well?]
4. zijn er mensen die buiten moesten blijven omdat hun huis was omgevallen?
   [were there any people that had to stay outside because their house fell over?]
5. waar bleef u?
   [where did you stay?]
6. doet het pijn als er oorlog is?
   [does it hurt when there is a war?]
7. waneer was de oorlog s,avonds of smidag,s?
   [when was the war, during nights or afternoons?]
8. wat vorn wapens hadden ze?
   [what kinds of weapons did they have?]
9. was het op het jornaal?
   [was it on the news?]
10. op welke datum was het?
    [at what date did it take place?]

This questionnaire was written by a Dutch girl, 7 years old, as a school assignment. She probably wanted to find out about people's personal experiences during World War II, and obtain some sort of eye-witness account. Some of her questions could have been answered better outside of a questionnaire, by just looking up the information (at what date did it take place), but most of her questionnaire is about individual experiences in the past (did you see anybody drop dead) or feelings (does it hurt when there is a war). Those kinds of 'private' variables are essentially only accessible through verbal interaction with individuals (Bateson, 1984). For measuring those kinds of things, questionnaires can be used quite well: surveys are the "least cumbersome method" (Dijkstra & Van der Zouwen, 1982:2) when a researcher aims at measuring personal characteristics that are not directly observable (opinions and attitudes, for instance), or behaviour that is not otherwise visible (such as behaviour in the past).

Surveys are important and widely used methods to gather information on characteristics of large numbers of people. Information obtained from surveys is an important basis of much social science research, as well as of government planning and evaluating and commercial planning. Survey methods are also used in referendums, in order to find out whether citizens think a certain building should be taken down, or a road construction project should be allowed. At the same time, research using surveys is faced with problems that seriously threaten the validity and usability of the data obtained. This especially holds for surveys that deal with subjective phenomena, such as attitudes. It turns out that many subtle characteristics of the survey as a whole, or of specific questions in it, unintentionally influence the answers obtained.

This study revolves around one of these subtle characteristics: the use of the verbs 'forbid' or 'allow' in attitude questions. Although those verbs are considered to be each other's counterparts, the answers to questions worded with the verb 'forbid' prove not to be opposite to answers to equivalent 'allow' questions. Research has repeatedly demonstrated that respondents are more likely to answer 'no' to questions containing the verb forbid, than 'yes' to questions phrased with the verb allow. This phenomenon is known as the *forbid/allow asymmetry*. It was first discovered by Rugg in 1941 (see Table 1.1) and since this original finding the effect has been replicated in a variety of studies. Schuman & Presser (1981:296) note in reviewing this work it is the "largest wording effect we have discovered", producing differences in the answers obtained of up to 30 percentage points.

Aware of these findings, should a researcher who wants to measure respondents' attitudes towards abortion ask in her survey whether abortion should be forbidden, or whether it should be allowed?

Do you think the United States should forbid public speeches against democracy?		
yes	54%	
no	46%	
Do you think the United States should allow public speeches against democracy?		
yes	25%	
no	75%	

Table 1.1: *Forbid/allow experiment reported by Rugg (1941)*

In order to answer this question, it has to be understood why the answers to forbid/allow questions differ. Obviously, the true attitude the researcher is interested in cannot be recovered as long as it is unclear due to which circumstances the asymmetry occurs, and to what extent and into which direction the use of forbid/allow distorts respondents' answers. In order to decrease validity problems, researchers using questionnaire data need to get a grip on these and other variables unintentionally influencing responses. This book aims at obtaining that grip.

Previous forbid/allow research is not equipped to provide this understanding. The measurement procedure generally used, is an excellent method to find out whether the wording effect occurs in specific circumstances, but generalization of the results is limited. This causes difficulties in assessing, from the heterogeneous body of findings, whether the use of forbid/allow can be concluded to affect the answers in general. The explanations offered in previous research suffer from the consequences – being rather heterogeneous as well. Furthermore, the research designs used do not supply handles to detect the cognitive processes underlying the wording effect. Consequently, the explanations based on these designs are ambivalent in their cognitive status as well. The goal of this study is to unravel the cognitive mechanisms causing the forbid/allow asymmetry. Once insight is obtained into the relation between the answers respondents give and the attitudes they hold, this can serve as a basis to provide practical advice (Cicourel, 1982; Schuman, 1982). At least equally important, however, is the more fundamental goal of gaining insight into the cognitive processes underlying question-answering, as well as into the variables that affect responses in a relatively natural task (Jobe & Mingay, 1991).

As long as the mechanisms underlying the characteristics unintentionally influencing survey responses are unclear, no solid advice can be based on the research outcomes (Billiet, 1989). It merely boils down to the general recommendation to phrase survey questions carefully. Out of sheer necessity, the questionnaire designer is forced largely to ignore the body of research showing that many question characteristics unintentionally influence the answers, and to apply a naive model of survey research in designing her questionnaire and interpreting her data. This dilemma is elaborated on in Section 1.2, by describing the assumptions questionnaire designers thus implicitly hold in designing their questionnaires and interpreting the answers.

In order to conduct research on which practical advice can be based, an understanding of the mechanisms underlying the effects needs to be obtained: the relation between respondents' attitudes and their answers to survey questions should be made explicit. This can be achieved by viewing the question-answering process as a communication process between researcher and respondents, and by using a cognitive model of the question-answering process to unravel the relation between respondents' attitudes and their answers. The model to be used in order to explain the forbid/allow asymmetry will be discussed in Section 1.3.

At first sight, whether and why the use of 'forbid' or 'allow' in attitude questions affects the answers may seem of little general significance for researchers using surveys, or doing research on surveys. As will be shown in Section 1.1, however, the forbid/allow asymmetry is considered to be paradigmatic for a variety of wording effects.

1.1 OBTAINING BALANCE

Small variations in the question wording turn out to cause large differences in the answers obtained: according to a meta-analysis (Sudman & Bradburn, 1974), task variables, such as question wording, cause the largest response effects. Therefore, every survey handbook warns questionnaire designers to phrase their questions with care. A lot of wording effects research, as well as practical advice, focuses on *balance* – on trying to pose questions as objectively as possible. Practical advice about balance is concerned with the fact that within the restricted communicative setting of survey research no attitude question can be worded completely neutrally. According to survey handbooks, questions can vary in their neutrality by making the pro and anti choices more explicit, though. This means that the question "Do you think this restaurant is good, or do you think it is bad? good/bad" should be preferred to the question "Do you think this restaurant is good? yes/no" (Sudman & Bradburn, 1982; Bartelds et al., 1989).

In sets of questions about the same issue, balance can be obtained by varying positively and negatively phrased questions about the same issue. By applying this variation the researcher does not impose one perspective (only negative, or only positive) on the respondent. Furthermore, it helps the researcher to avoid answering tendencies: when responding to sets of questions about the same issue people may tend to answer 'yes' (yea-saying) or 'no' (nay-saying) to each question, independent of their attitudes. Varying the perspective on the same issue between a positive and a negative one makes this more difficult. This implies that a set of questions about the restaurant should include asking whether the food is 'good', as well as whether the service is 'bad', for example.

Such practical advice concerning balance, however, suffers from a relatively large gap between the pieces of advice and the outcomes of wording effect research. Looking at the practical advice, balance is basically obtained by varying the evaluative perspective of the question: sometimes using the perspective 'bad' when the researcher wants to know whether something is 'good'. Generally, the advice concerning balance has to do with the construction of contrastive questions. Hence, the assumption is that the use of those contrastive dimensions does not influence the answers obtained: respondents who would answer agreeingly to a question using the evaluation 'good', will answer disagreeingly when the evaluation 'bad' is used. Nevertheless, a large variety of wording effects research shows that this assumption underlying the balance advice does not hold.

1.1.1 Research concerning balance

No attitude question can be entirely neutral. Yet questions can be more or less neutral in the way they are posed by making the pro and anti choice more explicit or by additions to the negative side of an issue – this can be done, for example, by providing additional substantive alternatives or counterarguments that may have been implicit for most respondents. For the forbid/allow asymmetry, the use of contrastive questions is relevant.

In order to achieve a questionnaire that is balanced, one could alternate between positively and negatively phrased questions about the same issue, so that respondents will not be assigned high or low scores by simply saying 'yes' or 'no' to each question. This procedure is often advised in survey handbooks, and can be obtained by using *contrastive questions*. Yes/no questions are usually worded in such a way that the predicate that is written out is linguistically positive (p, 'alive', as in 'I believe Jim Morrison is alive. yes/no'), whereas the predicate that is implied by the 'no' answer is its formal negation (-p, 'not alive'). One could also phrase the question using the negation (-p, 'not alive') written out ('I believe J.M. is not alive. yes/no'), whereas the implied meaning of 'no' is the formal negation of this negative predicate (--p, 'not not alive'). These two questions are logically equivalent, and the answers to both questions should be opposite to each other. The effect of this wording variable has been investigated in connection with acquiescence (yea-saying). Falthzik & Jolson (1974) found that the linguistically positive versions yielded more affirmations than their negatively formulated counterparts in experiments on unit pricing of food products, which could indicate acquiescence tendencies. Similar results were found by Blankenship (1940) in questions about local and national politics (Molenaar, 1982).

Questions containing a linguistic negation are difficult to process, however, and the answers, especially the negative ones, are difficult to interpret. Therefore, the specified negative predicate can be replaced by a linguistically positive predicate (q, 'dead', as in 'I believe Jim Morrison is dead. yes/no') that is felt to mean the same as the original (-p, 'not alive'). So, if p and q are contradictory to each other, then the percentage of agreeing answers to question p should be equivalent to the percentage of disagreeing answers to question q. Blankenship (1940) posed a question on whether the government helps (p) business, and another one whether the government hurts (q) business, as well as two questions whether diplomatic relations with Germany should be continued (p) or broken off (q). In both cases, 'yes' to p yielded 5% more responses than 'no' to q (and q yielded 5%

more 'yes' responses than 'no' responses to p). This could be an indication of acquiescence tendencies (Molenaar, 1982).

Similar experiments using the verbs forbid/allow show effects in the opposite direction. Rugg (1941) asked whether the government should 'forbid' (p) speeches against democracy, or 'allow' these speeches (q). In this case, 'no' to forbid was answered much (21%) more often than 'yes' to allow (and 'no' to allow much more often than 'yes' to forbid, see Table 1.1). Molenaar concludes from the conflicting results concerning contrastive questions that items expressing an attitude in a favourable direction tend to yield just 'other' reactions than the contrastive counterparts expressing the same attitude in an unfavourable direction, but that no general tendencies can be found (Molenaar, 1982:62). In the next subsection, it will be argued that the forbid/allow asymmetry is a good starting point for an attempt to build a theory explaining wording effects found in contrastive questions.

1.1.2 The forbid/allow asymmetry as a paradigmatic case

Despite the relatively large number of experiments conducted on contrastive questions, no general tendencies have been found. The effect of the use of contrastives is unexpected: if the questions are opposite, one would expect the answers to those questions to be contradictory as well. Therefore, it is interesting from a theoretical point of view, as well as important for practice, to concentrate on wording effects related to balance.

The effect of the use of 'forbid' and 'allow' is specifically interesting. Respondents are generally assumed to prefer agreeing to a question (acquiescence, or yea-saying). Therefore, one would expect a higher percentage of 'yes forbid' compared to 'not allow', rather than the nay-saying tendency found by Rugg. Because of this, the forbid/allow asymmetry has been subjected to a relatively high amount of theorizing and testing. In almost every handbook the warning to phrase questions carefully is pressed home by pointing at the huge effect of the use of forbid and allow as found by Rugg, causing it to be probably the best-known wording effect in the literature. However, despite the number of forbid/allow experiments conducted, the asymmetry has not yet been explained – so no sound advice can be based on the data apart from the widespread warning in survey handbooks to be vigilant in phrasing the questions.

Schuman & Presser (1981) discuss the forbid/allow asymmetry outside the scope of balance, as part of their chapter 'Tone of wording'. According to these authors, research on choice or tone of wording is relevant when the verbal variation appears to have implications beyond the single item involved. This is especially true for key words that occur in surveys time and again. According to Schuman & Presser (1981:276), this is why the forbid/allow asymmetry is one of the most interesting examples of the apparent impact of tone of wording. Many opinion polls and surveys inquire into moral issues such as abortion, or the use of marijuana. All such issues can be phrased in terms of whether a particular phenomenon should be forbidden or allowed. If the way the question is worded influences responses about free speech, it may do so about other issues as well.

Also, insights concerning the forbid/allow asymmetry may well provide a basis to generate hypotheses on other contradictory questions, or perhaps on other wording effects in general – especially now that a cognitive framework of question answering will be applied to explain this wording effect. Shortly: the forbid/allow asymmetry is an interesting phenomenon to explore further.

1.2 THE INADEQUATENESS OF THE NAIVE SURVEY MODEL

The forbid/allow asymmetry has been investigated relatively often. Yet, it has not been explained to such a level that practical advice can be based on it. This is due to the fact that forbid/allow research originates from a research tradition which focused on testing the implicit assumptions researchers use when designing surveys and interpreting the answers.

These implicit assumptions, which could be called the *naive model of survey research,* can be outlined most effectively by discussing the *black box model* (Van der Zouwen, 1974; Dijkstra & Van der Zouwen, 1977). This model describes that a researcher who wants to measure an unobservable variable (an attitude) assumes that there is a relation between the answer the respondent gives and the attitude of the respondent towards the issue that the question refers to. The 'real' value of this attitude is within the black box, unobservably within the heads of respondents.

A researcher working with questionnaires implicitly makes two types of assumptions. First of all, she holds *type-1 hypotheses,* which address the *response function* the respondent used to arrive at his answer. The response function refers to the relation between the answer of the respondent and the 'true' value of the underlying variable: it makes explicit which element of a set of answering options is connected to which element of the set of values of the variable she intends to measure. Several assumptions are connected to this response function:

1a) the response function does not change over time,
1b) the response function is the same for each respondent, and
1c) the response function is such that a change in the value of the variable intended to be measured leads to a change in the answer obtained.

Next to these the researcher holds *type-2 hypotheses*, that model the relation between the question and the variable within the black box intended to be measured. The question has to extract relevant information about the variable, without actually changing it. Type-2 hypotheses consist of three subhypotheses:

2a) the language of the theoretical variable is translated adequately into a concept-as-measured. That is, the respondent understands the question as intended by the researcher,

2b) alternative question wording will not lead to a change in the value of the intended variable as expressed in the answer, and

2c) changes in the research context (setting, interviewer, etcetera) will not change the value of the intended variable as expressed in the answer.

The black box hypotheses prove to be reasonably correct as long as factual information is asked for, no memory search is needed, and socially desirable answers are not possible. But especially in attitude research the hypotheses cannot be maintained. A vast body of research into response effects shows that respondents' answers are distorted by all kinds of factors[1].

The forbid/allow asymmetry violates implicit assumption 2b: alternative question wording does lead to a change in the value of the intended variable expressed in the answer. A large variety of other question wording characteristics proves to affect the answers as well. This concerns, for example, characteristics related to the linguistic complexity of the question, such as question length (e.g. Laurent, 1972; Converse, 1976), the use of syntactic negations or passives (e.g. Angleitner et al., 1986); the question form, such as open versus closed questions (e.g. Schuman & Presser, 1981; Houtkoop-Steenstra, 1991 and 1993, Wijffels, Van den Bergh & Van Dillen, 1992), assertions versus interrogatives (Petty, Rennier & Cacioppo, 1987), and the number and labels of answering options offered (e.g. Schwarz & Hippler, 1987; Krosnick & Alwin, 1987; Bishop, 1987). The implicit assumption that respondents understand the question as was intended by the researcher (2a) is undermined by research such as Belson's (1981), who showed that simple phrases, such as 'watching television', can mean different things to different people. Furthermore, the way respondents interpret the ques-

---

[1] The field of response effect research consists of a vast and heterogeneous body of findings, focusing on respondent characteristics, interviewer characteristics, task characteristics, as well as question characteristics that can unintentionally influence the answers to survey questions. Various reviews have appeared integrating these findings. Readers interested in an overview of research conducted in the field are referred to Sudman & Bradburn (1974), Schuman & Presser (1981), Dijkstra & Van der Zouwen (1982), Billiet, Loosveldt & Waterplas (1984), Molenaar (1986, 1991), Van der Zouwen & Dijkstra (1989), Jobe & Mingay (1991), or Sudman, Bradburn & Schwarz (1996).

tion is influenced by the order of questions about related subjects (e.g. Sudman & Schwarz, 1992). Research showing that the implicit assumption that changes in the research context will not change the value of the intended variable as expressed in the answer (2c) does not hold, concerns experiments into the effect of the administration mode used (e.g. Kiesler & Sproull, 1986; Schwarz, Strack, Hippler & Bishop, 1991), or the effects of interviewer characteristics or interviewer behaviour on the answers obtained (e.g. Billiet, Loosveldt & Waterplas, 1984; Reese et al., 1986; Bruinsma, 1987).

Experiments explicitly focusing on the tenability of the type-1 hypotheses have been conducted relatively less often. Research showing response effects' replication failures (e.g. Schuman & Presser, 1981) could be an indication that the response function changes over time (1a). Experiments showing that some types of respondents have a greater need of social approval, causing them to give answers that are socially desirable (e.g. Silver et al., 1986), or experiments testing whether respondents holding weak attitudes are more susceptible to subtle characteristics of the survey (see also Chapter 2), may show that the response function is not the same for each respondent (1b). Experiments concerning respondents' tendencies to overreport their behaviour, or to agree or disagree with questions independent of their content (e.g. Gove, 1982) could be an indication that the response function is not such that a change in the value of the variable intended to measure leads to a change in the answer obtained (assumption 1c).

Research testing the implicit assumptions as described in the black box model, is generally set up using a *split ballot design*: a random sample of respondents is randomly split into two groups. One group gets one variant of the question, the other group the other variant. Using this procedure the assumption is that both groups' opinions are roughly the same, so differences in the answers obtained can be attributed solely to the manipulated question characteristic. If one only manipulates one wording aspect, such as the use of forbid/allow, in two questions that are equivalent with respect to all other communicative characteristics, it is possible to pinpoint exactly which characteristic is responsible for the effect. All the other relevant variables within the communicative setting are either randomised over conditions (such as respondent or interviewer characteristics), or are held constant across conditions (such as question order and administration mode). These features make the split ballot design a suitable method to find out whether a question characteristic influences the answers and to test the implicit assumptions within the naive survey model.

At the same time, the effect of the use of forbid/allow found in *one* split ballot experiment for *one* question, only says something about the effect under these specific circumstances. It cannot be generalized to other question contents, other non-manipulated wording characteristics, other moments of data collection, a different position in the questionnaire, other data collection techniques, or other interviewers (Molenaar, 1986). Hence, the use of single split ballot experiments as the predominant research design, has resulted in a collection of heterogeneous response effects of which the implications beyond the specific question under study remains uncertain. The effect of the wording variable forbid/allow has been investigated relatively often, by the use of split ballot designs. Often an asymmetry occurs, though sometimes it does not. Sometimes researchers explain why the wording effect occurs, sometimes the non-occurrence is the focus of the explanation. Generally, these explanations are rather ad-hoc, due to the fact that each new forbid/allow experiment is not a systematic replication of previous experiments: too many communicative characteristics unintentionally vary in each new forbid/allow question posed. Furthermore, the cognitive status of the explanations is ambivalent. Assuming the forbid/allow asymmetry is caused by the connotations of 'forbid' as well as 'allow', as is hypothesized in the literature, then how does this explanation relate to the response functions and the 'true attitudes' within the black box? Does it mean that the true unobservable attitude towards abortion is not measured with either (or both) the forbid/allow question; or does it mean that the true attitude towards abortion is expressed differently in the answer due to the use of (either, or both) the forbid/allow question? Because of those conceptual ambiguities, as well as the generalization problem, the questionnaire designer has no handles to decide which question wording she should prefer: she is left with the naive model of survey research and the warning to be vigilant in designing her questionnaire.

1.2.1 Survey research is data construction

The inadequateness of the implicit naive assumptions underlying questionnaire design and data interpretation shows that large problems reside in the area that Bateson (1984:5) calls *data construction*, to stress the fact that data are not gathered, or collected like flowers waiting to be picked.

Researchers construct their data at three stages of their research process: a stage of content theory development, a stage of psychometric theory, and a stage of data-analytic theory (Mellenbergh, 1980). When a researcher wants to evaluate the communication quality within an organisation, she first of all chooses a content theory by which she describes and restricts the aspects of communication she thinks are important given her research goal. Also, she has to chose definitions of these theoretical aspects in such a way as to make them operational. These choices are made at the expense of other possible definitions. Second, the researcher designs an instrument through which the content theory defined is confronted with the reality of the organisation. For each relevant aspect of communication one or more survey questions have to be developed. In a psychometric theory, which is usually left implicit, the researcher assumes that the questions measure what the content theory prescribes them to do. Once the data have been collected, the researcher's final step is to choose the data-analytic techniques that correspond to the type of information obtained from the respondents, as well as to the research questions defined. By making these choices at each stage of the research process, the researcher constructs definitions of the kind of information she is aiming at. Furthermore, these three stages are inextricably bound up with one another: a choice at one stage clashing with choices at one of the other stages, inevitably leads to uninterpretable or improper results.

This study focuses on the choices at the psychometric level that may affect the validity of the research process. Psychometric theory describes and explains the reaction of persons to stimuli, and the utility and consequences of measurement instruments in view of the research questions. So it is on the level of psychometric theory that the black box assumptions of survey research prove to fail. But the questionnaire designer has no model available to replace that naive psychometric theory – at least not a model that accounts for wording effects such as the for-bid/allow asymmetry.

It is possible, though, to design research by way of which insight into the causes of the forbid/allow asymmetry can be obtained to a level that is also relevant for practice. This can be done by relating the asymmetry to a model describing the cognitive processes respondents go through from reading the question to providing an answer. What are respondents' cognitive processes when answering survey questions? And how and when do variations in question word-ing cause differences in the answers? If it is known what is being measured by questions that are worded differently, the researcher can infer in which circum-stances she will be drawing valid conclusions based on her data. These issues will be addressed in the next section.

1.3 EXPLANATORY APPROACHES

This is the first study which tries to unravel the question-answering processes underlying the forbid/allow asymmetry through the application of a systematic cognitive approach. Of course this is not the first study that tries to explain response effects. Especially in the area of question order effects quite some headway has been made already by applying communication and cognitive theories. Departing from that research area, the cognitive approach that will be used to explain the forbid/allow asymmetry will be described.

In 1982, Howard Schuman argued that more insight into the causes of re-sponse effects was needed in order to deepen our understanding of responses and respondents. In addition, Cicourel (1982) pleaded for research aiming to gain insight into the mechanisms behind response effects. According to these authors the interpretation of question and answer frames lacked of a clear theoretical perspective: communication and cognitive theories were needed in order to understand and theoretically integrate response effects. Furthermore, researchers realised that such theories could be used not only as auxiliary sciences in survey research, but that social sciences and linguistics could also benefit from insights obtained from a survey context. Since then there has been a revival of interest in response effect research among cognitive psychologists, sociologists, and psychometricians. Thus, it is only relatively recently that the cognitive and communicative processes underlying question answering in surveys receive theoretical attention. Drawing on psychological theories of language comprehension, memory and judgement, researchers have begun to formulate explicit models of the question-answering process and have tested these models in laboratory experiments and in split ballot experiments (see edited volumes like Hippler, Schwarz & Sudman, 1987; Jobe & Loftus, 1991; Schwarz & Sudman 1992, 1995; Tanur, 1992; or Sudman, Bradburn & Schwarz, 1996).

The factors that cause response effects seem to be so diverse, that for many researchers they seem impossible to account for. From the perspective of language use, however, many of these factors are less mysterious. The survey is a social situation in which language is used, and the interactions in the survey can be described by general theories of language use. If language use is viewed as a social activity, pragmatic theories explain the ways in which language is used and how it is understood (Clark & Schober, 1992). The main pragmatic principle is the Gricean principle of speaker's meaning: speakers and their addressees assume that the addressees will recognise what the speakers mean by what they say and do (Grice, 1975). All utterances have alternative interpretations or readings. Yet, in a given language use situation, readers rarely notice the alternatives and infer the intended readings quickly, unconsciously and without apparent effort.

The Gricean framework is useful in order to account for the general occurrence of response effects. Suchman & Jordan (1990, 1992) show how question answering processes in surveys differ from questions and answers in 'normal' conversations. First of all, there is no recipient design in surveys. They are highly standardised instruments, creating the possibility to aggregate data to describe a population and compare subgroups within that population. Because of these goals of aggregation and comparison, survey questions are not tailored to each individual respondent. Second, the interpretation of the question is left to the respondent, while the researcher cannot check whether the respondent understands the question as intended. Third, in surveys the form of the answer is externally restricted, and might fail to covary with the form in which the respondent wishes to answer the question. As a last point, interactional procedures for identification and correction of problems in question interpretation or answering are excluded, and therefore the survey situation does not provide the opportunity to interactionally correct lacks in presumed background knowledge. These kinds of restrictions cause the survey instrument to be a form of communication that is 'ecologically invalid'. Ecological validity refers to the degree to which an instrument captures the daily life conditions, opinions and knowledge base of the persons that are studied as expressed in their natural habitat (Cicourel, 1982:15). The Gricean framework can account for the inferences respondents make that cause response effects to occur. It is the ecological invalidity of surveys that causes response effects to arise and to remain unrepaired.

For a variety of phenomena, the Gricean framework proves to lead to insightful and testable hypotheses. In research focusing on question order effects, for example, Grice's cooperative principle and maxims can explain why questions are interpreted differently once their order is changed. In a study by Strack, Martin & Schwarz (1988), respondents were asked how happy they were about their life in general, as well as how often they normally went on a date. If the first question was asked first, the questions were perceived to be about unrelated topics and the answers were almost uncorrelated. If the second question was asked before the first one, respondents interpreted the second question to be a summary in which the information given in answer to the question about dating had to be included: 'Considering what you just told me about dating, how happy are you with your life in general?' (Clark & Schober, 1992). Grice's framework can account for these inferences being made: due to differences in the common ground caused by differences in the question order, respondents infer other speaker's intentions based on the maxim of Relevance or the maxim of Relation – causing a difference in the answers obtained.

For a great deal of wording effect research, however, and more specifically for the forbid/allow asymmetry, the Gricean framework does not seem to provide the tools to analyse why the answers to one question differ from the other. It predicts that respondents will infer that a certain question wording was chosen by the researcher for good reasons, because respondents assume that the researcher is obeying the Gricean maxims. It does not describe, however, the specific types of inferences respondents make that explain why forbid questions are answered disagreeingly by more respondents than allow questions are answered affirmatively.

1.3.1 A cognitive model of question answering

In order to explain the forbid/allow asymmetry, the application of a more general cognitive framework seems to be more fruitful – starting from the respondents' interpretation of the question and ending with communicating an answer.

Several models of the question-answering process have been developed, some describing the question-answering process for questions on events and actions (for example Cannell, Miller & Oksenberg, 1981; Graesser & Murachver, 1985; Graesser & Franklin, 1990), others aiming more specifically at describing the answering process for attitudinal questions in a survey context (Tourangeau, 1987; Tourangeau & Rasinski, 1988). The latter models are especially relevant for the forbid/allow asymmetry, because they focus on those mechanisms within the question-answering process that are focal issues within the field of attitude surveys, for example: How and when does language influence attitude formation? How and when do existing attitudes influence text interpretation?

In the latter models, the following stages are usually distinguished in the answering process: interpreting the question and locating the relevant attitude structure (if it already exists) in long term memory; retrieving an evaluation, or constructing an attitude (if it did not exist already); rendering a judgement; and reporting the answer by mapping the judgement onto one of the precoded answering categories. Clearly, within this type of cognitive approach communication theories have to be incorporated as well, as the first and the last step obviously involve language use, causing a complex interplay of social communication and individual thought processes (Sudman, Bradburn & Schwarz, 1996)[2]. So the first step, interpreting the question, is discussed in the cognitive survey literature using the Gricean framework sketched in the previous section. This will not be discussed in great detail here. Rather, the basic question-answering process as described by Sudman et al. (1996), Tourangeau (1987) and by Tourangeau & Rasinski (1988), will be elaborated on below (and summarized in Box 1.1).

As said, the first step is that respondents have to *interpret the question*. This is done using general communication assumptions, as described in pragmatic theories[3]. Tourangeau and Rasinski theorize that locating the relevant attitude

---

[2] Sudman, Bradburn & Schwarz refer to the Gricean framework as a 'social communication theory'. Sperber & Wilson (1986) have thoroughly criticised Grice's theory – precisely because of its perspective on communication as a social act, instead of a cognitive activity. They developed 'Relevance Theory', claiming that the maxim of Relevance is the central principle governing communication processes and that it incorporates the other maxims. Furthermore, they have integrated this maxim within general cognitive theories, relating communication processes to concepts such as processing effort. Therefore, Sperber & Wilson's pragmatic theory can be integrated more easily within the cognitive models of question-answering processes than the Gricean framework. Sperber & Wilson's Relevance theory will be referred to throughout this book.

[3] In addition, Sudman et al. make a distinction between 'understanding the literal meaning' of the question (disambiguation, for example), and inferring the questioner's intention ('understanding the pragmatic meaning'). It seems plausible, however, to assume

structure is a key component of the interpretation process. In the case of well-formed, highly accessible attitudes, merely encountering the issue may be sufficient to activate the relevant structure.

---

interpreting the question: reading the question and locating the relevant attitude structure – which happens automatically when the attitude is highly accessible, and requires searching in LTM when the attitude is not.

retrieval of the attitude: what is retrieved depends on the respondent's beliefs and the demands of the question. Respondents with well-formed beliefs may retrieve an overall summary of their beliefs, whereas respondents who know or care little about the issue may construct an attitude from superficial cues in the present situation.

rendering a judgement: sometimes an answer can be retrieved directly, but most of the time a complicated process is needed to generate a judgement from a set of beliefs: scaling them, attaching weight to each one, and combining them into an overall judgement.

reporting an answer: mapping the judgement onto one of the response options offered with the questions. In addition answers may be edited for consistency with prior answers and social desirability.

Box 1.1: *The question-answering process for attitude questions*[4]

Once respondents have determined what the researcher is interested in, they need to retrieve or form a judgement. According to Sudman et al., whether respondents can recall a relevant judgement from memory depends on whether such a judgement has been formed already, and whether it is accessible at the time of the survey. An important factor determining accessibility is the degree of personal experience with the attitude object and the degree of personal importance of the issue. If respondents have been asked a related question before, the judgement formed at that time may still be accessible. Usually, however, respondents need to form a judgement, because the opinion retrieved does not entirely match the facet the question focuses on. Respondents are unlikely to retrieve all potentially relevant information. They truncate the search process as soon as enough information has come to mind to form a representation that is sufficient for the judgement that has to be made. Accordingly, respondents' judgements are usually based on the information that comes most readily to mind, while less accessible

---

that inferences of the questioner's intention are also necessary to decide how to disambiguate (see Relevance theory, Sperber & Wilson, 1986), so it is uncertain whether this distinction is necessary.

[4] For convenience' sake, this model will be referred to in this study as Tourangeau & Rasinski's (1988).

possible relevant information is less likely to be considered (compare Sperber & Wilson, 1986).

Tourangeau and Rasinski, contrary to Sudman et al., make a distinction between *retrieval of an attitude*, and *render a judgement* on the basis of the infor- mation that is retrieved. According to them, what is retrieved depends on the respondent's beliefs and on specific demands of the question. "An item on the use of abortion as a means of birth control may activate one set of beliefs; an item about abortion in the case of a threat to the mother's life may activate a different set. Respondents with well-formed attitudes may in some cases retrieve a general evaluation that serves as an overall summary of their beliefs about the issue rather than retrieve the underlying beliefs themselves [...]. At the other extreme respondents who know and care little about an issue may construct an attitude from superficial cues present in the situation, in persuasion settings, for example, such uninvolved and uninformed respondents may base their opinions on the attractiveness ôr credibility of the source of a persuasive message (Chaiken, 1980; Petty & Cacioppo, 1984)" (Tourangeau & Rasinski, 1988:300). Only in a next step the respondents use the information that is retrieved to render a judgement. If the question taps a facet of the information that is retrieved, respondents do not need to make a complex judgement in deciding to agree or disagree with the item. Usually, however, the question will not map directly onto an existing belief or a summary evaluation, and a more complicated process will be needed to generate a judgement. Tourangeau and Rasinski refer to Anderson's information integra- tion theory (1981) to describe how this process may involve weighting and scaling of beliefs and combining them to an overall judgement using an integra- tion rule.

When an attitude has been retrieved and a judgement is formed, respondents are usually not allowed to report it in their own words: they have to *format* their response in line with the answering options, they have to 'map' their judgement onto the response options offered. It is important to note, however, that the influence of the response options is not limited to the formatting stage: the response alternatives are also likely to influence the inferences on the intended meaning of the question. Finally, respondents may want to edit their responses before communicating them, due to considerations of social desirability and self- presentation (consistency, for example).

The above description of the question-answering process (summarized in Box 1.1) makes clear that a fine-grained description of the question-answering process is a description of complex intertwined processes which happen very quickly. Based on a framework like the one discussed above, hypotheses on processes or subprocesses can be generated and can sometimes be tested. Also, findings from response effects research can be integrated in those models afterwards. Tourangeau & Rasinski (1988) for example, discuss various stages at which question order effects can occur. Their theoretical analysis shows that these effects can arise because a) context may influence as to what object or issue is being judged, b) context can change the considerations and beliefs that enter into the judgement, c) context may change the standards or norms that are applied in making the judgement, and d) context may affect how the judgement is reported.

Hence, response effects can be explained afterwards by using a description of the question-answering process. It seems difficult, however, to design experiments in which these kinds of models and hypotheses can be tested within a survey context without simplifying the models of the question-answering process. The cognitive processes involved are far too complex to distinguish each of them in an experimental design that covers the question-answering process as a whole.[5]

The question is, though, whether a division of the question-answering process into tiny subprocesess is necessary in order to obtain an understanding of the communication processes within survey research. For response effects research and problems concerning the validity of the survey method, it seems sufficient to distinguish between two stages: the stage of attitude retrieval, and the stage of mapping the judgement onto one of the response options.

1.3.2 Attitude retrieval or mapping?

Taking the validity problem that is relevant to survey practice as a starting point, it does not seem necessary to distinguish between all the processes in such a fine-grained manner. The question-answering process is important insofar as it concerns the issue whether questions measure what they are intended to be measuring. This concept of validity can be refined by using the stages distinguished within the question-answering process. Measuring what one intends to measure is then determined by two basic issues: first, whether respondents can be assumed

---

[5] Also, it becomes obvious in the description of the answering process for attitude questions that the precise way in which the question-answering process is described depends to a huge extent on the precise definition of attitudes that is chosen. If attitudes are viewed as network structures in memory, there seems no reason to assume that the nodes of the attitude network are unrelated to nodes with similar labels in a semantic network, for example. Whereas the relation between language and attitudes is somewhat looser if attitudes are considered to be the resultant of some expectancy value system, with a strong emphasis on the belief structure that forms the basis for the attitudes (Fishbein & Ajzen, 1975). There is a vast amount of literature on the structure and measurement of attitudes, the difference between opinions and attitudes, and the relation between attitudes and behaviour (for reviews see for example Eagly & Chaiken, 1993; Van der Pligt & De Vries, 1995), and many researchers take different viewpoints on the relation between attitudes and language.

to have retrieved the attitude the researcher wanted to measure, reflecting the first two stages of the question-answering process; and second, whether the answers obtained from the respondents can be interpreted as an adequate 'translation' of the attitude that was retrieved, reflecting the last two stages of the question-answering process.

For forbid/allow questions this implies that it is important to find out whether the asymmetry is caused by the fact that different attitudes have been retrieved: when answering a forbid/allow question about abortion, respondents might retrieve their attitudes towards abortion, as well as towards forbidding (or allowing) in general. Alternatively, it could be the case that respondents only retrieve their attitudes towards abortion for both questions, but that they express their evaluation of abortion differently on the answering scale due to the use of 'forbid' or 'allow'. In that case the asymmetry results from the mapping stage in the question-answering process.

Theoretically this is relevant, as the latter option would imply that question answering is not necessarily a linear process starting with a full representation of the question text as a whole. Rather, it would imply that some aspects of the question text are used in order to retrieve an attitude, whereas other aspects of the text are used as a point of reference in order to express the evaluation.

The distinction between attitude retrieval and the mapping stage is important for practice as well. If forbid/allow questions measure different attitudes, they differ in validity. Either questions, or both questions, do not measure what they are intended to measure. On the other hand, if forbid/allow questions measure a similar attitude, they are equally valid, even though the answers to the questions may differ due to differences arising at the mapping stage. In that case, the questionnaire designer's problem is how to translate the yes/no answers back correctly to the true attitude. Hence, finding out whether the forbid/allow asymmetry is due to the stage of attitude retrieval or to the mapping stage, is a central issue of the current study.

A crucial theme of this study is the relationship between input variables and the cognitive representation language users have or make of a text. The two basic issues that this study addresses are: How do the answers to questions that are worded differently, differ exactly? And how can the forbid/allow asymmetry be explained in a way that allows for generalizations? So sender characteristics, the sender's intentions and her content theory (as well as the cognitive processes by which she translates these into questions) are left aside. The focus is on what is happening within the receiver due to differences in characteristics of the language use situation: the use of 'forbid' or 'allow'.

It should be noted that regular split ballot designs (see Section 1.2) cannot provide an answer to these central issues. Split ballot designs, as used by Rugg (see Table 1.1), merely show that the number of respondents answering 'yes forbid' differs from the number of respondents who answer 'yes allow' in a specific context. Furthermore, they do not provide the means to detect whether different attitudes are being measured due to the use of forbid/allow, or whether similar attitudes are mapped differently onto the answering scales. This can be found out through the use of correlational approaches. How this is done, will be elaborated on in Chapter 4.

1.4 OVERVIEW OF THIS STUDY

The remainder of this book consists of seven chapters. In Chapter 2, a detailed description of all experiments concerning the forbid/allow asymmetry will be provided, as well as a discussion of theoretical explanations formulated in previous research. These explanations focus on connotations of forbid/allow, answering behaviour of indifferent respondents, as well as facilitating factors, such as the grammatical complexity of the question text. It will become clear that problems in forbid/allow research are very similar to problems in other wording or response effects research: failures to replicate the effect cause generalization problems of the key phenomenon itself, as well as of the explanations offered. This discussion will lead to a more detailed outline of the unsolved issues concerning the forbid/allow asymmetry. The explanations offered for the forbid/allow asymmetry will be related to the cognitive framework described in the current chapter – resulting in a detailed research agenda for the current study.

Before starting to build a theory revolving around characteristics of 'forbid' and 'allow' that can explain the asymmetry, it should be established whether the use of forbid/allow has any general effect on the answers obtained. The lack of systematic replications and the number of equivocal findings in previous forbid/allow experiments, give reason first of all to find out whether the asymmetry can be generalized beyond specific questions. This will be at stake in Chapter 3. The effect of the use of forbid/allow on the answers obtained will turn out to be quite large, although it will also be shown to vary greatly over questions.

In Chapter 4, a first step towards a monocausal explanation for the asymmetry is taken: it is investigated whether the asymmetry is due to the stage of text interpretation and attitude retrieval, or to the stage of mapping an answer. A research design is proposed in which a combination of measurement approaches and the cognitive framework is achieved. This results in a cognitive description of the question-answering process underlying the forbid/allow asymmetry. It will be shown that the asymmetry arises at the mapping stage: similar attitudes are being retrieved, but due to the use of 'forbid' or 'allow' they are translated differently into the answering scales. The theoretical implications will be discussed, as well as the implications for the validity of forbid/allow questions. Furthermore, this finding is important for the way the search for explanations can be continued: once the asymmetry is shown to arise from the mapping stage, differences in percentages obtained for forbid/allow questions in split ballot experiments can be interpreted in meaningful ways.

In Chapter 5, a meta-analysis of previous forbid/allow research will be reported. A further understanding of the asymmetry's causes is obtained by analysing the factors contributing to variations in the size of the wording effect. This provides the opportunity to summarize and integrate explanatory hypotheses offered in previous forbid/allow research. It will be shown that the question-answering process for forbid/allow questions is quite complex: many input characteristics from the communicative setting interact with the key process of mapping the attitude onto the answering options to forbid/allow questions. Theoretical explanations will be developed describing why the asymmetry does not necessarily occur in each question, and why the effect of the use of forbid/ allow can vary due to the specific communicative context in which the verbs are used. Based on these analyses, two hypotheses on the cause of the asymmetry will be formulated, to be tested in ten experiments that are reported in Chapter 6 and Chapter 7.

In the sixth chapter, it is investigated whether the asymmetry is caused by the fact that respondents are restricted to answering 'yes' or 'no', and whether the wording effect disappears once less answering restrictions are imposed upon the respondents to map their attitudes. This proves not to be the case: the wording effect is due to the use of 'forbid' and 'allow' combined with any agree/disagree dimension. Following on Chapter 4, it is investigated how the scales to forbid/ allow questions differ exactly. It will be shown that forbid-questions are more reliable measurements of the underlying attitude than allow-questions: apparently, the cognitive difference between 'yes allow' and 'not allow' is smaller than the cognitive difference between 'not forbid' and 'yes forbid'.

In Chapter 7, a monocausal hypothesis for the asymmetry developed in the fifth chapter will be tested and developed further. It revolves around the connotations of 'forbid' and 'allow' as well as around the attitude strength of respondents. The difference in reliability, as well as the wording effect in general, is explained by analysing the meanings of the answers to forbid and allow questions.

The final chapter summarizes the main results within one theoretical framework explaining the forbid/allow asymmetry that can also account for variations in the wording effect obtained. Furthermore, the generalization of this explanatory theory to other wording effects will be discussed, as well as the practical implications of this study. In addition, some lines for future research will be mapped out.

Chapter 2

THE STATE OF THE ART
IN FORBID/ALLOW RESEARCH

2.0 INTRODUCTION

> "To 'tear down' a building, or 'demolish' it, according to the leading dictionary there is no real difference. Yet the socialists on Leiden City Council do not think the word 'demolish' is appropriate. It sounds so negative. It smacks of vandalism. The people in Leiden could answer 'no' to the referendum question just because of this one word. And then the demolition, or tearing down, of the dining hall and conservatory of the Royal Military Nursing home could well be abandoned."[1]

This fragment, which was taken from a small article in the Dutch national newspaper *de Volkskrant*, shows that small differences in question wording can generate a great deal of discussion. And rightfully so, since wording effect research has demonstrated time and again that seemingly equivalent question wordings can lead to substantial differences in the answers. According to the leading Dutch dictionary *Van Dale*, the words *slopen* ('demolish') and *afbreken* ('tear down') mean the same, but some people's linguistic intuition tells them that the connotations differ and this may cause the people of Leiden to respond differently to the question, depending on which word is used. How can the city council decide which of these words should be included in its referendum question to objectively measure public opinion on the demolition of parts of the Royal Military Nursing Home? There is no ready-made advice available to tell them what to do.

The city council could check to see whether these words make a difference. They could draw a representative sample of Leiden's inhabitants and ask half of the group a question using the verb *slopen* and the other half a question using the verb *afbreken*, within a split ballot design. If the versions are divided over the two halves of the sample, and the verbs *slopen* or *afbreken* are indeed equivalent, then the answers to these two questions should not differ significantly. But suppose the answers to both questions do turn out differently. What if 60% of the respondents

---

[1] From *de Volkskrant*, 14 January 1995. The original text was: "Een pand slopen of afbreken, het maakt volgens de Dikke Van Dale geen verschil: in beide gevallen gaat het gebouw tegen de vlakte. Toch valt de PvdA-fractie in de Leidse gemeenteraad over het woord slopen. Het klink zo negatief. Zo vandalistisch. De Leidse bevolking zou alleen al vanwege dat ene woord 'nee' kunnen zeggen op de vraag die ze moeten beantwoorden bij het komende referendum. En dan zou de sloop, of het afbreken, van de eetzaal en de serre van het Koninklijk militair Invalidenhuis wel eens niet door kunnen gaan. [...]".

say 'no' to the *slopen* question whereas 45% answer negatively to the *afbreken* question? Which of these percentages best reflects the true opinions of Leiden's inhabitants? An account of the deviations from the true values caused by each of these question wordings is necessary in order to decide this: we need a theory that describes the relation between the percentages obtained and the true value within the black box (the respondents' attitudes). As was outlined in the previous chapter, such a theory would help solve the practical problem faced by Leiden City Council. Furthermore, it would increase an understanding of the effects of language variation, the interaction between reader characteristics and seemingly superficial text characteristics, and the differences in meaning of words like *slopen* and *afbreken* within a fairly natural language use environment. A theory of this kind does not exist, however, and hardly any work has been carried out on developing such a theory – especially not for wording effect research.

In the previous chapter it was argued that a general cognitive framework describing the question-answering process for attitude questions would make a particularly good starting point for such a theory, because it is directly related to the validity issues relevant to survey practice. The previous chapter also outlined the body of heterogeneous findings produced by previous response effect research in general, and wording effect research in particular. A great number of experiments have been conducted focusing on many different wording effects. Most of these experiments consist of single questions only, making it difficult to generalize beyond specific communication contexts such as question characteristics, respondent characteristics and characteristics of the administration mode. Furthermore, theories that explain specific wording effects have usually been formulated in a reasonably ad-hoc manner, and have not been tested systematically in further research. In this respect, research into the forbid/allow asymmetry does not differ from research focusing on other wording effects, although the forbid/allow asymmetry has been investigated relatively often compared to other wording effects, and many explanations for this wording effect have been formulated. This chapter provides an overview of all forbid/allow experiments and the explanations formulated for this wording effect.

In Section 2.1, research concerning the effects of the use of 'forbid' and 'allow' in attitude questions will be described in detail, and various explanations for these effects will be presented. Despite the fact that the forbid/allow asymmetry has been studied quite often, it has yet to be explained satisfactorily. Section 2.2 argues that this is mainly due to a problem which dogs a great deal of wording effect research: the gap between theoretical explanations and ways of testing them on the one hand, and extrapolating from individual effects and integrating individual findings on the other. So many issues surrounding the explanation and generalization of this wording effect remain unsolved. By relating these issues to the general cognitive framework described in the previous chapter, the discussion of previous research will lead to an outline of the research questions to be answered in the present study.

2.1 PREVIOUS RESEARCH INTO THE FORBID/ALLOW ASYMMETRY

In 1941 Rugg reported the first forbid/allow experiment, carried out by Elmo Roper (in 1940). Support for free speech in the United States proved to be 21% higher when respondents were asked a question with the verb 'forbid' than when they were asked the same question phrased using the word 'allow' (see Table 1.1). As 'forbid' and 'allow' are considered to be opposites, one would expect the answers to forbid/allow questions to be opposite to each other: the number answering 'no' to the forbid question should be equal to the number answering 'yes' to the allow question. This is not the case: the term 'forbid/allow asymmetry' refers to the fact that the answer 'no' to one question is obtained more often than the equivalent affirmative answer to the other question.

Since Rugg's findings, many researchers have studied the forbid/allow asymmetry. This overview will begin with a chronological discussion of three studies which build on each other (Schuman & Presser, 1981; Hippler & Schwarz, 1986; Waterplas, Billiet & Loosveldt, 1988). This will be followed by a description of two studies of other response effects, which also discuss findings relating to the forbid/allow asymmetry (Bishop, Hippler, Schwarz & Strack, 1988; Krosnick & Schuman, 1988). This will complete the review of the forbid/allow research found in the literature (Table 2.1 provides an overview of the experiments in figures[2]). While much work has been done in this area, this survey will show that many questions remain concerning the generalization and explanation of this wording effect.

2.1.1 Schuman & Presser (1981)

Schuman & Presser (1981) started off replicating Rugg's experiment, once in 1974 and twice in 1976, using exactly the same question. They found a similar effect: respondents were much more willing to not allow speeches against democracy than to forbid them ($p<.001$).

Schuman and Presser first of all assumed that less educated respondents would be more easily misled by superficial variations in wording, such as the use of forbid or allow. They did indeed find an interaction between years of schooling

---

[2] In Chapter 3 (Table 3.2) an overview is given of the same experiments, providing statistical tests of the differences between the percentages 'not allow' and 'yes forbid' answers obtained.

and the tendency to answer 'no' to allow rather than 'yes' to forbid on two occasions. The interaction was not linear: the asymmetry was largest for persons with 0-12 years of schooling, but decreased for people with some college education. Schuman & Presser (1981:281) concluded from this that "it is verbal confusion rather than verbal precision that leads to a difference in response. At the same time, even college graduates show a significant form difference [...], so the effect must be considered both powerful and widespread."

no.	author cntry	year	question wording	percentage forbid	allow
a	Rugg VS	40	Do you think the United States should forbid/allow public speeches against democracy?	N 46.0 Y 54.0	Y 25.0 N 75.0
b	S&P VS	74	ditto	N 71.9 Y 28.1	Y 56.1 N 43.9
c	ditto	76	ditto	N 79.9 Y 20.1	Y 54.8 N 45.1
d	ditto	76	ditto	N 78.6 Y 21.4	Y 52.2 N 47.8
e	ditto	76	Do you think the United States should forbid/allow public speeches in favor of communism?	N 60.1 Y 39.3	Y 43.8 N 56.3
f	ditto	77	Do you think the government should for- bi-d/allow the showing of X-rated movies?	N 59.0 Y 41.0	Y 53.6 N 46.4
g	ditto	79	Do you think the government should forbid/allow cigarette advertisements on television?	N 49.4 Y 50.6	Y 45.1 N 54.9
h	H&S BRD	82	Meinen Sie, der Gesetzgeber sollte die sogenannten Peep-Shows, also das bezahlte Sichzurschaustellen nackter Frauen in aufreizenden Posen, generell verbieten/ erlauben?	N 72.3 Y 27.7	Y 50.3 N 50.0
i	ditto	83	Meinen Sie, der Gesetzgeber sollte die Vorführung von pornographischen Filmen in öffentlichen Kinos generell verbieten/ erlauben?	N 74.0 Y 26.0	Y 60.0 N 40.0
j	ditto	86	Durch das Streuen von Salz im Winter sind Pflanzen und Bäume in Strassenähe gefährdet. Sollte man das Salzstreuen generell verbieten/erlauben?	N 37.7 Y 62.3	Y 21.2 N 78.8

no.	author cntry	year	question wording	percentage forbid	allow
k	B. et al. VS	86	Do you think that smoking in public places, such as restaurants, should be forbidden/ allowed?	N 47.6 Y 52.4	Y 51.1 N 48.9
l	ditto	86	ditto	N 38.7 Y 61.3	Y 53.0 N 57.0
m	B. et al. BRD	86	Meinen Sie, dass das Rauchen in öffentlich-en Gebäuden, so wie in Restaurants, verbo-ten/erlaubt werden/sein sollte?[3]	N 72.4 Y 27.6	Y 66.7 N 33.3
n	ditto	86	ditto	N 67.4 Y 32.6	Y 47.1 N 52.9
o	W. etal. Belg	87	Do you think the government should for-bid/allow the screening of pornographic films in public cinemas?[4]	N 36.3 Y 63.7	Y 23.6 N 76.4
P	ditto	87	Do you think the government should for-bid/allow racist speeches in public?	N 22.1 Y 77.9	Y 14.7 N 85.3
q	ditto	87	In some schools there are many children from ethnic minority families. Do you think the government should forbid/allow sepa-rate classes for Belgian and ethnic minority pupils in those schools?	N 62.4 Y 37.6	Y 35.4 N 64.6
r	K&S VS	83	Do you think the United States should for-bid/allow public speeches against democ-racy?	N 80.1 Y 19.4	Y 62.8 N 37.2
s	K&S VS	84	Do you think the United States should for-bid/allow public speeches against democ-racy?	? ?	? ?

<u>Note:</u> no: numbers a-s identify the questions as referred to in Appendix II, author: (S&P) Schuman & Presser (1981), (H&S) Hippler & Schwarz (1986), (Bish.) Bishop et al., (W.et

---

[3] The literal question wording of the German questions in the experiments by Bishop et al. was not reported. These are German translation of the English question texts.

[4] The original Dutch question wording of the three Belgian forbid/allow questions shown here, is: "Vindt u dat de overheid het draaien van pornofilms in openbare filmzalen moet verbieden/toelaten?", "Vindt u dat de overheid racistische toespraken in het publiek moet verbieden/toelaten?", and "In sommige scholen zitten veel kinderen van vreemde-lingen. Vindt u dat de overheid afzonderlijke klassen voor Belgische en vreemde kinderen in die scholen moet verbieden/toelaten?".

al.) Waterplas et al. (1988), (K&S) Krosnick & Schuman (1988), B. et al. (Bishop et al., 1988); *country* = country of data collection; *year* = year of data collection.
From: Schuman & Presser (1981, pp. 277, 281-283), Hippler & Schwarz (1986, pp. 90, 93), Bishop, Hippler, Schwarz & Strack (1988, pp. 335), Waterplas, Billiet & Loosveldt (1988, pp. 402/403, 408); Krosnick & Schuman (1988, p. 944), Bishop et al. (1988, pp. 335). With thanks to Waterplas et al. (1988) for their overview of forbid/allow experiments (pp. 402/403).

Table 2.1: *Overview of forbid/allow research reported in the literature*

Schuman and Presser distinguish three possible causes for the asymmetry, which form the foundation for further research into this subject. The first possible cause focuses on the connotations of both verbs. "The verb 'forbid' sounds harsher and may therefore be more difficult to endorse, whereas 'allow' in some contexts might seem to encourage deviant behaviour and therefore may invite opposition. Thus what we have called tone of wording could be the sole source of the effect" (1981:280). Schuman and Presser did not test this hypothesis. It was tested in a small experiment by Hippler & Schwarz (1986, see below) and will play an important role throughout this book. In the rest of the book, this hypothesis will be referred to as the *connotations hypothesis*.

The second possible cause of the asymmetry Schuman and Presser distinguish, is that the two terms create different grammatical structures. To forbid speeches against democracy may be confused with forbidding democracy itself, according to Schuman and Presser. They tested this hypothesis by posing a question in which the words 'against democracy' were replaced with 'in favour of Communism'. Although this led to a decreased asymmetry, a wording effect of 16% more 'no, not allow' answers than 'yes, forbid' answers was still obtained: the grammatical hypothesis was not supported. At the same time, the interaction with education disappeared entirely, showing that a lower level of education is not a prerequisite for the occurrence of the forbid/allow asymmetry.

The third possible cause of the asymmetry, according to Schuman and Presser, may be the abstractness of the issue. They hypothesized that the meanings of the verbs may be the main determinants of the asymmetry, but that there is an additional effect caused by the abstractness of the issue the question is about. It could be the case that the asymmetry occurs in the Rugg item only because 'speeches against democracy' is an abstract phrase that is not salient or clear to respondents, whereas the effect would disappear with a more concrete issue, or one with more salience. This third hypothesis was tested by designing two experiments about more concrete issues: one on X-rated movies, which Schuman and Presser believed to be of fairly high salience to the respondents, and one about cigarette advertisements on television, thought to be of lesser salience. If a forbid/allow asymmetry was found with these two questions as well, the effect could be generalized to a wider range of issues. This was also meant as a test of the first hypothesis, on the connotations of forbid and allow: Schuman and Presser decided to reject the hypothesis that the connotations of forbid and allow in and of themselves are sufficient to produce a response effect regardless of issue, if no asymmetry was found in either or both these concrete questions.

It turned out that neither of their concrete forbid/allow questions revealed a clear wording effect. Differences were in the expected direction, but too small to reach significance (p<.1 and p>.1 respectively). Schuman and Presser conclude by asserting that the forbid/allow asymmetry can best be attributed to a subtle interaction between the verbs and the subject matter, with grammatical structure perhaps playing an additional role in creating an effect of educational level in some instances. "But these interpretations are too much after the fact to be offered with great confidence, and given the large size and uncertain scope of the effect, further work on it would be desirable. Indeed, its nonobvious nature offers a challenge to students of survey research" (1981:283).

2.1.2 Hippler & Schwarz (1986)

The challenge was taken up by Hippler and Schwarz (1986). Hippler and Schwarz started working from the explanations offered by Schuman and Presser. Reasoning from the connotations hypothesis, they theorized that the asymmetry is primarily caused by the response behaviour of indifferent or ambivalent respondents, due to the extreme connotations of forbid and allow. They also hypothesized that the wording effect was caused by respondents' cognitive bias towards focusing on positive instances of a behaviour rather than considering the implications of its absence.

Throughout the current study, their hypothesis will be called the *indifferent respondents hypothesis,* or the attitude strength hypothesis. The nature of this hypothesis and how it was tested by Hippler and Schwarz will be explained below.

Working from the connotations hypothesis, Hippler and Schwarz reasoned that if forbidding has a harsh connotation and allowing has an inviting one, this will mean that 'to forbid' something may imply stronger opposition than 'not to allow' something. Forbidding entails an active act of opposition against an issue, while not allowing something only entails abstaining from active support. Similarly, 'allowing' something entails active support, while 'not forbidding' something entails abstaining from active opposition. They therefore reasoned that respondents who do not hold strong attitudes may be especially unlikely to endorse either the forbid or the allow question, responding 'no' to both questions, endorsing opposing positions by doing so. They may respond differently in an interview situation, however, because they would be more likely to focus on the behaviour they are being asked about.

Hippler and Schwarz supported this hypothesis with results from the area of social cognition research, which demonstrated that individuals pay more attention to positive instances of a behaviour than to the absence of a behaviour (cf. Nisbett & Ross, 1980). For example, they felt that what a person actually does provides more information about the person than what the person does not do (e.g. Fazio et al., 1982). This "tendency of both animals and humans to exhibit greater difficulty in the processing of nonoccurrences than occurrences" (Fazio et al., 1982:404) is usually referred to as the 'feature-positive effect'. Based on this effect, Hippler and Schwarz reasoned that a similar process could be at work when respondents are answering forbid/allow questions. "Similarly, when asked if something should be done (allowed or forbidden), individuals may focus on the implications of the behaviour under consideration, and they may not consider the implications of the absence of this behaviour. Such a bias could contribute to the forbid/allow asymmetries by clouding the idea that not allowing or not forbidding something indeed amounts to forbidding or allowing it respectively, thus resulting in the feeling that one has only said it shouldn't be allowed without ever commenting on whether it should be forbidden" (Hippler & Schwarz, 1986:89-90). Hence, this explanation predicts that the asymmetry is primarily due to the behaviour of indifferent or ambivalent respondents and should not be obtained for respondents holding a clear pro or anti attitude. This hypothesis is in line with Schuman & Presser's (1981) results, who found the effect to be more pronounced for abstract issues and for respondents who were less educated – as both factors may affect the number of indifferent respondents.

Hippler and Schwarz proceeded by testing their indifferent respondents hypothesis. However they first investigated whether the forbid/allow asymmetry is cross-culturally stable, and occurs in German too ('verbieten' versus 'erlauben'). In a small scale face-to-face survey they asked whether peep shows should be forbidden or allowed, and in a second larger face-to-face survey they posed a question on X-rated movies. No wording effect was found for each single question, but a combined analysis of both questions indicated a significant forbid/allow asymmetry ($p < .01$).

They then went on to test the connotations hypothesis, the hypothesis that allowing or forbidding are stronger statements than not forbidding or not allowing, respectively. They asked 54 respondents in a self-administered questionnaire to rate the extremity of a fictitious person's opinion: they read a sentence stating that 'Mr Mueller feels the legislator should forbid (not allow/ allow/not forbid) peep shows' and were asked to rate this opinion on an 11-points scale labelled 'extremely in favour of peep shows' versus 'extremely opposed to peep shows'.

Each respondent read and rated only one statement. The results indicated that allowing peep shows was rated as representing a more favourable attitude (a mean score of 2.1) than not forbidding peep shows (mean of 3.1, p<.04). Similarly, forbidding peep shows indicated stronger opposition according to the respondents (mean of 10.5) than not allowing them (mean of 9.2, p<.01). Hippler and Schwarz concluded from these data that forbidding and allowing are indeed perceived as differing in their extremity, but at the same time there is no doubt that 'not forbidding' is seen as a statement in favour of the issue while 'not allowing' is seen as a statement opposing the issue.

Hippler and Schwarz's central hypothesis was that *indifferent respondents* are responsible for the forbid/allow asymmetry, due to the extremity of forbidding and allowing compared to not forbidding and not allowing, as well as to the feature-positive effect. They expected that more respondents overall would endorse 'not allow' than 'forbid' (and 'not forbid' than 'allow'), and that this would be primarily due to the responses of indifferent subjects. In other words, the asymmetry would not be obtained in the responses of subjects holding strong attitudes. This hypothesis was tested in a mail survey on environmental issues. Indifference was measured with a question early in the questionnaire, reading 'Salt should no longer be used to melt ice and snow on the roads' ('agree'/'don't agree'/'indifferent'/'don't care'). Later in the questionnaire, half of the respondents were asked whether the use of salt to melt ice should be allowed (yes/no) or forbidden ('The use of salt during winter is dangerous to plants and trees near the road. Do you think that one should generally allow/forbid the use of salt?'). The results showed that the forbid/allow asymmetry applied to the whole sample of respondents (16.5% more 'not allow' than 'yes forbid', p<.001). When the scores obtained were split into three groups, no asymmetry was found for respondents holding a pro or anti attitude, and a strong wording effect of 54.5% was found for the respondents who had reported an indifferent attitude (see Table 2.2). This finding supports the hypothesis that the asymmetry is primarily due to the response behaviour of indifferent respondents.

Hippler and Schwarz wondered whether these findings might have been distorted by consistency effects: respondents who reported that they were indifferent towards the use of salt, may have been unlikely to endorse a 'strong' affirmative option later on. This consistency effect might increase the size of the forbid/allow asymmetry for indifferents. Hippler and Schwarz conclude that the presence of consistency effects seems unlikely, however, since 32% of the respondents who initially reported a favourable attitude towards the use of salt, answered 'forbid' or 'not allow' to the second question. Similarly, 11.3% of respondents reporting an anti attitude, gave an opposite response later – suggesting that consistency pressures cannot have been very strong.

all respondents

Do you think that one should generally forbid the use of salt?
  yes   62.3%
  no   37.7%
Do you think that one should generally allow the use of salt?
  yes   21.2%
  no   78.8%

$\chi^2 = 23.2$, df=1, p<.001, N=694

----

attitude opposed to the use of salt

yes (forbid)   86.4%   yes (allow)   9.3%
no (not forbid)   13.6%   no (not allow)   90.7%

$\chi^2 = 2.0$, df=1, n.s., N=422

----

attitude in favour of the use of salt

yes (forbid)   25.8%   yes (allow)   61.3%
no (not forbid)   74.2%   no (not allow)   38.7%

$\chi^2 = 2.5$, df=1, n.s., N=128

----

attitude indifferent towards the use of salt

yes (forbid)   18.8%   yes (allow)   26.7%
no (not forbid)   81.2%   no (not allow)   73.3%

$\chi^2 = 37.3$, df=1, p<.001, N=124

Table 2.2: *The forbid/allow asymmetry as a function of people's attitudes (Hippler & Schwarz, 1986)*

Based on these data, Hippler and Schwarz concluded that a more pronounced wording effect can be predicted if the number of indifferent respondents in the sample is larger. The effect should therefore be larger when the issue is more abstract, less salient, and the number of respondents who are less educated increases, as these characteristics are related to the number of indifferent respondents likely to be in the sample. In addition, they suggested the asymmetry may vanish if indifferent respondents are provided with the possibility of expressing their indifference. This should not be a 'don't know' option, as respondents do know that they do not want to forbid or allow something. Instead an option such as 'don't care' or 'leave things as they are' should be included.

2.1.3 Waterplas, Billiet & Loosveldt (1988)

Research by Waterplas, Billiet & Loosveldt (1988) was conducted along very similar lines to the experiments of Hippler & Schwarz (1986). First of all, they wanted to find out whether the forbid/allow asymmetry would also occur in Dutch (*verbieden* versus *toelaten*), to a similar extent as in German and English. They also tested whether the asymmetry occurred solely with questions on an abstract issue (as found by Schuman & Presser, 1981). Lastly, they tested the indifferent respondent hypothesis. They conducted their research in face-to-face interviews about ethnic policies with 400 married women in and around the city of Ghent – a homogenous sample, instead of a heterogeneous one. They posed one question about an abstract issue (on racist speeches, comparable to Rugg's original question), and two on concrete issues (a replication of the X-rated movies question and a question on separate classes for Belgian children and children from ethnic minority families).

Their results revealed a forbid/allow asymmetry for the abstract item and for two of the concrete items (effect sizes varying from 7.4% to 27%, significance levels varying from <.001 to .07). The weakest effect was found for the abstract item. This led to two conclusions: first of all, the forbid/allow asymmetry was replicated in Dutch. Secondly, Schuman and Presser's hypothesis about item abstractness was not supported.

Waterplas et al. continued by testing the indifferent respondents hypothesis with four subsequent analyses. First of all, they posed one forbid/allow question on a concrete issue (admission of foreigners to discotheques), using an explicit 'no opinion' answering option in addition to the options yes and no. This also resulted in a slight tendency towards negative answers, but the difference between the percentages 'no' to forbid and 'yes' to allow was not significant.

Secondly, they analysed the extent of the asymmetry for the other three forbid/allow questions, splitting the respondents into two groups: one consisting of those who had answered 'no opinion' on the discotheque questions (n=114) and the other of those who had expressed an opinion on discotheques. For the racist speeches question and the X-rated movies question the asymmetry disappeared for respondents who had expressed an opinion on discotheques, and remained for the respondents who answered 'no opinion'. The question on separate classes showed an asymmetry for both groups of respondents, but it was larger for the 'no opinion' group.

Thirdly, they conducted a similar analysis, this time using three other items on ethnic groups that contained a 'no opinion' filter. Respondents who used this option at least once, were defined as 'indifferent'. This analysis produced similar results to the previous one.

Lastly, Waterplas et al. made a distinction between specific and general attitude strength: in the previous analyses, attitude strength was measured by isolating respondents answering 'no opinion' to a question on ethnic groups and discotheques, a specific measurement of attitude strength towards 'ethnic policies'. In contrast, general attitude strength was defined as general knowledge about current public issues (the number of unemployed, the name of the prime minister and so forth). Based on the answers to these general knowledge questions, respondents were labelled 'badly informed', 'moderately informed', and 'well informed'. For the three forbid/allow questions, the asymmetry remained for the badly informed respondents (effect sizes of 12% to 27%, p<.06), but disappeared for the well-informed respondents (effect sizes of 2% to 8%, p>.3). A large asymmetry only applied to the moderately informed group for the item on separate classes (effect size of 40%). The indifferent respondents hypothesis formulated by Hippler and Schwarz (1986) was therefore generally supported by these results.

2.1.4 Krosnick & Schuman (1988) and Bishop et al. (1988)

Two additional experiments with the verbs 'forbid' and 'allow' are reported in the literature: one by Bishop, Hippler, Schwarz and Strack (1988), who compared the size of several response effects in self-administered and telephone surveys, and one by Krosnick & Schuman (1988), who tested the effect of attitude crystallization on the size of various response effects. As the forbid/allow asymmetry was not the primary focus of these studies, their experiments will be discussed jointly in this section.

Krosnick & Schuman (1988) embarked upon their research with the widely held assumption that response effects are largest when attitudes are uncrystallized, weakly held or not central to a respondent. They tested this hypothesis for various response effects, including the forbid/allow asymmetry. They posed the same forbid/allow question on public speeches against democracy twice, in 1983 (503 respondents) and in 1984 (435 respondents).

Krosnick and Schuman used a different cognitive theory to the one adopted by Hippler and Schwarz. Krosnick and Schuman defined attitude crystallization as certainty and intensity, whereas Hippler and Schwarz focused on indifference and Waterplas et al. also measured the general informedness of respondents.

In the first experiment, Krosnick and Schuman found a large overall wording effect (p<.01): fewer people were willing to forbid public speeches against democracy than not to allow them. Contrary to their hypothesis, however, atti-tude certainty (measured by the question: 'Some people are very certain about their feelings on this question of allowing/forbidding public speeches against democracy. Other people see this issue as a difficult one to reach a decision on. Would you say that you are more like those who are very certain, or that you are more like those who see this issue as a difficult one to reach a decision on?') did not influence the size of the asymmetry: respondents who said they were very certain of their attitudes on this issue were influenced just as much by the use of forbid/allow as those who stated they were relatively uncertain of their opinions.

In their replication they found a large overall response effect, although some-what smaller than in the first study (p<.03). This time, they defined attitude strength in terms of intensity (asking respondents how strong their feelings about the issue were). Contrary to their expectations, they found the asymmetry to be very large for respondents with more intense attitudes (21.7%) and small for those with less intense attitudes (-.1%) (p<.02). The effect of attitude strength as found by Hippler & Schwarz (1986) and Waterplas et al. (1988) for indifferent respondents, was not replicated in Krosnick and Schuman's research for certainty and intensity.

The expected relation between attitude strength and susceptibility to response effects was only found for the offering versus the omission of a middle alternative. For the other response effects investigated by Krosnick and Schuman (one form effect, two types of wording effects and two types of order effects), they did not find the expected relation. Krosnick and Schuman devoted an elaborate discussion to the absence of the expected effects of certainty, intensity and importance. More specifically for the forbid/allow experiments, they assumed the absence of the relation between attitude strength and the wording effect to be due to the fact that the operationalization of attitude strength as 'indifference' (as done by Hippler and Schwarz, Waterplas et al.) differs from 'intensity' and 'certainty'. Theoretically, various measures of attitude crystallization can be distinguished that are only weakly correlated with each other. Hence, Krosnick and Schuman concluded that both the evidence of Hippler and Schwarz and Waterplas et al., as well as their own findings, could be valid.

All forbid/allow data so far discussed were gathered in face-to-face or telephone interviews, except for the experiment on the effect of indifferent respondents by Hippler & Schwarz (1986). Bishop et al. (1988) replicated the forbid/allow asymmetry in a self-administered questionnaire. They reasoned that wording effects should be just as likely to occur in a self-administered survey as in a telephone or face-to-face interview, because the information presented to respon-dents in all of these modes of data collection is essentially equivalent. However, because respondents have more time to think about the meaning of the questions, subtle variations in how they interpret the question text may occur, resulting in significant differences between this and other modes of data collection (1988:322).

To test this hypothesis, and to test the cross-cultural stability of their findings, Bishop et al. designed an experiment using two modes of data collection that are most different from one another: telephone interviews (with more time pressure, probably, than face-to-face interviews), and self-administered questionnaires (where respondents can look over all the questions and responses before answering). The same questions were administered to 722 college students in the United States and to 331 students in West Germany. Their forbid/allow question was on 'smoking in public spaces, such as restaurants', because this issue was assumed to be more salient and comparable in meaning across the two societies than the ones used in previous investigations of the asymmetry. According to Schuman and Presser's (1981) hypothesis, the asymmetry should be small for a concrete issue like this.

The results obtained by Bishop et al. were rather difficult to interpret. Contrary to their expectations, no asymmetry was found in the telephone condition in the US or in Germany. They did find an asymmetry in the self-administered condition for both the US (p<.02) and Germany (p<.01), but in the US it was not in the expected direction (more affirmative answers in one condition than negative in the other). The authors made no attempt to explain these findings and recommended further replications. For other response effects their findings suggest that effects relating to question order and response order are less likely to occur in self-administered surveys than in a telephone survey, whereas question form and wording effects are probably equally likely to occur in either data collection method.

2.1.5 The state of affairs

The previous sections cover all forbid/allow research found in the literature. Despite the fact that 'forbid' and 'allow', as well as 'yes' and 'no', are considered to be opposites, respondents generally seem to prefer to answer 'no' to a question with the verb 'allow' rather than 'yes' to a question with the verb 'forbid'.

The results are not unequivocal, however. Like Rugg, Schuman and Presser found large asymmetries for abstract issues (speeches against democracy/in favour of communism), but they did not find an asymmetry for two concrete issues (X-rated movies, cigarette ads). On the other hand, Hippler and Schwarz did find asymmetries for three concrete issues (X-rated movies, peep shows, use of salt), although for two concrete issues the effect was only significant in a combined analysis. Waterplas et al. found asymmetries for two concrete issues (X-rated movies, separate classes) but, surprisingly, not for an abstract item (racist speeches). Krosnick and Schuman found an asymmetry twice using the same question Rugg and Schuman and Presser had already found an asymmetry for (the abstract issue 'speeches against democracy'), whereas Bishop et al. only found an asymmetry on a concrete issue (smoking in public buildings) in one self-administered questionnaire and not in a telephone survey. In another self-administered questionnaire they found an opposite asymmetry to the one they expected.

As to the explanations for the asymmetry, two would appear to be of particular importance: the connotations hypothesis and the indifferent respondents hypothesis. As will be argued in the next section, the connotations hypothesis is rather vague as to its cognitive status and is therefore vague with respect to its practical implications as well. One of the problems with the indifferent respondents hypothesis is the wide range of definitions of indifference, attitude strength or attitude crystallization from which to choose.

The connotations hypothesis states that 'forbid' and 'allow' both have extreme connotations, influencing respondents to say no to both questions. A small scale test of this hypothesis confirmed that people judge someone who wants to forbid something to be more extreme than someone who allows something and vice versa. In addition to the connotations hypothesis the grammatical explanation has been put forward: the verb 'forbid' would create an underlying negative structure, which yields a double negative if other negations are included ('speeches against democracy'). This could cause processing difficulties, especially for those respondents who are not highly educated. This specification of the connotations hypothesis implies that the problem lies in the verb forbid, instead of in the extremity of both verbs. However as a positively worded forbid/allow question also led to an asymmetry (Schuman & Presser, 1981), this hypothesis was not confirmed.

The explanation focusing on the answering behaviour of indifferent respondents is another specification of the connotations hypothesis. It predicts that respondents who are indifferent towards the issue (that is, people who have no specific attitude towards forbidding/allowing the issue at hand) only think about the consequences of answering affirmatively. Due to the extreme connotations of 'forbid' as well as 'allow', they feel that an affirmative answer is too extreme and do not realize the implications of a negative answer. Results generally seem to confirm this hypothesis: the asymmetry disappears once the 'indifferents' (or the 'uninformed') are excluded from the sample of respondents. However, if attitude strength is measured differently, the relation between attitude strength and the wording effect obtained vanishes. This casts doubt on the tenability of both the indifferent respondents hypothesis and the connotations hypothesis. Furthermore, the effect of issue abstractness is puzzling: the number of indifferent or ambivalent respondents is hypothesized to be larger for questions about abstract issues.

Yet the findings for questions about abstract versus concrete issues are far from unequivocal.

In conclusion, the discussion of forbid/allow experiments shows that research faces two main problems. These concern the generalizability of the wording effect, and the explanation of the asymmetry. In the next section, it will be argued that both of these difficulties in interpreting and generalizing the findings can be solved to a considerable extent by using designs and statistical techniques that permit generalizations above the level of specific questions. Furthermore, it will be argued that the explanations for the forbid/allow asymmetry can be integrated and made testable by relating them to the general cognitive framework outlined in the previous chapter.

2.2 UNSOLVED ISSUES AND PRECISION OF THE RESEARCH QUESTIONS

At first sight, the forbid/allow experiments may seem systematic replications contributing to an explanatory theory of asymmetry. Looking more closely, however, many questions remain unanswered. As Waterplas et al. note (1988: 405), "the circumstances under which the asymmetry may be expected to occur are not all too clear. Considering the contradictory findings discussed above, it is not surprising that each article ends with a plea for replications. These replications however are less systematic than they may seem, as all too often several variables are varied at the same time: the content of the question, the place and time of data collection, the mode of data collection, and other questions surrounding the manipulated question, which causes difficulties in interpreting the differences in findings". Furthermore, comparison of the answers to forbid/allow questions does not provide counsel as to which question wording is preferable. At best, this type of research increases knowledge of the way in which respondents react to aspects of question wording and warns questionnaire designers of the possible effects of subtle differences in question wording (Waterplas et al., 1988: 413).

Practical advice can only be given if it is known exactly how and why the answers differ. In order to achieve this understanding, forbid/allow researchers seem to be looking for a monocausal theory related to 'forbid' and 'allow', such as the connotations hypothesis. However, this explanatory hypothesis cannot be tested by checking the existence of the asymmetry alone. Therefore, research continued by focusing on the issue of whether the occurrence of the asymmetry is related systematically to certain respondent characteristics relevant to the research question: the indifference, uninformedness or attitude strength of respondents. Unfortunately, this does not seem to have led to unequivocal results either.

The problems related to finding explanations for the asymmetry can be converted into a variety of research questions. How can the hypotheses offered in previous forbid/allow research be made testable? How can the explanations be related to the more general model of the question-answering process, in such a way that the validity of forbid/allow questions and answers can be assessed? Can a monocausal explanation for the forbid/allow asymmetry be developed, despite the variation in asymmetry sizes obtained?

The generalizability issue is also related to a variety of questions. If the use of 'forbid' and 'allow' is supposed to systematically influence the answers, does this mean an asymmetry should be found for each forbid/allow question posed? In other words, given the equivocal results of previous forbid/allow research, would it be justifiable to conclude that 'forbid' and 'allow' cause a wording effect in and of themselves, independent of their context?

In the following sections, these questions will be related explicitly to the general cognitive framework discussed in the previous chapter. This will then be used as a basis for describing how this study will go about answering these questions.

2.2.1 Relating the explanations to the cognitive framework

Before an attempt to explain the asymmetry can be warranted, it needs to be established whether the use of forbid/allow affects the answers beyond the level of specific questions. Given the equivocal findings in previous forbid/allow experiments, this cannot be presupposed. If 'forbid' and 'allow' do not show an effect that can be generalized beyond question level, the primary focus of any explanation should be the communicative circumstances under which wording effects occur. If, on the other hand, the use of 'forbid' and 'allow' proves to have some general effect, explanations should first of all focus on the use of those verbs.

As will be reported in Chapter 3, a meta-analysis summarizing the results of previous forbid/allow research reveals that the use of forbid/allow does affect the answers to a level that can be generalized beyond question level. Accordingly an explanation for the effect of the use of 'forbid' and 'allow' is in order.

As discussed in Chapter 1, Grice's theory predicts that respondents will infer that the use of 'allow' (or 'forbid') is the optimal question wording, given the researchers' communicative and research goals. However, this does not reveal much about the precise inferences respondents make, or about the meanings they assign to these verbs. Instead, some kind of theory focusing on the differences between 'forbid' and 'allow' is called for.

Semantically, 'forbid' and 'allow' seem to be each other's counterparts: in terms of relational semantics (Chaffin & Herrmann, 1984; 1988) both verbs are contradictory antonyms, similar to word pairs such as married/unmarried or alive/dead. Contradictories are dichotomous: they do not allow for degrees as do contraries (like sweet/sour) which are opposed symmetrically on a continuous dimension: one cannot be 'very married', nor can one 'very forbid' something. In the same way is it not possible for something to be 'a little bit forbidden' or for someone to be 'a little bit dead'. The words 'yes' and 'no' are also contradictory: 'not no' implies 'yes', and the other way round. Yet respondents seem to treat the verbs as if they are not truly contradictory, and so a straightforward analysis from relational semantics fails to account for the forbid/allow asymmetry.

The connotations hypothesis may therefore provide an alternative explanation for the asymmetry. The idea that the connotations of both verbs are extreme ('forbid' might suggest harshness, while in some contexts 'allow' might be interpreted as encouraging deviant behaviour), could at least explain why the wording effect is in this specific direction (i.e. why more negative answers to the allow question are obtained than affirmative answers to the forbid question). This naysaying tendency is in contrast to the preference for agreement mechanisms usually found in response effects research (cf. Sacks, 1987).

The connotations hypothesis, however, is ambiguous in its cognitive status and this makes it difficult to test. The hypothesis does not clarify whether different attitudes are expressed by the use of forbid/allow or whether the answers express similar attitudes differently. In their test of the connotations hypothesis, asking respondents to rate the extremity of a fictitious opinion, Hippler and Schwarz leave the same ambiguity. At the same time, several authors who discuss the forbid/allow asymmetry clearly interpret the connotations hypothesis as being about the differing translations of similar attitudes in the answering options. Clark and Schober (1992:31) present the connotations hypothesis as "to answer 'no' to forbid does not mean the same as 'yes' to allow – to agree to 'forbid' implies a real act of opposition, but to disagree with 'allow' means merely to abstain from support". Krosnick & Schuman (1988:940) interpret the explanation along similar lines, assuming the asymmetry results from slight changes in perceptions of the meanings of response options in attitude questions: "[...] 'not allowing' is perceived as a less extreme stance than is 'forbidding'." In the same article, however, they argue that response effects can also arise at the stage of attitude retrieval. It is therefore obvious that the connotations hypothesis should be specified as to whether it means that different attitudes are being measured due to the extreme connotations of forbid/allow, or whether it means that similar attitudes are being expressed differently on the answering scales. Chapter 4 gives an account of an experimental investigation to identify the stage of the question-answering process at which the wording effect arises: during attitude retrieval or during the transla-

:ion of similar attitudes into the answering options. Based on the outcomes of this analysis the connotations hypothesis will be reformulated, to be tested and developed further in Chapters 6 and 7.

The question-answering process underlying forbid/allow questions cannot be unravelled through a comparison of the percentages 'yes forbid' and 'not allow' as performed in split ballot designs, however. To find out whether or not forbid/allow questions measure similar attitudes, a correlational design is needed. By comparing percentages, one already assumes that forbid/allow questions address similar attitudes. If this assumption holds true, a comparison of observed scores makes sense, as the answers obtained can be viewed as different expressions of the same attitudes. If forbid/allow questions measure different attitudes, however, a comparison between percentages obtained is like comparing apples with oranges or like carrying out a direct comparison between the scores on a questionnaire about happiness and the scores on an intelligence test. Hence, the question-answering process underlying forbid/allow questions not only needs to be untangled for theoretical reasons, but it also needs to be clarified to make sure whether a comparison of answering percentages in split ballot experiments is the appropriate analysis method for forbid/allow questions. Accordingly the experiments reported in Chapter 4, which seek to unravel the underlying question-answering process in forbid/allow questions, are very important to this study.

The above discussion of explanations focuses on the search for general patterns underlying the asymmetry. However, the variation in occurrence and nonoccurrence of the wording effect has also yet to be explained. Previous forbid/allow research has shown that the size of the asymmetry varies considerably across different questions and experiments. It seems researchers try to explain each nonoccurrence of the asymmetry by defining facilitating factors for the occurrence of the asymmetry, focusing on such aspects as the number of indifferent respondents or the number of respondents holding weaker attitudes in the sample.

It is questionable, however, whether the immediate formulation of such additional hypotheses for explaining variation in the occurrence and nonoccurrence of the wording effect is warranted. The inadequacy of the naive survey model (Chapter 1) shows that many variables can influence the answers. This influence is to be expected once question-answering is viewed as a communication process between a researcher and the respondents. When interpreting the question and retrieving an attitude, respondents use many clues from the communication setting, characteristics of the question wording and the interviewers' behaviour. In addition, respondents differ in the attitudes they hold, as well as in the strength of those attitudes. All these aspects of the language-use situation may affect the answers obtained. To complicate matters further, these various factors may also interact with one another. In the past, forbid/allow researchers immediately isolated one of those characteristics, the attitude strength of respondents, and in doing so may wrongly have neglected the influence of the other communicative characteristics.

In fact, the indifferent respondent hypothesis assumes an interaction between the respondent characteristic of attitude strength and the effect of the use of 'forbid' or 'allow'. Similarly, Schuman and Presser (1981:283) note that "the forbid-allow effect can best be attributed to a subtle interaction between words and subject matter, with grammatical structure perhaps playing an additional role in creating an educational difference in some instances. But these interpretations are too much after the fact to be offered with great confidence [...]".

Such interactions between the effect of forbid/allow and other characteristics from the communicative setting can only be interpreted once insight has been obtained into what the forbid/allow effect actually does. Does it cause different attitudes to be retrieved or does it exert an influence during the stage of mapping similar attitudes onto the answering scales? The hypothesis concerning attitude strength, for example, builds on the connotations hypothesis and is therefore plagued by similar ambiguities as to its cognitive status. On the one hand, it could imply that respondents holding strong attitudes retrieve similar attitudes when answering forbid as well as allow questions, whereas respondents holding weak attitudes towards the issue retrieve an attitude not only towards the issue itself but also towards forbidding (or allowing) things in general. On the other hand, the hypotheses could imply that all respondents are expected to retrieve similar attitudes when answering forbid/allow questions, but that the translation of this evaluation into the answering options 'yes' and 'no' causes more difficulties for respondents holding weak attitudes than for respondents holding strong attitudes towards the issue. Before the interaction between respondent, question or other communicative characteristics and the use of forbid/allow can be investigated (Chapter 5), the subprocess within which the question-answering process the forbid/allow asymmetry arises must first be identified (Chapter 4).

Many of the additional explanations for the asymmetry were offered after the event, in order to explain nonoccurrences of the wording effect obtained for a single question. To find out whether these explanations also hold for other questions, summarizing techniques should be used to generalize the effects of communicative setting characteristics on the occurrence of the asymmetry. The body of previous forbid/allow experiments will be analysed to find out whether, for example, oral administration modes are systematically related to larger asymmetry sizes. If so, this could indicate that this retrospective hypothesis for explaining variations in asymmetry size should be taken into account in designing further experiments, or in building a theory explaining the asymmetry. However, before such an analysis of previous forbid/allow research can be conducted, it must be ascertained whether the asymmetry is due to the retrieval of different attitudes (Chapter 4). If this is not the case, the differences in percentages of yes/no answers to forbid/allow questions cannot be interpreted, let alone be related to communicative characteristics influencing these differences. It can be revealed at this stage, though, that the analyses focusing on the cognitive processes in which the wording effect arises will show that the asymmetry occurs during the mapping stage. A meta-analysis of factors related to variations in the asymmetry size obtained will therefore be reported in Chapter 5.

This analysis will provide some theoretical understanding of the interplay between various aspects of the communicative setting. More importantly, however, it will provide hypotheses on which aspects of the language-use situation play a role in the occurrence of the wording effect, and how constructing the meaning of 'forbid' and 'allow' interacts with other contextual clues within the language environment and the accessible knowledge and attitudes of the respondents. Accordingly, it will provide further insight into the issue of whether a monocausal theory to explain the forbid/allow asymmetry can be developed and the aspects of the communicative setting which should be incorporated in such a theory. This will supply further input for a reformulation of the connotations hypothesis in order to test and develop it further (in Chapters 6 and 7).

To sum up, the explanatory research questions that will be answered in this study build on each other. First of all, the question of whether the asymmetry arises during attitude retrieval or during the translation of an attitude into a response option will be answered in Chapter 4. This will lead to a reformulation of the connotations hypothesis, stating that the asymmetry arises from changes in the perception of what the answering options mean, due to the extreme connotations of 'forbid' and 'allow'. The focus will then shift to the interactions between the effect of forbid/allow and other characteristics from the communicative setting: which retrospective explanations remain valid in a summarizing analysis of all forbid/allow research? This will generate a variety of explanatory hypotheses, that will be tested and developed further in Chapters 6 and 7, together with the connotations hypothesis.

2.2.2 Aiming for generalizability

The overview of previous forbid/allow research reveals that the wording effect was not found for each forbid/allow question. Yet the connotations hypothesis suggests that this should be the case: if 'forbid' sounds too harsh, and 'allow' can be seen to encourage deviant behaviour, one would expect an asymmetry to be found for each forbid/allow question. On the other hand, Schuman and Presser's account of the connotations hypothesis states that 'allow' may seem to encourage deviant behaviour "in some contexts", which implies that an asymmetry will not be obtained for those contexts in which the verb allow does not carry this connotation. In general, however, Schuman and Presser assume some sort of monocausality in noting that "tone of wording [that is, the use of forbid and allow] could be the sole source of the effect".

Bearing this in mind, it is worth focusing on the generality of the wording effect caused by the use of 'forbid' and 'allow' before starting to look for explanations for the nonoccurrence of the asymmetry. Previous forbid/allow research does not provide statistical evidence that the findings can be generalized beyond the specific sample of language materials selected by the researchers. How can general statements on the forbid/allow asymmetry for questions on concrete issues be based on one question about X-rated movies posed to a specific sample of American respondents, within a specific survey at one specific time of measurement? Similarly, if three forbid/allow questions are posed to three different samples of respondents in Germany, and a significant asymmetry is found for one of those questions, why should this allow general judgements on the definitive use of forbid/allow for all attitude questions in the German language?

Split ballot designs, such as those used in all previous forbid/allow research, provide the opportunity to check whether and to what degree answers to a question are influenced by the question wording. At the same time, the generalizability of findings in split ballot experiments in which just one question is manipulated, is limited to the specific variables that were held constant (see Section 1.2). This generalization problem is similar to the Language-as-Fixed-Effect-Fallacy (Clark, 1973). In order to arrive at general statements about the effect of the use of forbid/allow in attitude questions, evidence is needed that the findings of separate forbid/allow questions posed in specific settings can be generalized to the hypothetical universal collection of forbid/allow questions in a universal set of communicative settings.

Ideally, one should draw a random sample of forbid/allow questions from a hypothetical universal collection of communicative settings (varying in respondent characteristics, issues being questioned, interviewer characteristics, administration modes, etc.) in which forbid/allow questions could occur. Based on the findings in that sample, general conclusions can be drawn about the effects of the use of 'forbid' and 'allow'. Unfortunately, drawing such a representative sample from the 'population' of forbid/allow questions is hardly possible. However, it is possible to employ general strategies in order to enhance the possibilities for generalization: one strategy for the design of new experiments and two strategies for the analysis stage.

In the *design stage* of new forbid/allow experiments, generalization problems can be diminished to some extent by posing various forbid/allow questions to the same respondents at the same time. By doing this, at least some variation is incorporated in the communicative setting. The same group of respondents (differing in their attitudes, attitude strength and other possibly relevant characteristics) answers several forbid/allow questions. These questions are on a variety of issues, and each one differs from the other in terms of complexity, abstractness or other possibly relevant wording characteristics.

Of course, posing several forbid/allow questions to the same respondents at the same time cannot fully solve generalization problems. The number of pragmatic, semantic and content-related variables which might possibly influence the question-answering process is too large, and the situation is compounded still further by the lack of clarity about the characteristics which are minimally relevant to explain the forbid/allow asymmetry. Hence, large numbers of forbid/allow questions have to be posed to many different respondents about many different subjects by many different senders in various different task settings in order to obtain enough data to really generalize about the effect of forbid/allow. However, posing several different forbid/allow questions to the same respondents within the same experimental setting at least increases the possibilities for generalizing beyond the level of single questions. This design strategy will therefore be used in two new forbid/allow experiments conducted to unravel the question-answering process (Chapter 4), as well as in a variety of new experiments performed to test the connotations hypothesis (Chapters 6 and 7).

An effective *analysis strategy* for designs in which several forbid/allow questions are posed to the same group of respondents involves focusing on the general patterns that occur, as well as on the variations in the wording effect. The overall pattern found across a set of questions provides possibilities for formulating general conclusions about the wording effect. At the same time, insight into the variation between questions can lead to hypotheses on the effects of the characteristics of the issues addressed or linguistic characteristics of the questions other than the use of forbid/allow. Furthermore, a grasp of the differences between respondents can lead to hypotheses about the effects of respondent characteristics on the wording effect obtained, such as differences in attitude strength. These basic design and analysis strategies will be employed in the new forbid/allow experiments conducted for the current study and described in Chapters 4, 6 and 7.

The use of meta-analytic techniques in the *analysis stage* is a strategy that facilitates generalization above the level of questions and communicative settings for previous forbid/allow research. A statistical meta-analysis of existing forbid/ allow research can indicate whether an overall asymmetry exists for that specific set of forbid/allow questions. At least this provides possibilities for raising conclusions to the level of all forbid/allow research, instead of having to focus on each individual question posed (Chapter 3). This will then form the basis for conclusions on the generality of the effect of 'forbid' and 'allow'. A more general determination of characteristics of the communicative setting under which the asymmetry is likely to occur can subsequently be derived (Chapter 5). As discussed in the previous section, meta-analytic techniques can be used to relate variations in the occurrence of the asymmetry to more general question characteristics, so that the effect of circumstances similar for different forbid/allow questions can be generalized to some extent.

2.2.3 Outlook

The remainder of this book consists out of four main steps, each contributing to an integrated cognitive analysis for explaining the forbid/allow asymmetry. The types of experiments and analyses that will be conducted have already been described in the previous sections. Below a more chronological overview of the research questions to be dealt with in each chapter is provided.

Chapter 3 uses meta-analytic techniques to investigate the claim that the use of 'forbid' and 'allow' has some general effect on the answers obtained and establishes whether the effect is large enough to warrant investigating its causes.

Chapter 4 reports on two experiments conducted to discover whether forbid/allow questions measure different attitudes or whether the asymmetry arises in the mapping stage of the question-answering process. This will not only be investigated for the group of respondents as a whole but will also be explored for respondents holding weak attitudes.

Chapter 5 reports on a meta-analysis of forbid/allow research, trying to trace the characteristics of the communicative setting relevant to the occurrence of the asymmetry. Explanatory hypotheses are formulated by analysing the factors contributing to variations in the asymmetry size.

In Chapter 6, experimental research will be reported focusing on one of the hypotheses resulting from Chapter 5: is the asymmetry due to the use of 'forbid' and 'allow' associated with any agree/disagree dimension or is it caused by the communicative restriction of only offering the possibility to express the evaluations by choosing between 'yes' or 'no'? Differences between the answering scales to forbid/allow questions will also be subjected to further analysis, following on from the outcomes of Chapter 4.

The meta-analysis in Chapter 5 will serve as the basis for the hypothesis that the asymmetry is due to a combination of the extreme connotations of forbid/allow and the extremity of respondents' attitudes. This hypothesis will be tested and developed further in Chapter 7, by focusing on the meanings of 'yes' and 'no' to forbid/allow questions. This will also provide a further grasp of the differences between the answering scales to forbid/allow questions.

3.0 INTRODUCTION

Quite a few researchers have studied the forbid/allow asymmetry. Their results are not unequivocal, however: sometimes a large wording effect is found, sometimes none at all (see Tables 2.1 and 3.2). Explanations for the occurrence and the nonoccurrence of the asymmetry are difficult to provide, as most experiments in forbid/allow research consist of only one manipulated question. The same applies to research on many other wording or response effects. This creates difficulties in terms of generalizing the wording effect to questions other than the one posed, and to communicative settings other than the one used. The main goal of the current chapter is to establish whether the effect of forbid/allow can be generalized beyond question level, and whether it is large enough to warrant an investigation of its causes.

When computing differences between responses to variants of single questions, it is impossible to generalize above the level of the specific linguistic variables used in an experiment (Molenaar, 1986). The wording effect found in one specific question is the result of a combination of factors within the distinct communicative setting in which the question was posed. On the one hand this is determined by the use of either 'forbid' or 'allow' and on the other hand by a variety of other linguistic characteristics of the question, such as respondent characteristics and perceptions of the senders' intentions or goals. Computing and experimenting on the basis of single questions gives rise to generalization problems comparable to the language-as-fixed-effect fallacy (Clark, 1973). In order to generalize on the effect forbid/allow, the chosen operationalization of possible question content, wording variation, administration modes and so forth has to encompass a good sample of possible variations in forbid/allow contexts. By definition this is not the case when analyses are only performed for each question separately. While this does not imply that split ballot designs should be avoided, it does mean that generalization problems require special attention (see Section 2.2.2).

From the discussion of previous forbid/allow research, it is clear that the wording effect obtained for forbid/allow questions varies greatly. Many hypotheses for explaining this variation have been offered after the fact but this has often been done prematurely. It is difficult to identify the right theory to explain the

---

[1] Most parts of the meta-analysis presented in this chapter (and in Chapter 5) were published in the *Journal of Quantitative Linguistics* (1999) and in *Taalgebruik ontrafeld, verslag van het 7e VIOT-congres* (1997).

variation as long as the data do not indicate which characteristic of the communicative setting causes the variation. It could be caused by differences in the experimental setting (e.g. the administration mode used), but it could also be caused by respondent characteristics (e.g. attitude strength).

One way of finding out which type of characteristic causes this variation is to pose several forbid/allow questions to the same respondents. If different asymmetry sizes are obtained for two forbid/allow questions on abortion posed to the same respondents, the variation should be attributed to specific characteristics of each question (e.g. grammatical complexity), rather than to respondent characteristics (e.g. the strength of the attitude towards abortion) or characteristics of the experimental setting (e.g. the administration mode). It is also possible that the variation in the wording effect obtained for different questions will disappear if these questions are posed to the same respondents. In that case, the variation in asymmetries should be explained by variation in the characteristics of the experimental setting or by question characteristics that were unintentionally varied, rather than by respondent characteristics. In order to be able to make this distinction, two new forbid/allow experiments were conducted in which several forbid/allow questions were posed to the same respondents within one questionnaire (see Section 3.1).

The results of these experiments show, however, that the variation in the wording effect found within these two new experiments is also very large. Combined with the sizeable variation in the wording effect found in previous forbid/allow research, this is a direct impetus for raising another generalization issue: can the effect of 'forbid' and 'allow' be generalized beyond the level of single questions posed within a wide variety of communicative settings?

An initial examination of all the experimental results fails to provide a clear conclusion as to whether the use of forbid/allow in questions has a general effect on the answers, since the wording effect varies in size and in its occurrence and nonoccurrence. Waterplas et al. (1988: 405) note that given these contradictory findings, the researchers' desire for replications is hardly surprising. A careful study of the experiments shows, however, that the replications were less systematic than they initially seemed, as many factors were varied in each experiment. These included the content of the question, the place where the data was collected and particularly the data collection methods. This meant that there were always a number of different explanations available for the occurrence or nonoccurrence of the effect. In addition to these aspects, it is worth considering whether or not wording variables other than forbid/allow are also varied unintentionally, making comparison between the experiments even more difficult. For example, the act of 'forbidding' or 'allowing' is sometimes attributed to a nation as a whole (the United States) and sometimes to the legislator, or an unidentified actor.

National or moral obligations, or legal prohibitions, are therefore difficult to distinguish from each other.

First of all, these considerations make it necessary to find out whether the use of forbid/allow causes a wording effect that can be generalized beyond question level. This will be done by using meta-analytic techniques to summarize the results obtained in single split ballot experiments. Molenaar (1986) adopted meta-analytic techniques to analyse seventeen experiments on the answers to one-predicate versus two-predicate questions. These are questions like 'Do you favour a law which would require a police permit to buy a gun' (one predicate), versus 'Do you favour a law which would require a police permit to buy a gun, or do you oppose such a law' (two predicates). For several single experiments using this and similar question pairs (see Schuman & Presser, 1981) a significant wording effect was found. In a summarizing variance analysis, Molenaar (1986) found that one or more experiments showed a wording effect that differed significantly from the effect found in other experiments. The main effect of the wording variable was nonsignificant, however. Molenaar concluded that a wording effect for one-predicate as opposed to two-predicate questions can be found under specific circumstances, but observed large variations in the wording effect between questions posed under different experimental conditions or on different issues. Indeed, these variations were so large that this wording variable cannot be seen as affecting the answers in general. Hence, for one-predicate versus two-predicate questions, it seems that explanations should focus on the communicative circumstances facilitating the effect, instead of solely on specific characteristics of this wording variable.

In the same vein, it is interesting to examine whether the effect of the use of forbid/allow can be generalized above the level of experiments and individual questions and also whether this effect is large enough to explore further in an attempt to explain it. Furthermore, in the light of Clark's warning about the language-as-fixed-effect fallacy, not only is it interesting to know the main effect of the use of the verbs 'forbid' or 'allow', but it is also important to analyse the variation in the asymmetry sizes obtained.

Section 3.1 will discuss two new forbid/allow experiments conducted in the Netherlands. Contrary to previous forbid/allow research, both experiments consisted of several forbid/allow questions posed to the same respondents. Repeated measurements were also used. The results of these experiments show that the wording effect obtained varies greatly between questions posed at the same time of measurement, but also between equivalent questions posed at different times of measurement. Meta-analytic techniques were therefore employed in order to find out whether the asymmetry can be generalized beyond question level when analysed for the new experiments as well as for previous forbid/allow research. Is the wording effect large enough to justify a further investigation of its causes (Section 3.2)? In the last section (Section 3.3) some general conclusions are drawn with respect to the analyses.

3.1 TWO NEW FORBID/ALLOW EXPERIMENTS

Research into the forbid/allow asymmetry and on response effects in general usually starts by checking whether the asymmetry can be found in the specific country or language area the researcher is working in. In most cases, forbid/allow questions concern something that is allowed at the moment the question is posed. In order to replicate Rugg's original findings with regard to the asymmetry, forbid/allow questions often deal with the subject of public speeches. Sometimes this is a literal replication (public speeches against democracy), sometimes the theme is altered slightly (public speeches in favour of communism, racist speeches in public), or other questions on racism or integrational issues are posed (separate school classes for ethnic minority pupils, Waterplas et al., 1988). There are also questions on pornography (X-rated movies, peep shows), smoking (smoking in public places, cigarette advertisements on television), or on an environmental issue (salt on roads). The questions are usually posed to a random national sample of respondents, but sometimes they are posed to a quota sample (one question of Hippler & Schwarz, 1986), or to a more homogenous sample (of students, by Bishop et al., or of women in a certain area of the country, by Waterplas et al.). Questions in the early experiments were posed in oral administration modes, either by telephone or face-to-face, while some of the later experiments were conducted using self-administered questionnaires.

For the present research project two new forbid/allow experiments were carried out: one on nature and environmental issues, and one on ethnic and integrational issues. They were designed in order to obtain an understanding of the cognitive processes underlying the wording effect (which will be discussed in Chapter 4). In order to address this specific research question, an extended split ballot design was used involving repeated measurements, and it was possible to use a smaller sample of respondents than in most other forbid/allow experiments.

The two new experiments differed from existing forbid/allow research in that a four-point answering scale (yes!/yes/no/no!) was used instead of the regular yes/no answering scale.The answers were recoded to a two-point yes/no scale, in order to achieve maximum comparability to previous studies. The issue of whether the use of these four-point answering scales confounded the results will be addressed in Chapter 6.[2]

In this section, the data obtained for each question will be reported. Here, the main question is whether the asymmetry can be generalized above question level when a variety of questions on two issues are posed to the same respondents. Although each experiment was about a different issue, both questionnaires were administered to the same respondents. Since this was the first time that so many forbid/allow questions were included in one experiment, the data shown here give some indication as to whether an asymmetry found for one question can be generalized to other questions posed to the same group of respondents. Furthermore, as the experiments consisted of repeated measurements, the data presented here provide some indication of the stability of the wording effect over time.

3.1.1 Questionnaires and procedure

For both experiments a written self-administered questionnaire was developed containing several questions formulated with either 'forbid' or 'allow', separated by fillers about related issues in order to obscure the research goals for the respondents. The questionnaire in the first experiment covered nature and environmental issues, as a literature search (in Dutch newspaper databases and policy papers) showed that a lot of recent discussions within this domain have dealt with the notion of whether a particular practice should be forbidden or not (e.g. driving on Sundays, the use of disposable batteries).

The questionnaire consisted of 36 questions: 12 questions about whether practices relating to environmental issues (e.g. the use of disposable batteries), or nature policy (e.g. road construction through nature conservation areas) should be forbidden (version 1) or allowed (version 2) and 14 questions on related subjects but without the verbs 'forbid' or 'allow'. All of the issues addressed in the forbid/ allow questions in the questionnaire concerned practices which were allowed at the time the experiment took place. Table 3.1 shows the question wordings of the forbid/allow questions.

The questionnaire developed for the second experiment generally focused on public opinion issues relating to ethnic groups. The questionnaire consisted of 32 questions, 12 about whether practices relating to discrimination (racist speeches in public, separate classes for Dutch children and children from ethnic groups) and about integrational issues (female circumcision, nightly call for prayers from

---

[2] Four-point scales were used because a two-point scale requires more complex correlational analyses, which can be avoided by using more scalepoints. The research objective for which the experiments were developed (see Chapter 4) requires correlational analyses. Furthermore, the use of such a scale is in line with Hippler & Schwarz's (1986) advice to offer respondents the opportunity to express more moderate opinions instead of just a 'yes' or a 'no'.

the mosque) should be allowed (version 1) or forbidden (version 2).[3] Again issues were selected from Dutch newspaper discussions, television debates and policy papers. Contrary to the first experiment, all issues were forbidden at the moment the questions were posed. Two questions were an almost exact replication of existing forbid/allow questions in the literature: the question on separate classes and the question on racist speeches in public (both used by Waterplas et al.). A variety of questions about related issues were posed, not using the verbs 'forbid' or 'allow'. Table 3.1 contains the question wordings of the forbid/allow questions used.

The experiments were carried out simultaneously in May 1996. The questionnaires were administered twice to the same respondents, with a four-week period between the first and the second administration. Four weeks was considered sufficient to diminish memory effects to a reasonable extent.

Subjects were students in languages and the arts. The questionnaire was administered during visits to five different university classes. Students were asked to fill in a questionnaire about environmental issues and policies on ethnic groups. The students were told that the study would contribute to research on the informativeness and feasibility of referendums, a hot issue among the general public at that time. The questionnaire was filled in during classes. On the first occasion, the different versions of the questionnaire were randomized within classes. Students were asked to put their names on the empty front page of the questionnaire but were told that their answers would be stored and processed anonymously. Their names were needed to keep track of who was given which version of the questionnaire but the respondents were not notified that the questionnaire would be administered again several weeks later to avoid memory effects. The total number of students present on the first occasion was 300, and 297 questionnaires were filled in and returned.

After four weeks the same classes were visited again. The students were asked to fill in the questionnaire once more. The reason given this time was to test whether it would make a difference when a referendum is held. Questionnaires were handed out on the basis of the students' names: half of the students who filled in version 1 the first time, received version 1, while the other half received version 2. The same applied to the students who filled in version 2 the first time, thereby creating a four-group design (see Table 4.1). The subjects were not notified that there were different versions of the questionnaire, nor that they

---

[3] In other words, 24 forbid/allow questions were included in the two experiments. However, seven questions were left out of the analyses, for reasons discussed in Chapter 4. Here, the results of 17 forbid/allow questions will be addressed, the answers obtained for the 7 remaining questions are provided in Appendix I.

might have received a different version to the previous occasion. After the second administration, the goals of the research were explained to the students. On the second occasion, some of the students (98) who took part in the first phase of the study did not attend the class and a small number (4) refused to cooperate a second time, which meant that 195 respondents filled in the questionnaire twice and 136 students filled in the questionnaire at T1 or T2. Only the subjects who cooperated twice were included in the analysis (see also Table 4.1).

3.1.2 Results

Table 3.1 shows that 28.7% of the 101 respondents who answered the first question in a forbid version chose the answer 'not forbid', whereas 22.6% of the 93 respondents who answered this question in the allow version the first time chose the answer 'yes allow'. These percentages show an asymmetric tendency (as higher percentages are obtained for 'not forbid' than for 'yes allow' and therefore also for 'not allow' compared to 'yes forbid') but the wording effect is nonsignificant (χ^2=.95, p=.33, df=1). On the second occasion, once again no significant wording effect was found for this question (p=.99). A combined analysis of the data obtained on both occasions shows that this question generally does not lead to a significant wording effect (p-com=.33).

no.	question wording "Do you think ...	T	N F	A	percentage NF	YA	χ^2	p	p com
1	[...] the government should forbid/allow urban expansion at the expense of agricultural areas or nature conservation areas?[4]	1	101	93	28.7	22.6	.95	.33	.33
		2	95	99	23.2	23.2	.00	.99	
2	[...] the government should forbid/allow military exercises in or near nature conservation areas?	1	102	93	26.5	15.4	3.53	.06	.05
		2	96	98	19.8	23.5	.39	.53	

---

[4] The original Dutch questions texts are presented in Appendix I.

no.	question wording "Do you think ...	T	N F A	percentage NF YA	χ^2	p	p com
3	[...] parliament should forbid/allow the expansion of Schiphol Airport by a fifth runway?	1	102 93	61.8 55.9	.69	.41	.41
		2	95 97	64.2 53.6	2.23	.14	
4	[...] the government should forbid/allow the extraction of natural gas from the Wadden Sea if it affects the natural characteristics of the area?	1	101 91	20.8 18.7	.13	.71	.71
		2	94 99	14.9 14.1	.02	.88	
5	[...] parliament should forbid/allow the construction of roads through nature conservation areas?	1	100 90	17.0 8.9	2.73	.10	.10
		2	95 99	22.1 15.2	1.55	.21	
6	[...] the government should forbid/allow speeds of over 90 km/h on motor ways?	1	102 93	90.2 90.3	.00	.98	.98
		2	96 99	91.7 83.8	2.77	.10	
7	[...] the government should forbid/allow the increase of railway fares by the NS [Netherlands Railways]?	1	102 93	21.6 10.8	4.15	.04	.05
		2	96 99	22.9 16.2	1.42	.23	
8	[...] the government should forbid/allow driving cars on Sundays?	1	102 92	86.3 96.7	6.63	.01	.02
		2	96 97	89.6 89.7	.00	.98	
9	[...] the government should forbid/allow the use of disposable batteries?	1	102 91	40.2 49.5	1.67	.20	.31
		2	96 98	44.8 46.9	.09	.76	
10	Some people do not wish to sell their house to people from ethnic minorities. [...] the government should forbid/allow this?	1	93 101	23.7 17.8	1.01	.32	.96
		2	99 94	20.2 10.6	3.36	.07	

no.	question wording "Do you think ...	T	N F A	percentage NF YA	χ^2	p	p com
11	In some schools there are many children from ethnic minority families. [...] the government should forbid/allow separate classes for Dutch and ethnic minority pupils in those schools?	1	92 102	29.3 7.8	15.13	.00	.00
		2	99 95	27.3 14.7	4.57	.03	
12	[...] the government should forbid/allow racist speeches in public?	1	92 100	19.6 14.0	1.07	.30	.30
		2	98 94	22.4 10.6	4.82	.03	
13	[...] the government should forbid/allow the exclusion of people from ethnic minorities for certain jobs?	1	92 100	45.7 13.0	24.99	.00	.00
		2	99 94	32.3 12.8	10.48	.00	
14	In Moslem cultures people find it important to slaughter their own animals rather than have it done by a butcher.[...] the government should forbid/allow home slaughter?	1	92 100	43.5 36.0	1.12	.29	.29
		2	99 96	39.4 37.5	.07	.79	
15	[...] the government should forbid/allow female circumcision?	1	91 101	30.8 28.7	.11	.76	.76
		2	99 95	25.3 22.1	.27	.61	
16	[...] the government should forbid/allow marriages to more than one woman for men from polygamous cultures?	1	91 102	42.9 25.5	6.49	.01	.01
		2	99 95	39.4 27.4	3.15	.08	
17	[...] the government should forbid/allow the nightly call for prayers from mosques?	1	92 98	53.3 41.8	2.48	.12	.11
		2	98 93	56.1 47.3	1.48	.22	

note: no= numbers 1-17 identify the questions as referred to in Appendix II, T= time of measurement, N= number of respondents, F=forbid, A= allow, NF=not forbid, YA=yes allow, p com= combined p for T1 and T2

Table 3.1: *Answers to 17 forbid/allow questions at two times of measurement*

As can be seen in Table 3.1, the asymmetry was only found 6 times for this set of 17 new forbid/allow questions, each of which was posed twice (on a significance level of p<.05). Hence, the same group of respondents answered 6 questions asymmetrically while no wording effect was found for 11 questions. However, 6 asymmetries out of 17 observations is more than should be expected solely on chance (p<.05).

Basically the results demonstrate that the wording effect does indeed exist, but that the same respondents do not answer separate questions on the same topics asymmetrically each time: there is considerable variance within respondents due to the characteristics of each specific question. For example, the question on different classes (question 11), which was a replication from previous research (Waterplas et al., 1988), is answered asymmetrically at T1 as well as T2. The same holds for the question on polygamy (question 16), whereas the question on female circumcision (question 15) does not produce a wording effect. So despite the fact that all the questions are about ethnic issues, some questions are answered asymmetrically, whereas others are not. This variance within respondents cannot be attributed to question order effects, as asymmetrical answers were not obtained for questions at a specific position in the questionnaire.

It is not the case that each question producing a wording effect does so at each time of measurement: some questions are only answered asymmetrically at T1 (e.g. question 2: military exercises). In view of the explanatory hypothesis of Hippler & Schwarz (1986), which states that weak attitude strength is an important cause of the asymmetry, one might consider whether respondents who held weak attitudes on the topics covered by the questionnaires during the first time of measurement, started forming an attitude on various subjects due to the measurement procedure, which caused the asymmetry to diminish four weeks later. This does not seem to be the case, however, as no consistent time effects were found: for example, the question on racist speeches (again a replication from Waterplas et al., 1988), was only answered asymmetrically at T2. Furthermore, in the experiment on nature and environmental issues, cumulative asymmetry sizes do not differ between the first and second time of measurement. In the experiment on ethnic issues, meanwhile, the asymmetry size is somewhat smaller at T1 than at T2 (see Table 4.2).

If each question is viewed separately at each time of measurement, a wording effect is only found 7 times out of 34 observations. This is more than should be expected on chance, however (p<.05). For one question (driving on Sundays) a significant wording effect is found, but in a direction opposite to that expected (more 'yes allow' than 'not forbid'). If the level of significance is set at <.1, a significant wording effect emerges five more times, in the expected direction. Questions not showing a significant wording effect tend to differ in the expected direction but the differences are too small to reach significance. The fact that a number of questions do not lead to significant wording effects may be attributable to the fact that all respondents are highly educated and therefore less susceptible to response effects (cf. Schuman & Presser, 1981). However, the fact that some questions do produce an asymmetry casts doubt on this account.

Overall, the asymmetry is larger for the experiment on ethnic issues than for the experiment on environmental issues (see Table 4.2). The size of the wording effect not only differs within respondents for several questions on the same theme, but also within respondents over different questionnaire themes. This might indicate that the asymmetry size is related to issue characteristics in combination with characteristics of the attitude or strength of the attitude towards the issue. All in all, the results presented in this section stress the importance of analysing whether the effect of forbid/allow can be generalized beyond question level. This analysis will be discussed in the following section.

3.2 Generalization of the Asymmetry Beyond Questions

Taking the new experiments reported in Section 3.1 together with previous forbid/allow research (summarized in Tables 2.1 and 3.2), a total of 52 forbid/allow questions have been used to investigate this matter, administered in different languages and countries.[4]

Clearly, the wording effect does not occur in each question. The two new experiments show that the asymmetry size even varies over questions posed to the same respondents: one question about environmental issues is answered asymmetrically, whereas a related question about the same issue is not. Obviously, a large variety of characteristics within the communicative setting of the survey process can be expected to influence the occurrence of the forbid/allow asymmetry. But before dealing with this issue, it must be considered whether the asymmetry exists at all. Does the use of 'forbid' instead of 'allow' in attitude questions generally affect the answers?

---

[4] The total number of forbid/allow questions found was actually 53. Unfortunately, the last experiment by Krosnick & Schuman (1988), using another question on public speeches against democracy administered in 1984 (see Table 2.1) could not be included in the current analyses because the percentages 'not forbid' and 'yes allow' could not be recovered.

question wording "Do you think...	N	percentage forbid allow	χ^2 p (df=1)
[...] the United States should forbid/allow public speeches against democracy?	2600[5]	N 46.0 Y 25.0 Y 54.0 N 75.0	? ?
ditto	936 F 494 A	N 71.9 Y 56.1 Y 28.1 N 43.9	35.75 <.001
ditto	586 F 591 A	N 79.9 Y 54.8 Y 20.1 N 45.1	85.5 <.001
ditto	1475 F 1375 A	N 78.6 Y 52.2 Y 21.4 N 47.8	223.2 <.001
[...] the United States should forbid/allow public speeches in favor of communism?	409 F 432 A	N 60.1 Y 43.8 Y 39.3 N 56.3	22.73 <.001
[...] the government should forbid/allow the showing of X-rated movies?	547 F 576 A	N 59.0 Y 53.6 Y 41.0 N 46.4	3.33 <.1
[...] the government should forbid/allow cigarette advertisements on television?	607 F 297 A	N 49.4 Y 45.1 Y 50.6 N 54.9	1.48 n.s.
Meinen Sie, der Gesetzgeber sollte die sogenannten Peep-Shows, also das bezahlte Sichzurschaustellen nackter Frauen in aufreizenden Posen, generell verbieten/erlauben?	40 F 48 A	N 72.3 Y 50.3 Y 27.7 N 50.0	3.5 <.06
Meinen Sie, der Gesetzgeber sollte die Vorführung von pornographischen Filmen in öffentlichen Kinos generell verbieten/erlauben?	74 F 72 A	N 74.0 Y 60.0 Y 26.0 N 40.0	2.9 <.1
Durch das Streuen von Salz im Winter sind Pflanzen und Bäume in Strassenähe gefährdet. Sollte man das Salzstreuen generell verbieten/erlauben?	345 F 359 A	N 37.7 Y 21.2 Y 62.3 N 78.8	23.2 <.001
[...] that smoking in public places, such as restaurants should be forbidden/allowed?	187 F 188 A	N 47.6 Y 51.1 Y 52.4 N 48.9	0.32 >.25
ditto	174 F 173 A	N 38.7 Y 53.0 Y 61.3 N 47.0	6.61 <.02

[5] Exact Ns (numbers of respondents) were not provided by Rugg, but Schuman & Presser (1981) assume from Cantril (1940) that the percentages shown were based on about 1300 respondents per version.

question wording "Do you think...	N	percentage forbid allow	χ^2 p (df=1)
Meinen Sie, dass das Rauchen in öffentlich- en Gebäuden, so wie in Restaurants, verbo- ten/erlaubt werden/sein sollte?	77 F 77 A	N 72.4 Y 66.7 Y 27.6 N 33.3	0.59 >.25
ditto	89 F 88 A	N 67.4 Y 47.1 Y 32.6 N 52.9	7.42 <.01
[...] the government should forbid/allow the screening of pornographic films in public cinemas?	179 F 191 A	N 36.3 Y 23.6 Y 63.7 N 76.4	7.19 .007
[...] the government should forbid/allow racist speeches in public?	179 F 191 A	N 22.1 Y 14.7 Y 77.9 N 85.3	3.28 .07
In some schools there are many children from ethnic minority families.[...] the government should forbid/allow separate classes for Belgian and ethnic minority pu- pils in those schools?	179 F 191 A	N 62.4 Y 35.4 Y 37.6 N 64.6	26.8 <.001
[...] the United States should forbid/allow public speeches against democracy?	503	N 80.1 Y 62.8 Y 19.4 N 37.2	? <.001
[...] the United States should forbid/allow public speeches against democracy?	435	? ?	? <.03

Table 3.2: *Results of forbid/allow research reported in the literature*

In order to find out whether the asymmetry can be generalized beyond question level, ideally one should draw a select sample of forbid/allow questions from a hypothetical universal collection of communicative settings in which these questions could occur. As such a sample is difficult to obtain, an alternative strategy is to summarize the findings of the forbid/allow questions posed so far and at least obtain insight into whether the asymmetry can be generalized within that specific sample of questions.

Therefore, an analysis was done for all forbid/allow experiments that have been conducted: 15 forbid/allow experiments, consisting of 52 forbid/allow questions. For each question posed, the difference between the percentage 'not forbid' and 'yes, allow' answers was computed, resulting in a dependent variable that could be called the 'asymmetry size'. Since the sample size for each question varied, the asymmetry size obtained for each question was weighted relative to the number of respondents for that question: questions answered by 1500 respondents carry more weight in the analysis than questions answered by 40 respondents (cf. Wentland & Smith, 1993).

Results of a first analysis showed the overall existence of the forbid/allow asymmetry exists. The mean size of the wording effect was 14.2%: the answer 'no, not forbid' was given 14.2% more often than the answer 'yes, allow' (p<.001).

The important next question is whether the asymmetry size is substantial enough to warrant further investigation. In order to evaluate this, the effect size can be calculated, indicating "the degree to which the phenomenon is present in the population", or "the degree to which the null hypothesis is false" (Cohen, 1977:9-10). The effect size can be calculated by dividing the mean difference between forbid/allow (14.2%) by the standard deviation of that mean. The effect size obtained can then be evaluated using Cohen's criteria, which define an effect of about 0.2 of the standard deviation as small, an effect of about half a standard deviation as medium, and effects of about 0.8 of the standard deviation as large (Wolf, 1986). The standard deviation of the wording effect is 9.85, resulting in an effect size (d) of 1.44, which can be judged to be large (1.44 of the standard deviation). This indicates that the forbid/allow asymmetry is general and is rather substantial: 'forbid' and 'allow' do not function as real counterparts in attitude questions, as they have a general effect on the answers obtained.

At the same time, however, huge differences in the size of the wording effect exist. The overall standard deviation of 9.85 indicates that for 95% of the questions the difference between 'not forbid' and 'yes allow' lies between -6% (an asymmetry in the 'wrong' direction) and +34%: in some cases the asymmetry does not occur and in some cases it is considerable. Obtaining insight into these variations is important, because it offers opportunities for relating this phenomenon to factors within the communicative setting as a whole.

In order to gain more insight into the variation of the asymmetry size, the Iterative Generalized Least Squares method was used to distinguish between two sources of variation in the asymmetry obtained: variance between questions within experiments (Level I), and variance between experiments (Level II). This was done because questions within the same experiment can be expected to have more in common with each other than with questions administered in different experiments: questions from the same experiment were answered by the same respondents, for example, so the frequencies obtained can be expected to be more alike than the frequencies obtained for questions from different experiments posed to different respondents.[6]

---

[6] There are no strict criteria available for deciding what should be viewed as one experiment. For this research, questions were coded as being part of one experiment when they were posed within a single questionnaire (the three questions posed by Waterplas et al., and each of the two experiments conducted by Holleman). The questions on smoking posed by Bishop et al. (1988) were coded as being part of one experiment as well: although they were posed to different respondents using different methods of data collection (oral

A standard deviation of 9.85 implies that the overall variance of the asymmetry size is 97. A break down of this variance at the level of experiments and the level of questions within experiments, shows a variance in asymmetry size of 65 between experiments and 32 between questions within experiments (see Table 3.3).

The variation between experiments indicates that the asymmetry sizes obtained in each experiment varies greatly between experiments. In some experiments the asymmetry size is less than zero, in others it is large. In fact the asymmetry size obtained varies between -1.5% (14.2-15.7)[7] and 29.9% (14.2+15.7). This variation between experiments could indicate that experimental conditions (e.g. administration mode), or respondent characteristics (e.g. educational level) are important factors facilitating the occurrence of the asymmetry.

mean asymmetry size	p	variance between experiments (II)	variance within experiments (I)	total variance
14.2%	<.001	65	32	97 (sd = 9.85)

Table 3.3: *Overall difference between 'not forbid' and 'yes allow' and its variation*

The variance between questions within experiments is 32, which means that depending on the mean difference between forbid questions and allow questions within a certain experiment, specific questions within that experiment can show an asymmetry size that is 11.1% smaller or larger than the mean for that specific experiment. This variation within experiments could indicate that question characteristics (such as linguistic features other than the use of forbid/allow) contribute to the occurrence of the wording effect as well.

As the variation between questions within experiments is smaller than the variance between experiments, one might conclude that differences in asymmetry size should mainly be explained in terms of communicative setting characteristics relating to the experimental setting, as experiments within this set of forbid/allow questions are reasonably homogenous with respect to those characteristics. On the other hand, as many experiments in this question set consist of one question only, it could also be the case that characteristics from the communicative setting other than sampling method or administration mode can explain variation in the asymmetry size. These might include respondent characteristics or linguistic characteristics of the questions other than the use of forbid/allow.

---

versus written), the exact same question was posed four times. The set of forbid/allow questions therefore consists of 15 experiments.

[7] This value is obtained by multiplying the standard deviation 8.06 (the root of variation 65) by 1.95 (the z-score belonging to a significance level of <.05).

Hence, an analysis of the variations in the asymmetry size that distinguishes between variance from one experiment to another and within experiments does not lead to a conclusive understanding of the possible causes of the variance. This is due to the specific composition of this sample of forbid/allow questions.

3.3 CONCLUDING REMARKS

In order to diminish generalization problems and to pinpoint sources of variation in the asymmetry sizes obtained, two new experiments were conducted posing a variety of forbid/allow questions about the same issues to the same respondents. Analyses of the answers obtained showed that the asymmetry size varies considerably for questions within respondents. This substantial variation found for forbid/allow questions posed within the same experimental setting to the same respondents threw the variation in asymmetry sizes in previous forbid/allow research further into relief, raising the issue of whether the effect of using 'forbid' and 'allow' in attitude questions can be generalized beyond question level at all.

This was investigated by employing meta-analytic techniques for the full set of forbid/allow questions reported in the literature as well as for the two new forbid/allow experiments. It was established that the forbid/allow asymmetry can be generalized beyond question level and is in fact quite large: the answer 'no, not forbid' is given 14.2% more often than the answer 'yes, allow'. Not only can the asymmetry be generalized beyond questions, it can also be judged substantial enough to make a further investigation of its causes worthwhile.

The asymmetry size varies considerably between experiments and between questions within experiments, which justifies the search for additional explanations over and above the connotations hypothesis or for factors facilitating the occurrence of the asymmetry. Meta-analytic techniques will therefore be used to discover which characteristics of the communicative setting can be related to variations in the size of the wording effect found (Chapter 5). Before any such analysis of forbid/allow data obtained from split ballot experiments can be conducted, however, it has to be established whether the asymmetry is due to the retrieval of different attitudes or is due to differences at the mapping stage of the question-answering process. The assumption underlying a comparison of observed scores in split ballot experiments is that forbid/allow questions measure similar attitudes, whereas the application of a cognitive framework for question-answering shows that this assumption does not necessarily hold.

In light of the above, the time has come to investigate whether the cause of the wording effect is due to processes at the stage of question interpretation and attitude retrieval within the question-answering process, or at the stage of mapping similar evaluations onto the answering options. Relating the forbid/allow asymmetry to the general cognitive model of question-answering will provide a basis from which to start looking for a monocausal theory to explain the asymmetry (see Section 2.2.1). Furthermore, the distinction between attitudes measured and answers obtained relates directly to the validity of forbid/allow questions, which in turn holds relevance for the way surveys are carried out.

In Chapter 4, the only monocausal theory available to explain the forbid/allow asymmetry (the connotations hypothesis) will be reformulated by relating it to the general framework of the question-answering process described in Chapter 1. This will result in two competing hypotheses: one stating that the asymmetry is caused during question interpretation and attitude retrieval, the other stating it arises at the stage at which similar attitudes are mapped onto the answering options. As the indifferent respondent hypothesis follow on from the connotations hypothesis, the same distinction will be made for the subgroup of respondents holding weak attitudes. The focus will be on distinguishing patterns within the question-answering process which can be generalized beyond question level, a goal similar to that of the analyses conducted in the current chapter.

Complicated design and measurement procedures are required in order to answer the research questions in the following chapter. Split ballot experiments cannot make a distinction between the attitudes being measured on the one hand and the translation of· these attitudes into answering options on the other. However, this can be done by means of a correlational design. If researchers want to know, for example, whether two psychological tests measure the same phenomenon, this is usually done by computing the correlation between those tests. If this correlation approximates 1.0, the tests can be said to measure the same thing. A similar line of reasoning can be applied to forbid/allow questions: if the correlation between a questionnaire with forbid questions and an equivalent questionnaire with allow questions is 1.0, it can be concluded that forbid/allow questions measure the same attitude. If this is the case but the percentages 'not forbid' and 'yes allow' differ, this would demonstrate that 'yes' to an allow question and a 'yes' to an equivalent forbid question actually reflect the same attitude.

Following this line of reasoning and employing a variety of techniques stemming from measurement approaches, the next chapter reports the results of two experiments which focus on the nature of the asymmetry. Is the asymmetry the result of different attitudes being measured, or of similar attitudes being mapped differently onto the answering scales?

Chapter 4

ATTITUDE RETRIEVAL VERSUS
MAPPING AN ANSWER[1]

4.0 INTRODUCTION

From the analyses conducted in Chapter 3 it can be concluded that the use of 'forbid' and 'allow' has a general effect on answers, although the asymmetry obtained varies greatly across questions. Overall, more negative answers are obtained for forbid questions than affirmative answers for the allow questions, despite the fact that forbid/allow, as well as 'yes' and 'no', are counterparts. An explanation of this wording effect is therefore called for.

This is not only necessary to generate practical advice for questionnaire designers, which is the traditional goal of wording-effect research (Billiet, 1989). Equally important is the more fundamental goal of gaining insight into the cognitive processes underlying question-answering and the variables that affect responses (Cicourel, 1982). What is more, this latter goal has to be fulfilled before recommendations for questionnaire designers can be formulated. An understanding of exactly how wording variation causes differences in responses, and in precisely what respect two seemingly equivalent questions measure something different, is a prerequisite for judging the validity of survey questions.

Two general explanations for the forbid/allow asymmetry have been offered in the literature. The most general explanation is the *connotations hypothesis*, which focuses on the extreme connotations of both 'forbid' and 'allow': "the former sounds harsher and may therefore be more difficult to endorse, whereas the latter in some contexts might seem to encourage a deviant behavior and therefore may invite opposition" (Schuman & Presser, 1981:296). A second explanation takes the form of a specification of this hypothesis and concentrates on the answering behaviour of indifferent respondents. Due to the extreme connotations of 'forbid' and 'allow', those respondents holding weak attitudes may be particularly unlikely to endorse either the 'forbid' or the 'allow' statement, responding 'no' to both question forms (Hippler & Schwarz, 1986). This *indifferent respondent hypothesis* predicts that the forbid/allow asymmetry is primarily due to indifferent or ambivalent respondents, and should not be obtained for respondents holding a definite opinion for or against. Results of the experiments by Hippler & Schwarz (1986) and Waterplas et al. (1988) are consistent with this explanation: when subjects with a weak or indifferent attitude towards the issue were removed from the

---

[1] A slightly adapted version of this chapter appeared in *Sociological Methods and Research* (1999). Results were also presented at the Fourth International Conference of Social Science Methodology (1996).

sample, the wording effect disappeared. However, Krosnick & Schuman (1988) used other measures for attitude strength (certainty and intensity of the opinions) and did not find the expected relationship between attitude strength and the answering behaviour (Section 2.1.4).

As discussed in Chapter 2, both hypotheses are promising, but do entail some problems. The indifferent respondents hypothesis may be the result of premature isolation of one characteristic from the communication process. It focuses exclusively on respondent characteristics, whereas it is just as likely that other characteristics relating to the communicative task of question-answering may at least influence the asymmetry size. On the other hand, the focus on attitude strength relates directly to the extreme connotations that 'forbid' and 'allow' are supposed to carry. As a logical extension of the connotations hypothesis, the indifferent respondents hypothesis might indeed go a long way towards explaining the variation in the asymmetry sizes obtained. By building on the connotations hypothesis, however, the indifferent respondents hypothesis also has to deal with the same problem as the connotations hypothesis: it does not provide any real insight into the cognitive mechanisms underlying the asymmetry, thereby remaining a retrospective explanation rather than a testable hypothesis. Nevertheless, the connotations hypothesis can be transformed into a testable theory by relating it to the general cognitive framework of the question-answering process. This will also provide opportunities to address the validity issue that is relevant to the practice of survey design (see Section 2.2.1).

Generally speaking, the question-answering process can be divided into four stages (Section 1.3.1): interpretation of the question, location of the relevant attitude structure, retrieval of the attitude (or formation of the attitude), and mapping the judgement onto one of the precoded answering categories (Tourangeau, 1987; Tourangeau & Rasinski, 1988; Sudman, Bradburn & Schwarz, 1996). The connotations hypothesis does not explicitly state whether the difference between forbid/allow answers has its roots in the first two stages of the question-answering process (during attitude localization and retrieval or formation) or whether similar attitudes are being measured and the asymmetry stems from the last stage, in which the opinion is mapped onto the answering options 'yes' or 'no'.

According to Krosnick & Schuman (1988), research on attitudes and response effects suggests a number of reasons why reported attitudes can be 'distorted' by response effects. One possible approach is to view response effects as a result of slight changes in perceptions of the meanings of the answering options. These changes presumably lead respondents to map their attitudes onto the response options in different ways. Hence, when answering a forbid/allow question on X-rated movies, a general attitude towards X-rated movies is formed or retrieved, similar for both the forbid and the allow question, but while mapping this evalua-tion onto the response options, the meaning of 'no' to 'forbid' comes to differ slightly from the meaning of 'yes' to 'allow' (and similarly for 'no' to 'allow' and 'yes' to 'forbid'). In this case, the connotations hypothesis means that similar attitudes are retrieved with forbid and allow questions, but that the perceived extremity of the response alternatives 'yes' and 'no' will vary depending on the use of either 'forbid' or 'allow'. The answering options 'yes' and 'no' should not be viewed as nominal scales then, but essentially as interval scales that differ from one another due to the use of forbid/allow. On a more general theoretical level, this could imply that question-answering is not necessarily a linear process in which respondents only begin to locate and retrieve an attitude once the question text as a whole has been fully represented during the first stage. Rather, it would suggest that some aspects of the question text are used to retrieve an attitude, whereas other aspects of the question text are used as a point of reference when expressing the evaluation.

A second possible explanation for the occurrence of response effects focuses on the clarity and accessibility of attitudinal cues in memory. "Some attitudes are characterized by clear, univocal and highly accessible cues in memory (e.g. Fazio, 1986), whereas others are associated with weak, ambiguous and inaccessible cues (e.g. Bem, 1972, Converse, 1970), or with heterogeneous, conflicting cues that must be integrated into a summary evaluation in a piecemeal fashion (e.g. Fiske & Pavelchak, 1986). If a respondent is faced with ambiguous, conflicting, or inacces-sible internal cues, an attitude question wording or context that emphasizes one point of view more than others might influence the respondent's perception of what his or her own attitude is (Bishop, Oldendick & Tuchfarber, 1984). In contrast, if one's internal cues are clear and accessible, question wording, form and context are unlikely to distort self-perceptions" (Krosnick & Schuman, 1988:941).[2] Should this second explanation of response effects prove to be valid for the forbid/allow asymmetry, this would mean that answers to forbid questions reflect different attitudes than answers to equivalent allow questions. The general connotations or semantic fields of 'forbid' and 'allow', may be so strong that not only the attitude towards a specific issue (e.g. X-rated movies) is retrieved, but also a general attitude towards forbidding (or allowing) things. Theoretically, this would imply that the process of question-answering is more linear: the linguistic input as a whole affects the tasks of attitude retrieval and rendering a judgement.

To sum up, the research question for the current chapter is whether the conno-tations hypothesis means that answers to forbid questions reflect different atti-

---

[2] According to Krosnick & Schuman response effects may also occur because aspects of question wording change respondents' attitudes. This may be the case when arguments for or against the issue are presented when posing attitude questions.

tudes from answers to equivalent allow questions. This will be called the *different attitudes hypothesis*. An alternative explanation for the forbid/allow asymmetry is that it results from slight changes in perceptions about the meanings of the response options for attitude questions. Krosnick & Schuman (1988:940) describe the asymmetry as being caused by differences in the way respondents map their answers onto the answering options due to the use of 'forbid' and 'allow': "[...] 'not allowing' is perceived as a less extreme stance than is 'forbidding'." This will be referred t as the *different scales hypothesis* (see Box 4.1).

This distinction between different attitudes being measured and similar attitudes being expressed differently in the response options, is not only important for a better understanding of the question-answering process, but it is relevant to the way questionnaires are designed as well. If forbid/allow questions measure different attitudes, they differ in validity and either or both may not measure what the researcher intends to measure. However, if forbid/allow questions measure a similar attitude, they are equally valid, even though the answers to the questions differ. In that case, the questionnaire designer's problem is how to translate the yes/no answers back into the true attitude correctly.

If applied to the stages in the question-answering process, the connotations hypothesis (Schuman & Presser, 1981) results in two competing hypotheses:
- different attitudes hypothesis: the use of forbid/allow in attitude questions causes respondents to retrieve or form different attitudes, not only towards issue X, but also towards forbidding (or allowing) in general
- different scales hypothesis: the use of forbid/allow in attitude questions does not influence the attitudes that are retrieved, but causes the attitudes to be expressed differently on the answering scales due to the use of forbid/allow.

Box 4.1: *Two competing hypotheses following from the 'connotations hypothesis'*

The vague nature of the connotations hypothesis means that the indifferent respondents hypothesis is also vague, as the latter is based on the former. Hence, it is first necessary to establish which version (if either) of the connotation hypothesis is correct: the *different attitudes hypothesis* or the *different scales hypothesis*. As will be discussed in the next section, psychometric criteria can be developed to test both hypotheses. Only when an understanding of the exact nature of the differences between forbid/allow answers is obtained, can the important issue of how the answers to forbid and allow questions differ for the subgroup of 'indifferent respondents' be addressed.

First of all, the different attitudes hypothesis and the different scales hypothesis have to be tested. The next sections will discuss why it is not possible to use a traditional split ballot design for this purpose. The test can be performed, however, using a more complex correlational design in which the data are analysed using the psychometric concept of 'congenericity'. Section 4.1 discusses the technical details of this design. Section 4.2 sketches the general procedure of the experiments that were conducted, as well as the planned analyses. An outline of the latter will take up quite some space, as various models have to be fitted to the data in order to test the hypotheses. In Section 4.3, the results of the analyses are discussed. These will show that forbid/allow questions are congeneric, which means that the different attitudes hypothesis has to be rejected. The interpretation of the connotations hypothesis should be that forbid/allow questions measure similar attitudes, but that those similar attitudes are mapped differently onto the answering scales due to the use of forbid/allow. Based on this finding, Section 4.4 explores how the attitude strength hypothesis should be interpreted. Do forbid/allow questions measure different attitudes for respondents holding weaker attitudes? Or do these respondents encounter mapping problems as well? Section 4.5 provides a general conclusion and discussion of the findings presented in this chapter.

4.1 MEASUREMENT PROBLEMS AND SOLUTIONS

In order to obtain precise insight into the nature and cause of the forbid/allow asymmetry, a research design that allows for detection of the exact differences between responses has to be applied. Furthermore, it is important to use a research design that facilitates generalization beyond the level of the specific questions used in a particular experiment.

The research design that is generally used in forbid/allow research does not meet these two demands. A different approach, proposed by Andrews (1984), draws on correlational techniques and can therefore distinguish between differences in the attitudes being measured and differences between the answering scales. His 'multitrait-multimethod' design, however, still suffers from generalization problems. In the current section, the problems associated with traditional split ballot designs and with Andrews' approach will be discussed. This will be followed by the proposition of an experimental correlational design that can comply with both demands: one that makes a distinction between differences in attitudes and differences in the mapping stages, and combines this with increased generalizability (Section 4.1.1).

In all experiments on the forbid/allow asymmetry, a split ballot design is used to analyse on the basis of single questions. Although the comparison of response percentages or frequencies can determine whether a difference exists at some stage in the question-answering process, it does not detect whether differences between forbid/allow answers reflect differences in the attitudes measured or differences in the answering scales due to the use of 'forbid' or 'allow'. The simple comparison of the observed scores in traditional split ballot designs is based on two assumptions which are not necessarily true. The first assumption is that the answers to both questions are represented on identical scales, so that differences in observed scores are interpreted as differences in true scores, in other words as differences in attitudes. An alternative assumption is that the answers reflect similar attitudes, so that differences in observed scores are interpreted as differences in the meaning of the answering options. Such assumptions should be tested and not simply identified. The second assumption made when comparing observed scores is that the reliabilities (and error score components) of both questions are the same. This is not necessarily the case either.

The question of whether similar attitudes are being measured can only be answered by comparing the true scores to forbid/allow questions. But true score components and error score components cannot be distinguished when analysing single questions measured at only one time. Accordingly, a traditional split ballot is not the appropriate research design.

The solution is to opt for a correlational design. The distinction between differences in attitudes measured versus differences in the answering scales can then be made based on a distinction between error scores and true scores. A correlational design of this kind has been used by Andrews (1984), among others, and stems from psychometric theory. It is sometimes referred to as a 'measurement approach' to wording effects or a 'structural modelling approach'. His correlational design will be discussed here, as there are some parallels between his proposal and the design adopted in the current research. Both use the concept of *construct validity*.

4.1.1 Measurement approaches

Within psychometric theory, answers to survey questions are viewed as composite scores that partly reflect a latent construct: an observed score combines a true score and an error score component. For example, if 10 questions are constructed to measure the attitude towards sailing, the answers to those 10 questions each consist of a portion that reflects the 'true scores', the actual evaluation of sailing, and a portion of measurement error, due to characteristics of specific questions and not related to the general latent sailing concept. Measurement approaches try to distinguish between true scores, random measurement error and systematic measurement error (the latter being an aspect of the true score). In other words, measurement approaches try to separate theoretical parameters (the content or true score being measured) from the measurement problems.

Within this structural modelling approach, research focuses on measurement error and not directly on effects. Furthermore, the focus is not on univariate distributions, but on the associations between several items: hence a correlational design. Ideally it would be possible to divide the total variance into three components for each answer obtained: valid variance, correlated error variance and random error variance. This would make it possible to ascertain the extent to which the true bivariate relationships (i.e. the relations between the concepts being investigated) are attenuated because of random measurement error and/or inflated because of correlated measurement error (Andrews, 1984: 410). In this approach, validity refers to *construct validity*, the extent to which an observed score or combination of scores reflects the underlying theoretical construct that the investigator intended to measure (Cronbach & Meehl, 1955). *Correlated measurement error* refers to deviations from the true scores on one measure (the scores that reflect the construct to be measured, i.e. the observed scores minus measurement error) which are related to deviations in another measure being concurrently analysed. For example, if 10 questions are posed about happiness, 5 of which are worded as questions and 5 as assertions, then a correlated error between the 5 assertions might be found, indicating that the question form leads to a systematic error or method effect. *Random measurement error* refers to deviations from the true scores that are unrelated to deviations in any other measure being analysed concurrently. This part of the score is not related to the 'happiness' concept as a whole, nor is it related to the method, and must therefore be related to characteristics of a specific question.

The concept of construct validity only means something if the items can be seen as indicators of a theoretical construct that is not measured directly (a latent variable) and if there is a theoretical model that contains hypotheses about the way these theoretical concepts relate to each other. Within Andrews' approach, the multitrait-multimethod data matrix (Campbell & Fiske, 1959) provides a basis for estimating the true correlations between latent variables assumed within the theoretical model. Furthermore the assumption is that the convergent validity is larger than the discriminant validity: correlations between different measures (several items) of the same variable (happiness) are larger than associations between similar measures (assertions) of different variables (happiness and health). It is also assumed that similar measures which vary due to the response effect under study, correlate as a result of correlated error and do not reflect 'true' correlations (Billiet, 1989).

The correlational design outlined here was proposed and used by Andrews. This resulted in recommendations on the number of answering options, the inclusion of an explicit 'don't know' option and so forth. Based on this design, Saris (1990) set up an international research project along similar lines. Outside of a survey context within the field of test research, Van den Bergh, Eiting & Otter

(1988) estimated the effects of open questions versus closed questions in science and geography exams at secondary schools. In wording effects research, measurement approaches are scarce and research questions or outcomes from measurement approaches have not been connected to insights or research questions stemming from cognitive frameworks. The research presented in this chapter aims to bridge this gap.

Measurement approaches permit the exact detection of differences between responses, whereas split ballot designs that analyse single questions cannot distinguish between true scores and error scores. The specific multitrait-multimethod design Andrews proposed can make this distinction, but it fails to provide an adequate solution to generalization problems as it focuses largely on single questions. This research combines these techniques in order to develop a design that complies both with the demand of generalizability and cognitive precision. It uses split ballot designs analysing several questions instead of single questions and employs correlational techniques.

A correlational design based on the concept of construct validity will be used. This is similar to the approach proposed by Andrews. It is basically a split ballot design consisting of several questions that measure one underlying content variable. One half of the group of respondents answers this set of questions in an allow version, the other answers them in a forbid version. The answers to the forbid/allow questions are not compared one by one but all at the same time. The result is a correlational split ballot design that can test the competing hypotheses formulated in this chapter, and that also goes a long way towards solving the generalization problem.

Two competing hypotheses are tested in the current chapter: the different attitudes hypothesis and the different scales hypothesis. The hypothesis concerning the difference in attitudes measured relates directly to the concept of *congenericity* (Jöreskog, 1971). Two tests or items are congeneric if they measure the same trait, irrespective of errors of measurement. In other words, two items are considered to be congeneric if the correlation coefficient between the true scores of those items equals unity (equals 1.0). The *different attitudes hypothesis* would be confirmed if forbid and allow questions are noncongeneric. If this is the case, the different scales hypothesis would have to be rejected because this hypothesis states that forbid/allow questions measure similar attitudes that are expressed differently on the answering scales due to the use of forbid/allow.

Conversely, if forbid and allow questions correlate unity (are congeneric), they do measure similar attitudes. In this case, the different attitudes hypothesis would have to be rejected. If the forbid and allow questions correlate unity but the observed scores to forbid and allow questions differ, the *different scales hypothesis* would be confirmed, indicating that an equivalent opinion is expressed differently on the answering scale, probably because the two verbs carry extreme connotations. In this case, it can be concluded that the answering scales to forbid/allow questions are dissimilar interval scales. The answering scales can differ in various ways: the midpoints of the scales can differ, or the midpoints to the scales can differ as well as the distances between the intervals. This has to do with differences in true scores and differences in error scores to forbid/allow questions and will be discussed in greater detail in Section 4.2.2.

This completes the outline of the research design needed in order to test the hypotheses formulated in this chapter. In the end it all revolves around the psychometric concept of congenericity. The next section discusses how the correlational measure needed to test the congenericity of forbid/allow questions can be obtained.

4.1.2 An experimental correlational design

The most important hypothesis in this research is the different attitudes hypothesis, which focuses on the congenericity of forbid/allow questions. The other hypothesis can only gain in importance if it turns out that forbid/allow questions measure the same trait. Only then does the concept of differences in scales between forbid and allow questions become meaningful.

In order to establish the congenericity of forbid/allow questions, a correlational measure between 'forbid' and 'allow' has to be obtained, corrected for random error. As discussed in the previous section, this can be achieved using the concept of construct validity, which requires the construction of a questionnaire that consists of several questions. If a cluster of questions measuring one underlying construct (the attitude towards abortion, for example) is constructed in a forbid version and in an allow version, the random error inherent in the specific question content can be distinguished by computing the reliabilities of each question within its forbid or allow factor respectively. Subsequently, the correlational measure between the 'forbid abortion' factor and the 'allow abortion' factor can be computed, indicating congenericity when the correlation is unity.[3]

The correlational measure needed in order to test congenericity of forbid and allow questions is most easily obtained by posing one cluster of forbid questions and an equivalent cluster of allow questions to the same sample of respondents. However, this design faces two classical validity problems: memory effects and time effects. If the forbid and allow cluster are posed at the same point in time,

---

[3] As discussed in the previous section, this design solves generalization problems to some extent, because it achieves variation in question wording (apart from the manipulation on forbid/allow) and in the nature of the subissues addressed in each question.

the correlational measure can be inflated by memory effects. On the other hand, if forbid and allow questions are posed at different times it is impossible to determine whether low correlations should be attributed to attitude change or to the wording effect.

A solution to these problems is to apply a design that allows the congenericity of forbid and allow questions to be tested at the same point in time and avoids memory effects by including several groups of respondents. In addition, the design can be extended to measure congenericity over time, using the correlation between similarly worded clusters as a measurement of time effects. This would then allow time effects influencing the correlational measure between differently worded clusters to be interpreted. To this end, Jöreskog's concept of congenericity has to be generalized to an experimental correlational design involving several groups (Van den Bergh, Eiting & Otter, 1988; Van den Bergh, 1990).

Congenericity means that a forbid factor and an allow factor correlate unity. If forbid and allow questions are congeneric, it follows that the correlation between two allow factors should equal the correlation between two forbid factors. This inference can be used to construct a design in which the congenericity between forbid and allow questions is tested while avoiding interference from time or memory effects. Note however, that the reverse is not necessarily true. If the correlations are similar, this would mean that the congenericity hypothesis for allow and forbid questions cannot be rejected, but it does not automatically imply congenericity.

A more direct test of congenericity can be obtained by comparing correlations between forbid and allow questions over time. However, it is not very likely that unity correlations will be found in such a case. Although congenericity refers to a unity correlation of true scores, this by no means implies that a respondent's attitude cannot change over time. If congenericity is tested over two consecutive measurement occasions, the definition of congenericity should be relaxed to some extent. Instead of looking for a unity correlation between a cluster of forbid questions posed at one time of measurement and a cluster of equivalent allow questions at a different time of measurement (i.e. an 'absolute' definition of congenericity), a 'relative' definition of congenericity can be established. Two sets of forbid and allow questions answered on different occasions can be defined as congeneric if the correlations between forbid and allow questions (and between allow and forbid questions, for that matter) equal the correlation between allow and allow questions (and between forbid and forbid questions). The correlation between two successive measurements using different question wordings does not differ from the correlation between two successive measurements using similar question wordings. Or, to put it differently, the question wording does not influence the magnitude of the relation over time.

In this study, the test on congenericity within time will be combined with the comparison over time. The test on congenericity within time will be used to answer the basic question asked by wording effect researchers: do forbid and allow measure the same attitude? If forbid and allow questions prove to be congeneric, then the test on congenericity within time will give a *strong indication* for that congenericity and in that case it is unnecessary to compare correlations over time to obtain further evidence. If forbid and allow questions are noncongeneric, then the test on congenericity within time will give direct *statistical falsification* of congenericity. In that case, a comparison of correlations between forbid and allow over time with correlations between questions that were formulated similarly at T1 and T2, will provide a touchstone for evaluating the size of the effect. If the effect of the use of 'forbid' and 'allow' is smaller than the time effect found, then the wording effect might be evaluated as not very important or meaningful for questionnaire designers, in spite of the statistical evidence for the effect provided by the test on congenericity within time. Another advantage of combining these two measures of congenericity is that congenericity within time can be tested twice within this design, at both times of measurement separately, thereby providing a replication of the method effect.

4.1.3 Summarizing the goals of the two experiments

The first goal of this research is to test whether forbid and allow questions measure the same attitudes. This question of congenericity will be tested using the correlational design outlined in the previous section. This provides a direct test of the *different attitudes hypothesis*, an explanation of the forbid/allow asymmetry which predicts that 'forbid' and 'allow' are noncongeneric for all respondents.

If 'forbid' and 'allow' prove to be congeneric and yet the observed scores differ, the *different scales hypothesis* is confirmed. Further analyses will show whether differences in the observed scores on forbid and allow questions can be attributed to consistent differences between the answering scales. If this is the case, explanations of those differences can and should be formulated. This is where the extremity of the connotations may become relevant.

The *indifferent respondents hypothesis* will also be explored. This hypothesis predicts that forbid and allow questions are congeneric for respondents with stronger attitudes, but noncongeneric for respondents who are indifferent towards the issue. This exploration will also provide an additional check on the congenericity of forbid and allow questions, to be discussed in Section 4.4.

4.2 QUESTIONNAIRES, PROCEDURES AND DESIGN

For both experiments a written self-administered questionnaire was developed containing several questions formulated with either 'forbid' or 'allow', separated by fillers about related issues in order to obscure the research goals for the respondents. Most of this has already been outlined in Section 3.1.

The subject of the questionnaire in *Experiment 1* was 'Nature and Environmental Issues'. The questionnaire contained 36 questions: 12 questions about whether practices relating to the environment or nature policy should be forbidden (Version 1) or allowed (Version 2); 13 fillers on related subjects but without the verbs 'forbid' or 'allow' and 11 questions measuring attitude strength at the end of the questionnaire. None of the practices included were subject to any kind of ban at the time the questions were posed.

The questionnaire developed for *Experiment 2* dealt with matters of public opinion on the subject 'Ethnic Groups'. The questionnaire consisted of 12 questions about whether practices related to discrimination and integrational issues should be allowed (Version 1) or forbidden (Version 2). Again issues were selected from Dutch newspaper discussions, television debates and policy papers. In contrast to Experiment 1, all the questions concerned practices which were forbidden at the time the questionnaire was administered. There were 12 fillers on related issues and 8 questions measuring attitude strength at the end of the questionnaire. The exact wording of the forbid/allow questions used in the two experiments was presented in Table 3.1[4]. The questions measuring attitude strength will be discussed jointly with the results concerning attitude strength (Section 4.4).

4.2.1 Procedures and design

The two experiments were carried out simultaneously. The questionnaires were administered twice to the same students of languages and the arts, with a four week interval between the first and the second time of administration. The length of time between the first and the second measurement was set in order to diminish memory effects as much as possible. The procedure used has been described in detail in Section 3.1.1.

A total of 195 respondents filled in the questionnaire on both occasions and 136 students participated either at T1 or T2. Only subjects who filled in the

---

[4] Except for the questions that were excluded from the analyses because they turned out not to load on the theorized factors. This is discussed in Section 4.3. Appendix I contains the observed scores and exact wording for these questions.

questionnaire twice were included in the analysis, resulting in a four-group design with about 50 subjects per group (see Table 4.1).

gr	experiment 1				experiment 2				N = 195
	T 1		T 2		T 1		T2		
	EI	NP	EI	NP	DM	IG	DM	IG	
I	F	F	F	F	A	A	A	A	47
II	F	F	A	A	A	A	F	F	55
III	A	A	F	F	F	F	A	A	49
IV	A	A	A	A	F	F	F	F	44

<u>Note</u>: *gr*=group number, *EI*=Environmental Issues, *NP*=Nature Policies, *DM*=Discrimination, *IG*= Integration, *N*=number of respondents in each condition, *F*= forbid, *A*= Allow

Table 4.1: *Conditions and the number of respondents per condition*

In each experiment this four-group design will be applied to assess whether 'forbid' and 'allow' are congeneric, and, if so, to identify the aspects which cause the observed scores to forbid and allow questions to differ.

Two experiments were conducted on two separate occasions. The second time of measurement provides a replication of the first, as similar questionnaires were administered to the same group of respondents. Both experiments applied the same research design and method, but the manipulated questions were on different issues. Converging results from both experiments and both times of measurement will support generalizability of the findings.

The method of analysis employed was a structural modelling approach (using LISREL). Models are constructed in which all the variables and relations among them are defined, allowing a statistical test of hypothesized relations between variables (Jöreskog & Sörbom, 1986; Bollen, 1989). Under the assumption of a multivariate normal distribution, maximum-likelihood parameter estimates can be calculated, which are then compared to the observed data. If the difference between the observed data and the computed estimates is small, the model fits the data. The fit of the model is expressed as a likelihood ratio, which is approximately χ^2 distributed. This χ^2 measure, combined with the number of degrees of freedom, can be used as a measure of relative fit compared to the other models (Jöreskog & Sörbom, 1986).

Several models are fitted to the data, all of which are nested within each other. The first model is extremely restrictive, the last model hardly puts any restrictions upon relations between variables within the data set. The strictest model (the parallel model) implies that there are no differences in either means, true score variances or error score variances[5] between forbid and allow questions. If this model fits the data best, there is no wording effect due to the use of 'forbid' and 'allow'. The least restrictive (noncongeneric) model describes forbid and allow questions as measuring underlying constructs, which differ to some extent at least. In this model all aspects of the scores to forbid and allow questions are allowed to differ. If this model fits the data best the different attitudes hypothesis is accepted. The three models between the most and least restrictive ones imply that the different scales hypothesis is true, each offering a more refined step-by-step definition of how exactly the scales for forbid/allow questions differ. This will be explained in the next section. For now it is important to note that the differences between the answers to forbid and allow questions can be analysed step-by-step by fitting these 5 nested models.

4.2.2 Planned analyses: congenericity

The planned analyses for both experiments consist of three steps. Firstly, descriptive analyses will be conducted per cluster of questions: Environmental Issues (EI) and Nature Policies (NP) in Experiment 1; Discrimination (DM) and Integration (IG) in Experiment 2. This is done in order to check whether the key phenomenon was replicated and whether a construct, an underlying attitude, has indeed been measured by a set of forbid questions and a set of allow questions. The next stage is to fit the models onto the data obtained in each experiment. This is done to answer the question of whether forbid/allow questions are congeneric, and if so, how the answering scales for these questions differ due to the use of forbid/allow. The fit of a model can be evaluated by means of a χ^2 testing statistic. The fit of two nested models is compared by means of the differences in χ^2 in relation to differences in the number of degrees of freedom. The aim of this kind of structural modelling approach is to describe the actual data with the maximum number of restrictions (i.e. with the minimum of parameters), because it is this model that describes the data with the highest degree of economy and accuracy. Finally, an exploratory analysis focusing on the answering behaviour of indifferent respondents will be conducted, providing an additional check on the congenericity of 'forbid' and 'allow'. As the analyses do not differ between the two experiments, this section describes the method of analysis for both experiments simultaneously.

---

[5] As the focus is not on individuals but on groups of people, analysis is done for error score and true score *variances*, instead of for the actual component of error score or true score.

All of the examples given here are taken from Experiment 1 but can easily be applied to Experiment 2.

Firstly, reliabilities will be computed for both clusters of questions (EI and NP) in each version to check whether the questions do indeed measure an attitude related to the subjects dealt with in 'Environmental Issues' or 'Nature Policies'. This is necessary in order to make a distinction between true scores and measurement error (see Section 4.1). If a question in both the forbid and allow version does not load on the theorized factor, the item will be excluded from further analysis. Secondly, in order to gain some insight into the degree to which the results of these two experiments are comparable with the asymmetries found in previous forbid/allow experiments, a series of split ballot analyses (of each question, for each time of measurement) was carried out (see Section 3.1.2). Thirdly, covariance matrices will be computed for each group in each experiment containing the covariances of the observed scores[6] obtained at T1 and T2. These four covariance matrices per experiment form the input for testing the two competing hypotheses. The four matrices will be analysed simultaneously for each experiment using LISREL models for multi-sample analysis (Jöreskog & Sörbom, 1986).

The models will be analysed one after another, each nested within the other. In each successive model one restriction is relaxed. All models are defined beforehand to avoid the risk of models being changed during analysis according to the results obtained. The models contain restrictions for the relations between clusters of questions (EI and NP), as well as the relations between questions and the content variable they reflect (the true score variances and error score variances for the questions). These relations are modelled within time as well as over time (between T1 and T2), resulting in 25 (5 x 5) models.

The randomization procedure used means there is no reason to assume that characteristics of answers to similarly worded questions on the same issue should differ between groups. Two invariant restrictions therefore apply to all identically formulated questions on the same issue (either forbid or allow) and administered at the same time: the regression of observed scores on true scores ($\lambda^s_{i,j}$) is the same and the error score variances ($\theta_{\epsilon}{}^s_{i,i}$) are the same. A similar restriction holds for the correlations between the factors: the correlations between the clusters have to be the same if they were administered in the same version at the same time (for example, $\psi^1_{2,1} = \psi^2_{2,1}$). Furthermore, the factor variance is required to be the same for all groups and for all factors, in order to be able to compare the

---

[6] The observed scores of the forbid questions are reversed in order to facilitate comparison between forbid and allow answers.

value for $\lambda^s_{i,j}$. Without loss of generalizability the true score variances can be standardized to unity ($\psi^s_{j,j}=1$) (Van den Bergh & Eiting, 1989).[7]

These invariant restrictions for λ, θ_ϵ and ψ are theoretical assumptions about the relations between variables that hold for all 25 models and will not be tested. Next to these invariant restrictions, variable restrictions are defined, which will be described in the following section. Readers are also referred to Figure 4.1 for a visual presentation of the design and the models.

The variable restrictions are used to test hypotheses about the possible differences between answers to forbid and allow questions. For each experiment 25 models are specified, all containing restrictions within time and over time. The restrictions within time are the most important, because it is by these restrictions that the exact differences between forbid/allow questions can be analysed without a complicating time factor. The various restrictions within time result in 5 models that are nested within one another. The restrictions over time are each nested within those 5 models, resulting in a total of 25 models. The 5 models containing restrictions within time will first be described, followed by the 5 models containing restrictions over time.

Restrictions within time

Five different models restricting relations within time are specified. If the first model (the parallel model) fits the data best, then no wording effect is present. If the last model (the noncongeneric model) fits the data best, the different attitudes hypothesis is confirmed. Should the second, third or fourth model fit the data best, this means that the different scales hypothesis is confirmed. The second, third and fourth models indicate exactly how the answering scales to forbid/allow questions differ. The answering scales can differ in a number of ways, but whatever the difference, 'forbid' and 'allow' are still congeneric.

The first model is a parallel model. *Parallelism* within time (Ia-Ie) implies the following restrictions (within and across groups): correlations (ψ) for a given time of measurement (at T1 and at T2) between factors (EI and NP) are the same in all groups, independent of the wording of the questions; the regression of observed scores on true scores (λ) is the same for all equivalent EI questions and for all equivalent NP questions, independent of the wording; error score variances (θ_ϵ) are the same for all similar questions independent of the wording of the questions; and mean scores for all equivalent EI questions and all NP questions are the same, independent of the question wording. If one of the parallel models within

---

[7] If the factor variance differs between groups or factors, these differences will be reflected in differences between the true score variances due to this restriction on the factor variances.

time fits the data best, this means there is no difference at all between forbid and allow questions.[8]

The *essential tau-equivalent* model within time (IIa-IIe) does away with the restriction that the mean scores have to be the same for equivalent EI or NP questions that are worded differently. If a model of this kind fits the data best, question means differ at one time of measurement, but all other aspects of the score are equal. This means that the wording of the questions causes a difference in scales: the same attitude is measured with forbid and allow questions, leading to the same true score and error score variance but the attitude is expressed on a different scale due to the question wording. The answering scale to forbid and allow questions should not be viewed as a scale on which 'yes' means 'yes' and 'no' means 'no', but essentially as an *interval scale* with different psychological scale midpoints due to the question wording. If one of these essential tau-equivalent models fits best, this would support the *different scales hypothesis*. Further analysis of the means should indicate whether there are consistent patterns in the scale differences for forbid and allow questions.

The *tau-equivalent* model within time (IIIa-IIIe) does away with the restriction that error score variances (θ_ε) have to be the same for questions that are worded differently at the same point in time. If this type of model fits best, differences in means for forbid and allow questions are caused by differences in the scale point that is chosen to express similar attitudes, as in the essential tau-equivalent model. In addition, differences in error score variances show that the perceived width of the scale differs due to the use of 'forbid' and 'allow': the cognitive distance between 'yes' and 'no' to forbid questions is different from the distance between 'yes' and 'no' to allow questions.

In the *congeneric* model within time (IVa-IVe) all restrictions on question level are done away with, apart from the invariant restrictions. Only the restrictions for ψ remain: correlations between EI and NP are required to be the same across groups. If a model of this kind fits best, this too is an indication that forbid and allow questions measure the same underlying construct: the same attitude is measured with forbid and allow questions at one time of measurement. In this case, however, not only do the means and the error score variances differ, but so do the true score variances. If tau-equivalent or congeneric models fit the data best and consistent patterns can be found between the differences in true score variances and error score variances, explanations should focus on the differences in reliabilities between forbid and allow questions.

---

[8] In fact, in split ballot designs the parallel model is compared to all other models in one go.

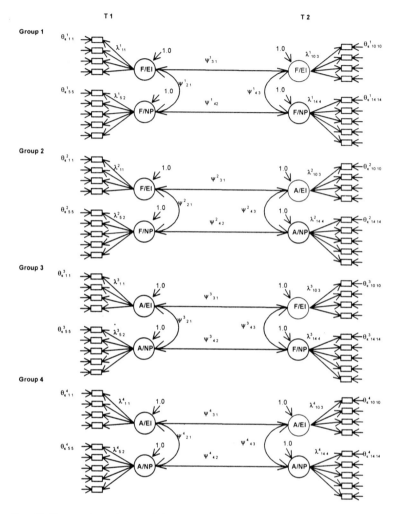

Note: To illustrate the variant restrictions of the models, model restrictions for the essential tau-equivalent model within time and the noncongeneric model over time are:

ess.tau-equivalent within time: $\theta_{\varepsilon}^1{}_{11}$ to $\theta_{\varepsilon}^1{}_{99} = \theta_{\varepsilon}^2{}_{11}$ to $\theta_{\varepsilon}^2{}_{99} = \theta_{\varepsilon}^3{}_{11}$ to $\theta_{\varepsilon}^3{}_{99} = \theta_{\varepsilon}^4{}_{11}$ to $\theta_{\varepsilon}^4{}_{99}$
and $\theta_{\varepsilon}^1{}_{10\,10}$ to $\theta_{\varepsilon}^1{}_{18\,18} = \theta_{\varepsilon}^2{}_{10\,10}$ to $\theta_{\varepsilon}^2{}_{18\,18} = \theta_{\varepsilon}^3{}_{10\,10}$ to $\theta_{\varepsilon}^3{}_{18\,18} = \theta_{\varepsilon}^4{}_{10\,10}$ to $\theta_{\varepsilon}^4{}_{18\,18}$
And as the models are nested within each other, the restrictions from less restrictive models apply for this model as well:
tau-equivalent: $\lambda^1{}_{11}$ to $\lambda^1{}_{9\,2} = \lambda^2{}_{11}$ to $\lambda^2{}_{9\,2} = \lambda^3{}_{11}$ to $\lambda^3{}_{9\,2} = \lambda^4{}_{11}$ to $\lambda^4{}_{9\,2}$
and $\lambda^1{}_{10\,3}$ to $\lambda^1{}_{18\,4} = \lambda^2{}_{10\,3}$ to $\lambda^2{}_{18\,4} = \lambda^3{}_{10\,3}$ to $\lambda^3{}_{18\,4} = \lambda^4{}_{10\,3}$ to $\lambda^4{}_{18\,4}$
congeneric: $\psi^1{}_{21} = \psi^2{}_{21} = \psi^3{}_{21} = \psi^4{}_{21}$ and $\psi^1{}_{43} = \psi^2{}_{43} = \psi^3{}_{43} = \psi^4{}_{43}$

Figure 4.1: *The research design and some models*

Differences in true score variances also support the different scales hypothesis. Not only do the psychological midpoints to the scales differ, but the distances between intervals also differ due to the question wording.

In the *noncongeneric* model within time (Va-Ve) all variable restrictions for one point in time are lifted, even the restrictions for ψ. If a model of this type fits best, this means that forbid and allow questions measure a different attitude, to some extent at least. If this is the case, there is no use in comparing the means or other score characteristics for one time of measurement, as it would be like comparing apples and oranges. If one of the noncongeneric models fits best, this supports the *different attitudes hypothesis*.

Restrictions over time

The restrictions over time are defined by the same types of models. In *parallel* models (a) all aspects of the scores are the same over time: answers to equivalent EI questions have the same mean scores, error score variances and true score variances, irrespective of wording and independent of time (the same applies to all NP factors). Furthermore, correlations between EI and NP factors at T1 are similar to those correlations at T2, and correlations between EI (or NP) at T1 and EI (or NP) at T2 are similar between groups. If a parallel model over time fits the data best, there is no attitude change over time. Nor is there any difference in the answers to forbid and allow questions over time: answers obtained at T1 and T2 are exactly the same, irrespective of the similarity or difference in question wording at each time of measurement. In *essential tau-equivalent* models (b) error score variances do not have to be the same over time for equivalent questions, worded differently or similarly. In *tau-equivalent* models (c) restrictions for λ are relaxed. In *congeneric models* (d) only the correlations between EI and NP are required to be the same over time; in *noncongeneric* models (e) there are no restrictions over time, as restrictions for ψ are relaxed as well.

Note that the restrictions over time make no distinction between similarly worded questions at T1 and T2 (Group I and IV) and questions that were worded differently at T1 and at T2 (Group II and III). This implies that the model that fits best over time not only says something about the relation between forbid and allow over time, but also about the relation between similarly worded questions over time. If a parallel model over time fits the data best, this means two things: there is no difference between forbid and allow, and there is no attitude change due to the time interval. If a noncongeneric model fits the data best over time, this could either mean that forbid and allow are noncongeneric, or that all questions (those worded similarly and those worded differently) are noncongeneric due to attitude change over time.

4.3 RESULTS

Two questions in *Experiment 1* did not measure 'Environmental Issues' reliably in both the forbid and the allow version and were excluded from further analysis. This results in an EI factor consisting of four questions. Similarly, one question did not load very well on the theorized factor 'Nature Policies', resulting in a NP factor consisting of 5 questions[9]. In *Experiment 2*, both theorized factors contained two questions that did not load very well in both versions. These questions were excluded, resulting in a 'Discrimination' factor and an 'Integration' factor both consisting of four questions.[10]

For each question posed at T1 or T2 a separate split ballot analysis was conducted, resulting in 18 split ballot analyses for Experiment 1, and 16 split ballots for Experiment 2. These analyses indicate that the forbid/allow asymmetry does exist in the present data. The key phenomenon itself was replicated, although not for every question at each time of measurement (see Section 3.1.2).

The issue of whether the design used may have confounded the results was also explored, as it might have been the case that answering the questions for a second time increased attitude strength, causing smaller asymmetry sizes at T2. As already stated in Chapter 3, this was not the case. Both experiments showed an asymmetry at T1 as well as at T2. In Experiment 2 the asymmetry is smaller at T2 than at T1, in Experiment 1 it is the other way round (see Table 4.2).

experiment and time	cumulative percentage 'not forbid'	cumulative percentage 'yes allow'
experiment 1, T1	393.1%	368.8%
experiment 1, T2	393.2%	366.2%
experiment 1, totals	786.3%	735.0%
experiment 2, T1	288.8%	184.6%
experiment 2, T2	262.4%	183.0%
experiment 2, totals	551.2%	367.6%

Table 4.2: *Cumulative percentages of 'not forbid' and 'yes allow' answers per experiment per time*

---

[9] These questions were not included in Table 3.1. The question texts and the answering percentages obtained are included in Appendix I.

[10] Preliminary analyses showed that reliabilities of the questions were not very high in either experiment. This is discussed further in Note 12 and in Section 4.5.

In addition to these preliminary analyses, the models described in the previous sections were fitted to the resulting data set.

4.3.1 Model fitting: congenericity over time

Since the models are nested within each other, model fit is compared by keeping one restriction constant, either over time or within time. In this case, the logical step is to first keep restrictions within time constant, as these are the most important in relation to the research goals. As will be discussed in the next subsection, within time forbid/allow questions prove to be at least congeneric. Accordingly, Table 4.3 contains fittings of the congeneric model within time for both experiments, while restrictions over time are varied in submodels. The fit of each model is described with a χ^2 testing statistic, while model fits are compared by looking for the model with the lowest ratio of χ^2 and degrees of freedom: the aim is to find the model that describes that data with the maximum amount of restrictions.[11]

mo-del	restrictions		experiment 1			experiment 2		
	within time	over time	df	χ^2	comparison result	df	χ^2	comparison result
IVb	con	ess-tau	636	999.02	IVb-IVc: p=.014	501	721.02	IVb-IVc: p<.001
IVc	con	tau	591	930.71	IVc-IVd: p=.524	461	644.08	IVc-IVd: p=.093
IVd	con	con	573	913.72	IVc-IVe: p=.011	445	620.24	IVc-IVe: p=.001
IVe	con	noncon	558	876.27	**best fit: IVe**	430	583.13	**best fit: IVe**

***Table 4.3**: Comparison of models, restrictions over time varied*

Comparison of the model fits (applying a level of significance of .05) shows that the model that is noncongeneric over time fits the data best in both *Experiment 1*

---

[11] Not surprisingly, the parallel models turned out not to comply with this demand: the parallel models differ about 1000 χ^2 with a maximum of 70 df compared to less restrictive models (for example, the parallel-parallel model (Ia) in *Experiment 1* had 2649.98 χ^2 with 724 df; in *Experiment 2* it was 1543.15 χ^2 with 579 df), so a comparison of the fit for all parallel models (Ia-Ie, and all a-models) with the less restrictive models will not be reported in more detail here.

and *Experiment 2*. The model fits in Table 4.3 illustrate this for the model that is congeneric within time and noncongeneric over time: for Experiment 1, the model fit of Model IVb (the model that is congeneric within time and essential-tau equivalent over time) differs significantly from the fit of the less restrictive Model IVc. The less restrictive Model IVc should therefore be preferred over Model IVb. The fit of Model IVc does not differ from the fit of Model IVd, hence the most restrictive model is preferred. A comparison between this more restrictive Model IVc and the least restrictive Model IVe shows, however, that the fit of Model IVe is significantly better. Model IVe should therefore be regarded as fitting the data best.

Does the fact that the noncongeneric models fit better than the other models over time mean that 'forbid' and 'allow' are noncongeneric? Or does it mean that the attitudes towards the issues were generally subject to change over time, thereby affecting the correlational measures between 'forbid' and 'allow' measured at different times? This can be checked by comparing the correlation between questions that were worded similarly at both times ('forbid x' (or 'allow x') at T1 and 'forbid x' (or 'allow x') at T2) to questions that were worded differently at T1 and T2 (see Table 4.1). This criterion was not specified in the models, however, so the correlation matrices have to be examined in order to discover the exact meaning of noncongenericity.

For *Experiment 1*, correlations between factors over time are quite high. Correlations between Environmental Issues (EI) (or Nature Policies, NP) at T1 and EI (or NP) at T2 vary between .75 and unity. The lowest correlation between NP at T1 and NP at T2 is found in Group II (forbid at T1, allow at T2), but the lowest correlation between EI at T1 and EI at T2 is found in Group IV (.77), where respondents answered the allow version on both occasions. This means that differences in correlations cannot be attributed to wording.

This is even more clearly visible in *Experiment 2*, where the correlation between Integration (IG) at T1 and IG at T2 in Group IV (.64) and the correlation between Discrimination (DM) at T1 and DM at T2 in Group I (.66) are much lower than the correlations obtained in Group II and III (.72 for DM at T1 and DM at T2 in Group II, to .89 for the correlation between DM at T1 and DM at T2 in Group III), whereas Groups II and III were given different versions at T1 and T2, and Group I and IV answered either the forbid or the allow questions on both occasions.

It can therefore be concluded that the noncongenericity over time in both experiments is basically caused by instability of the attitudes measured and by instability of the relations between these attitudes (between EI and NP, and between IG and DM), independent of the wording that was used. The next section looks at whether congenericity is found within time. If 'forbid' and 'allow' turn out to be noncongeneric within time, the size of that wording effect can be evaluated by comparing it to the general time effect found.

4.3.2 Model fitting: congenericity within time

A way of measuring the congenericity of 'forbid' and 'allow' without a disturbing influence was built into this research, as its design anticipates the influence of time on the attitudes measured. Congenericity within time was operationalized by the restriction that the correlation between the two factors in each experiment (EI and NP in Experiment 1; DM and IG in Experiment 2) should be similarly independent of the wording of the questions in those factors. The fit of more restrictive models was of course also tested. These models are a refinement of the different scales hypothesis, requiring the true score variances to be similar for forbid and allow questions (tau-equivalent) and requiring the true score variances and error score variances to be equivalent (essential tau-equivalent). Table 4.4 shows the results of the analyses.

In *Experiment 1*, the essential tau-equivalent model fits the data best: forbid and allow questions are not only congeneric and measure similar attitudes, they also yield the same true and error score variances. This result was obtained for all questions included in this experiment, independent of the specific issue addressed in each equivalent forbid or allow question. The observed scores for equivalent forbid and allow questions differ, however. This implies that the answering scales for forbid and allow questions are interval scales with dissimilar midpoints – the psychological turning point between 'yes forbid' and 'not forbid' is different from the turning point between 'not allow' and 'yes allow'. Hence, the results of Experiment 1 support the different scales hypothesis of the forbid/allow asymmetry.

Experiment 2 was an almost exact replication of Experiment 1, apart from the different subject matter of the questions and the fact that the practices addressed in the questions were forbidden at the time the questionnaire was administered. Experiment 1 differs from Experiment 2 however in that the congeneric model fits the data best for Experiment 2 (see Table 4.4).[12]

---

[12] As can be seen in Table 4.4, none of the models fitted the data very well. Other indicators of model fit (not reported here) show the same. For Model IIe, which fitted best in *Experiment 1*, the GFI=.665 and the RMS=.090. For Model IVe, which fitted best in *Experiment 2*, the GFI=.721 and the RMS=.119. Lisrel parameter estimates show reasonably low values for lambda in both experiments. These weak factor loadings seem to be the main reason for the lack of fit.

This implies that the attitudes in this study have been measured unreliably. This is not a problem, however, because the goal of this research was not to develop questionnaires that measure attitudes towards 'Nature and Environmental Issues' or 'Ethnic Groups'. The goal was to investigate the differences in responses caused by differences in question wording,

Again forbid and allow measure similar attitudes, but in Experiment 2 the error score variances, true score variances and observed scores differ. Closer inspection of the parameter estimates (which are not reported here), however, indicated no systematic patterns in differences between the error score variances and true score variances for forbid and allow questions.

mo-del	restrictions		experiment 1			experiment 2		
	within time	over time	df	χ^2	comparis-on result	df	χ^2	comparis-on result
IIe	ess-tau	noncon	621	949.48	IIe-IIIe: p=.189	486	736.55	IIe-IIIe: p<.001
IIIe	tau	noncon	567	886.56	IIe-IVe: p=.178	438	621.70	IIIe-IVe: p<.001
IVe	con	noncon	558	876.27	IIe-Ve: p=.164	430	583.13	IVe-Ve: p=.104
Ve	non-con	noncon	552	869.08	**best fit: IIe**	424	572.61	**best fit: IVe**

Table 4.4: *Comparison of models, restrictions within time varied*

This shows that, in both Experiment 1 and Experiment 2, questions worded with 'forbid' or 'allow' are at least congeneric, because in both experiments the correlation between 'forbid x' and 'forbid y' is similar to the correlation between 'allow x' and 'allow y'. This is the case at both T1 and T2. Conceptually speaking, these results indicate that the equivalent questions worded differently (either with 'forbid' or 'allow') measure the same underlying construct. In other words, the hypothesis that equivalent questions worded differently measure the same underlying construct cannot be rejected. As a result the *different attitudes hypothesis* has to be rejected. It also means that it is not necessary to use the measure of congenericity over time as a touchstone for evaluating the effect size.

The results are ambivalent as to whether error score variances and true score variances differ for forbid and allow questions. They are similar in Experiment 1, but differ in Experiment 2, which may be an indication of issue dependency. However, the congenericity in Experiment 2 and the essential tau-equivalence in

---

by comparing *differences* in model fit. However, low reliabilities could influence the power of these analyses. The order of the fitted models and the fact that some models can indeed be rejected, it may be concluded that this lack of power is not a major problem for this study. Due to the bad model fit, however, caution is warranted in interpreting or comparing the parameter estimates.

Experiment 1 both indicate support for the *different scales hypothesis*. In Experiment 1 only the midpoints of the scales for forbid and allow differ, while in Experiment 2 the midpoints of the scales differ and the distances between the intervals are dissimilar. The results of Experiment 2 also indicate another problem, as the reliabilities of forbid and allow questions differ.

4.4 EXPLORATION: THE EFFECT OF ATTITUDE STRENGTH

So far, most of this chapter has been devoted to testing two competing hypotheses following on from the connotations hypothesis (Schuman & Presser, 1981). In the introduction to this chapter, another hypothesis was also mentioned: the *indifferent respondents hypothesis*. This hypothesis predicts that the forbid/allow asymmetry is primarily due to indifferent or ambivalent respondents and should not be obtained for respondents with a definite attitude for or against an issue.

As this indifferent respondents hypothesis is an extension of the connotations hypothesis, it can be reformulated into equivalent competing hypotheses. One possibility is that respondents holding weak opinions are more susceptible to superficial cues in the question than respondents holding stronger opinions, causing forbid/allow questions to measure different attitudes (towards the issue as well as towards forbidding/allowing) for the 'indifferents', while measuring similar attitudes for respondents holding stronger attitudes. The other, competing hypothesis, would be that 'indifferent respondents' are more prone to mapping problems than respondents holding stronger attitudes. A third hypothesis would be that indifference is not related to the wording effect at all.

As the focus of the experiments was on the congenericity of forbid/allow questions and not on the models specifying the way the answering scales to forbid/allow questions differ, it is difficult to test the 'different scales' version of the indifferent respondents hypothesis. This different scales hypothesis predicts that the 'indifferents' cause the larger part of the difference in scales and respondents holding stronger opinions do not. This cannot be tested here, because the moment a subgroup of respondents (the 'indifferents' in this case) is isolated from the other respondents, the variances are expected to change, thereby clouding a clear view of the difference in scales.[13] Nevertheless, the 'different attitudes' version of the indifferent respondents hypothesis will be tested in this section, as

---

[13] On the other hand: if attitude strength does turn out not to be related to the congenericity of forbid/allow, this suggests it should not to be related to the error score variances and true score variances either, for they can hardly be different for the 'indifferents' and the others, without affecting the congenericity of forbid/allow questions.

well as the competing hypothesis that there is no relation whatsoever between indifference and the wording effect.

Establishing the congenericity of forbid/allow questions for the subgroup 'indifferents' will not affect the finding of congenericity for the group of respondents as a whole. The experiments found that forbid and allow questions measure the same attitudes (are congeneric) for the whole group of respondents, but that the scales for forbid/allow questions are different. If forbid/allow questions are noncongeneric for the 'indifferents', then logically they should be noncongeneric for the sample as a whole, because the correlation coefficients for the subsample would influence the correlation coefficients for the whole sample. Hence, it would be an indication of power problems if forbid/allow questions should turn out to be noncongeneric for 'indifferents'. If, on the other hand, forbid/allow questions had been noncongeneric for the whole sample of respondents, it would have been interesting to test whether this was attributable to the answering behaviour of the indifferent respondents. In that case, forbid and allow questions might have been noncongeneric for the subgroup of 'indifferents', while being (at least) congeneric for respondents holding stronger attitudes.

Nevertheless, testing this 'different attitudes' version of the indifferent respondents hypothesis remains an interesting proposition. If the research does suffer from power problems, it is important to at least be aware of this aspect. Furthermore, this analysis provides an additional test of congenericity within time by exploring whether the correlation between a forbid factor and a variable 'x' is similar to the correlation between an allow factor and the same variable 'x'. If forbid and allow are congeneric this should indeed be the case. In this exploration, the 'x' variable is the variable 'attitude strength'.

4.4.1 Instruments and models

Basically, the only hypothesis that will be put to the test in this exploration, is the 'different attitudes' version of the indifferent respondents hypothesis. The next section outlines the results. First, however, some attention should be devoted to the questions that were used to measure attitude strength and to the models that were developed to find out whether forbid/allow questions are congeneric for the subsample of indifferent respondents.

Instruments

The discussion of forbid/allow research showed that many researchers use different ways of defining and measuring attitude strength. According to several experts on attitude strength, the concept consists of various dimensions. The dimensions identified include: the degree of ambivalence towards the issue, the degree of certainty or confidence with which one holds an attitude, the degree of elaboration regarding the issue (how long and carefully has a respondent thought about the information relevant to the attitude object?), the extremity of the attitude, the personal importance of the attitude, the knowledge of the issue (the amount of knowledge stored in memory regarding the attitude object), the personal relevance of the issue (the extent to which people believe that the issue holds significant consequences for some aspect of their lives), and the structural consistency of the attitude object (the degree to which the attitude is evaluatively consistent with other attitudes) (see Wegener et al., 1995). This suggests that attitude strength is probably a multidimensional construct. The current research took this into account by using a combination of attitude strength measures.

In Experiment 1 the following dimensions of attitude strength were addressed in the questions: certainty ('If I was an environment minister I wouldn't know how to develop good environmental policies', 'I had strong doubts about my answers to these questions on environmental issues'), personal importance ('I feel very strongly about policies on environmental issues', 'I am prepared to pay more for an environmentally friendly product', 'I am willing to spend more time in order to live in an environmentally friendly way'), elaboration ('If television programmes deal with nature or environmental issues, I tend to switch to another channel', 'I have a subscription to a magazine on nature or environmental issues'). In the second experiment similar dimensions were measured but fewer of them: involvement ('I feel very involved in policies on ethnic groups'), certainty ('If I was a minister, I would not know how to develop good policies concerning ethnic groups'), personal importance ('I can get very upset about discrimination', 'I am very interested in the customs and cultures of people from ethnic groups'). In accordance with research literature on attitude strength (Krosnick & Schuman, 1988; Wegener et al., 1995; Krosnick & Petty, 1995) which shows the relations between dimensions such as these to be neither very stable nor strong, a sum score for attitude strength was used[14]. Scores obtained for questions to which a positive answer indicated a weak attitude ('If television programmes deal with nature or environmental issues, I tend to switch to another channel') were reversed, so that high sum scores indicated strong attitudes.

A problem when measuring attitude strength, is that the strength measure should be unrelated to the content of the attitude itself. In other words, some respondents can hold very strong attitudes that are positive towards the issue,

---

[14] The measure used for attitude strength is therefore rather general and beyond the level of the specific issues raised in each forbid/allow question. Previous research indicates that attitude strength does not have to be measured for each specific act to be forbidden or allowed. In Waterplas et al. (1988), for example, a relation is even found between the degree of general informedness and the answers to specific forbid/allow questions.

others can hold very strong attitudes that are negative towards the issue. Both of these groups hold strong attitudes, the only respondents holding weak attitudes are the ones who really do no care about the issue. It is especially difficult to avoid a reference to the content of the attitude if one wants to address attitude-behaviour consistency, which is also related to attitude strength. Respondents who hold strong attitudes are supposed to reflect the content of their attitudes more consistently in their behaviour than respondents whose behaviour is based on weak attitudes. For this reason, using attitude strength measures that refer to a behaviour or intention that is based on the attitudes (e.g. 'I am prepared to pay more for an environmental friendly product') is often recommended. The answers obtained for such a question reflect attitude strength as well as attitude content: a positive or negative evaluation of the importance of the protection of the environment. A few questions that were used as attitude strength measures in the current experiments suffer from this bias ('I am willing to spend more time in order to live in an environmentally friendly way', 'I can get very upset about discrimination', 'I am very interested in the customs and cultures of people from ethnic groups'). These ambiguities in the measure of attitude strength used in the current experiments are the reason for referring to the following analyses as 'exploration'.

The measurement problem was solved to some extent, by using a sum score of attitude strength. Homogeneity measures of the answers obtained to the attitude strength questions indicated that reasonably homogeneous constructs had been measured. The sum of scores obtained are therefore interpreted as reflecting attitude strength.

Models

Section 4.3 described two reasons for exploring the effect of attitude strength on congenericity. The first is to provide an extra check on the congenericity found for forbid/allow questions. The second is to establish whether forbid/allow questions also cause the subgroup of 'indifferent respondents' to retrieve similar attitudes.

These two issues can be examined by comparing the model fit of three models. Once again, the models are nested within each other. The first model (Model 1) requires the effect of attitude strength on the factors (EI, NP) to be the same for each factor across the different groups, independent of the use of forbid/allow. The second, less stringent, model (Model 2) specifies that the effect of attitude strength will differ for factors that are worded differently. The third model allows the effect of attitude strength to be estimated freely, varying according to factors that are worded differently and different groups (Model 3). These three models are modifications of the model that fitted best for the whole sample: essential tau-equivalent within time and noncongeneric over time for Experiment 1 and congeneric within time and noncongeneric over time for Experiment 2. The effect of attitude strength was not required to be the same at T1 and T2, because the noncongeneric restrictions fitted best over time in both experiments.

The comparison of fit for these three models will be used to explore the effect of attitude strength, as well as for the additional check on congenericity. For both analyses the answers to the questions measuring attitude strength will be combined to form one score for each respondent per experiment. The attitude strength at T1 and the attitude strength at T2 will be combined into one variable, the variable 'attitude strength of respondent x towards the issues (NP/EI) in Experiment 1' (and similarly for Experiment 2).

In order to explore the different attitudes version of the *indifferent respondents hypothesis*, the attitude strength variable will be dichotomized on the median, thereby creating a dummy variable which separates respondents with a weak attitude from those who hold a strong attitude. If the second or third model fits the data best when the dummy variable for attitude strength is used, this would indicate that low attitude strength causes 'forbid' and 'allow' to be noncongeneric. If the effect of attitude strength differs for factors that are worded differently, or differs for different groups, then it follows that the correlations between 'forbid EI' and 'forbid NP' factors cannot logically be similar to the correlations between 'allow EI' and 'allow NP'. Forbid and allow questions would therefore have to be regarded as noncongeneric for the subsample of 'indifferent respondents'. If the first model fits best, this would indicate a lack of support for the hypothesis that forbid and allow questions measure a different attitude for 'indifferents'.

In order to perform an extra test on the congenericity of forbid/allow questions, undichotomized mean scores of the attitude strength variable are used. If the observed scores on the attitude strength variable are used, and the first model fits the data best, this would provide additional evidence for the congenericity of 'forbid' and 'allow'. If the second or third model fits best, 'forbid' and 'allow' have to be regarded as noncongeneric.

4.4.2 Results

For the exploration of the effect of attitude strength, as well as for the extra test on congenericity, three models were fitted to the data, with varying degrees of restriction on the influence of attitude strength. First, the model fit for the attitude strength variable as a dummy variable was tested. This tests the different attitudes version of the *indifferent respondents hypothesis*. For both experiments the first, most restrictive model fitted the data best (see Table 4.5).

This means that the influence of attitude strength is the same for both forbid and allow questions and the same in every group. It can therefore be concluded that 'forbid' and 'allow' are also congeneric for the 'indifferent respondents': for this group too, the answers to these differently worded questions reflect the same traits. Furthermore, the results of this exploration indicate that this research is not plagued by power problems.[15]

restrictions	experiment 1			experiment 2		
	df	χ^2	comparison result	df	χ^2	comparison result
Model 1	677	982.28	1-2 p=.800	482	659.14	1-2 p=.418
Model 2	673	980.63	1-3 p=.516	478	655.23	1-3 p=.121
Model 3	665	971.13	**best fit: 1**	470	641.32	**best fit: 1**

***Table 4.5**: The effect of (the dummy variable) attitude strength (level of significance used: .05)*

The effect of attitude strength was also built in as an extra test of the congenericity of forbid and allow questions. The same three models were therefore compared using the observed scores to the 'attitude strength' variable. Again, the first model fitted the data best: the correlation between forbid questions and attitude strength did not differ from the correlation between allow questions and attitude strength in both experiments. In addition to the test on congenericity within time, this is another strong indication that forbid and allow factors correlate unity and that forbid and allow questions measure the same trait.

4.5 CONCLUSIONS AND GENERAL DISCUSSION

The results of the two experiments reported in this chapter show that attitude questions worded with either forbid or allow are at least congeneric. The hypothesis that questions containing one of these verbs measure different attitudes from

---

[15] This means that, within time forbid/allow questions measure the same attitudes for the group of respondents as a whole, as well as for the subgroup of 'indifferents'. It is interesting to note, however, that an effect of indifference was found on the relations over time. For example, the answers to NP at T1 were shown to be noncongeneric to the answers to NP at T2 for the group as a whole, whereas for the subgroup of 'indifferents' the correlations over time were even lower than those for the respondents holding stronger attitudes.

questions containing the other must be rejected. Strong indication for this was provided by the test on congenericity within time and it was confirmed by the extra test on congenericity using the variable 'attitude strength'. Questions containing either 'forbid' or 'allow' measure the same attitude if random measurement error is filtered out.

The design and analysis procedure used allows this finding of congenericity to be generalized over 17 forbid/allow questions, over two times of measurement and for the two general issues addressed in the current experiments. In terms of the implicit hypotheses of the black box model (Section 1.2), this research shows that the response function does not change over time for the forbid/allow questions included in these experiments: sets of forbid questions measure similar attitudes to sets of allow questions at the first time of measurement, as well as at the second time of measurement (Assumption 1a). It shows that a change in the variable to be measured leads to a change in the answers obtained (Assumption 1c). Regardless of the use of 'forbid' or 'allow', the attitudes measured in both the experiments were shown to have changed.

Accordingly, by relating the connotations hypothesis to the general cognitive framework of question-answering, a fundamental understanding of the cause of the forbid/allow asymmetry can be established. The results of both experiments show that the connotations hypothesis can be specified in line with the interpretation of the hypothesis by Clark & Schober (1992, see Section 2.2.1): "to answer 'no' to forbid does not mean the same as 'yes' to allow". The forbid/allow asymmetry does not originate during question interpretation or attitude localization, it originates from the stage at which the opinion is mapped onto the answering options 'yes' or 'no'. The first hypothesis offered by Krosnick & Schuman (1988), stating that the asymmetry is caused by differences in the way respondents map their answers onto the answering options (see Section 4.0) due to the use of 'forbid' and 'allow' is borne out by the data. Forbid/allow questions measure similar attitudes that are expressed differently on the answering scales due to the use of 'forbid' or 'allow' (see Box 4.2). This means that the *different attitudes hypothesis* has to be rejected.

Forbid and allow questions prompt respondents to retrieve or form similar attitudes, sometimes general in nature (e.g. 'What do you think of abortion?'), and then require them to translate a general negative or positive evaluation into a much more specific form: 'yes or no forbid' or 'yes or no allow'. The asymmetry results from slight changes in the perception of the meanings of the response options to attitude questions during this translation process.

Box 4.2: *The nature of the forbid/allow asymmetry*

Although forbid/allow questions measure similar attitudes, the observed scores to forbid and allow questions differ. This is shown by the results of split ballot analyses and the bad fit of the parallel models: the forbid/allow asymmetry is present in both experiments. The nature and cause of that difference cannot be allocated unequivocally, however. The *different scales hypothesis* is clearly supported by the present data but it works out differently in both experiments. In Experiment 1 only the midpoints of the answering scales differ, while in Experiment 2, the distances between scale points also differ. What is more, in Experiment 2 reliabilities of forbid and allow questions differ too, but no consistent patterns in those differences were shown to exist.

The connotations hypothesis predicts that the meaning of an affirmative answer to either 'forbid' or 'allow' is more extreme than a negative answer. Similarly, Clark & Schober (1992) say "[...] to agree to forbid implies a real act of opposition, but to disagree with allow means merely to abstain from support". Accordingly, the perceived extremity of the response alternatives 'yes' and 'no' is hypothesized to vary depending on the use of 'forbid' or 'allow'.

The experiments reported here cannot determine whether this is indeed the case. The results show that the asymmetry reflects a mapping problem, a difference in the answering scales to forbid/allow questions, but they are ambivalent as to the precise nature of the difference between the scales for forbid/allow questions. The differences in results between Experiments 1 and 2 as regards the essential tau-equivalence of 'forbid' and 'allow' may indicate a certain degree of issue dependency. In addition to this, results reported in Chapter 3 show that the asymmetry size may not only be dependent on the issue being addressed in the questions, but on question characteristics as well, as large variances in asymmetry size were shown between as well as within experiments. With this in mind, Chapter 5 goes on to focus on the question of whether these variations can be systematically related to a variety of characteristics of the communicative setting. Experiments reported in Chapter 6 and 7 were designed to find more uniform tendencies in the differences between the answering scales for forbid and allow questions. This will also shed light on the exact interpretation that should be given to 'yes' and 'no' answers to forbid/allow questions.

An exploration of the effect of attitude strength did not support the hypothesis based on the feature-positive effect that predicts 'forbid' and 'allow' to be noncongeneric for respondents with a weak attitude towards the issue. As the analyses reported here focused on the congenericity of forbid/allow questions, this study did not directly test the alternative interpretation of the *indifferent respondents hypothesis*, which predicts that the mapping problem will be larger for respondents with weak attitudes than for respondents with stronger ones. It is not likely, however, that the current research would have provided any support for this hypothesis, had it been tested explicitly. However, the exploration of attitude strength did provide additional evidence for the congenericity of 'forbid' and 'allow'.

Theoretically, attitude strength is an interesting background variable. In the experiments reported here, no effect of attitude strength on the relations between 'forbid' and 'allow' was found. Accordingly, a direct measure of respondents' attitude strength found no difference between the answering behaviour of respondents with a weak or a strong attitude: respondents' self-reports of 'certainty', 'intensity' or 'importance' do not seem to be related to forbid/allow answers. Attitude strength could have been operationalized differently, however. Instead of defining the indifferents group by splitting the results around the median, indifferents could have been identified as those who did not systematically select the extremes of 'yes!' and 'no!' or the extremes on the agree-disagree scale. Other direct measures of attitude strength could also have been used or the measures used in this research could have been split up into several factors each with different effects (Krosnick & Abelson, 1992; Waterplas et al., 1988), instead of treating the attitude questions as belonging to one factor. It seems that more research into the nature of the attitude strength construct is called for in order to come to a robust operationalization of attitude strength and the way it may influence the relations between questions that are worded differently. Chapter 5 reports analyses in which attitude strength is operationalized differently and is deduced from judgements relating to question characteristics.

For now, the advice to questionnaire designers based on the experiments here is to either use 'forbid' or 'allow', but to be careful not to interpret the answers in terms of defined scale points, as the meaning of the scale points and the distance between scale points depend on question wording. Both forbid and allow questions are equally valid, but the conclusions based on the answers are not necessarily so.

Another piece of practical advice can be extrapolated from the fact that the policy issues addressed in the questions turned out to be noncongeneric over time. This does not imply that respondents answered the opinion questions posed in the two experiments in a more or less random fashion. Had that been the case, reliabilities would have been much lower. It does mean, however, that public opinion (i.e. the opinions expressed in response to each single question, as well as the relations between those opinions, the underlying attitudes) can change quite drastically over time. This constrains the generalizability of findings over time and makes it worthwhile considering repeated measurements in opinion polls.

A number of topics associated with the research reported here merit further discussion. First of all, research carried out according to the correlational design

described here is in itself highly complex. It would have been even more complicated if two-point answering scales had been used, as was the case in previous
forbid/allow research. Such an approach would have called for the computation
of polychoric correlations. As outlined in Chapter 3, the current experiments used
a four-point scale (yes!/yes/no/no!), which meant that this research was not an
exact replication of previous research. The use of four-point scales might have
affected the outcomes, as research demonstrates that the number of response
alternatives might influence the answers (e.g. Cox, 1980). On the other hand,
respondents still had to choose between a 'yes' or a 'no' and analysis of the observed scores does indicate that there was a forbid/allow asymmetry present in
the data used in this research. Chapter 6 contains reports of experiments in which
forbid/allow questions were asked in conjunction with a two-point yes/no scale,
as well as with an agree-disagree scale involving a larger number of points. These
experiments tested whether the finding of congenericity using four-point scales is
supported when questions with a two-point answering scale are posed. This does
indeed turn out to be the case.

Secondly, it would be interesting to repeat this research in a more heterogeneous population, since it is quite possible that students in languages and the arts
have a heightened sensitivity to language which might decrease wording effects.
This should preferably be done using a questionnaire which measures the theorized constructs more reliably. In the current chapter, the concept 'attitude' was
defined rather pragmatically as 'that which four to five questions about an issue
commonly measure', a definition which does not do particular justice to the
complexity of this concept. However, this pragmatic approach was necessary in
order to define some underlying construct and compute the congenericity of for-
bid/allow questions. The constructs were not measured very reliably, causing
rather poor model fits. This was not a problem for the comparison of model fits
(as the models were nested within each other), but it did cause difficulties in
terms of interpreting the parameter estimates (the actual variances and reliabilities). In Chapter 6, the differences between the scales for forbid/allow questions
will be investigated again, with less of a presupposition about the reliable measurement of an underlying attitude. These investigations allow for a more adequate interpretation of the parameter estimates (i.e. the differences in variances
and reliabilities between forbid and allow questions), thereby providing a basis
for a refinement of the different scales hypothesis.

Thirdly, as discussed earlier, it would be revealing to relate the extremity of
respondents' opinions to the answers to forbid/allow questions they give. This can
be done by the use of a within-subjects design, in which the attitudes as expressed
on an answering scale with more than two points for forbid/allow questions are
related to the answers given on a two-point scale for forbid/allow questions. This

will be done in Chapter 7, providing possibilities for comparing the extremity of yes/no answers to forbid/allow questions.

As a final point, some comments on the use of split ballot experiments can be made. First, the noncongenericity over time found in this research stresses the methodological importance of taking time effects into account when measuring wording effects. The manipulated questions should be administered at the same point in time, or a criterion should be introduced for the allocation of time effects during the analysis stage. Apparently, attitudes can be subject to change even over a period as short as four weeks or this would at least seem to apply to the traits measured in the current research. If attitude change is not taken into account in the experimental design, the results of wording effect research will basically indicate attitude instability (that is, changes in the true scores) instead of wording effects.

A more fundamental comment should also be made on the use of split ballots. At the beginning of this chapter, as well as in previous chapters, it was posited that split ballot designs may not be suitable for this type of research design, as they do not distinguish between differences in the attitudes measured and differences in the way similar attitudes are expressed on the answering scales. The support for the different scales hypothesis reported here implies that split ballot designs are adequate research designs after all, at least for forbid/allow questions. It is now known how the differences between the percentages of affirmative and negative answers to forbid/allow questions should be interpreted: as a different expression of similar attitudes on the answering scales, due to the use of 'forbid' and 'allow'.

This means that the forbid/allow data obtained from split ballot experiments can be used in the further search for explanations after all. In the light of this reassurance, the next chapter employs meta-analytic techniques in order to identify the question and respondent characteristics which relate to a larger asymmetry, that is to say a more pronounced mapping problem when answering forbid/allow questions. Which circumstances are likely to give rise to the largest mapping problem when answering forbid/allow questions? Schuman & Presser (1981) name the extreme connotations of 'forbid' and 'allow' as the sole reason for the forbid/allow asymmetry. However, the large variation in the asymmetry size (Chapter 3) suggests that there is scope for additional explanations. This issue will be explored in the next chapter, which devotes special attention to the effect of attitude strength on the asymmetry.

Chapter 5

THE COMMUNICATIVE SETTING
AS AN INFLUENCING FACTOR[1]

5.0 INTRODUCTION

In the previous chapter evidence was obtained suggesting that the asymmetry results from slight changes in the perceived meaning of the response options due to the use of forbid/allow. Respondents retrieve or form similar attitudes, but during the mapping stage these general evaluations have to be translated into a specific response in the form of 'yes or no forbid' or 'yes or no allow'. The answering options 'yes' and 'no' to forbid/allow questions should not be viewed as nominal scales, but as interval scales which differ from one another.

Based on this understanding of the question-answering process, the connotations hypothesis can be reformulated into "to answer 'no' to forbid does not mean the same as 'yes' to allow – to agree to forbid implies a real act of opposition, but to disagree with allow merely to abstain from support" (Clark & Schober, 1992). The results in the previous chapter show that "to answer 'no' to forbid does not mean the same as to answer 'yes' to allow". But whether the second part of the hypothesis is true ("to agree to forbid implies a real act of opposition, and to disagree with allow merely to abstain from support"), will be investigated later (Chapter 6 and 7). It must first be established which of the other explanations for the asymmetry formulated in previous forbid/allow research remain valid. This is the focus of the current chapter.

Before we start looking for a monocausal theory to explain the asymmetry by focusing on characteristics of 'forbid' and 'allow', an explanation for variations in the asymmetry size should be found. In the previous chapters, the asymmetry was shown to vary greatly across questions. In spite of this, Schuman & Presser (1981:280) note that "what we have called tone of wording could be the sole source of the effect". If this is true, differences in the asymmetry sizes would only reflect random error and would not be systematically related to other question, respondent or experimental characteristics. However, there is likely to be a complex interaction between the process of answering forbid/allow questions and characteristics from the communicative setting. Insight into this interaction will provide hypotheses on which aspects of the language-use situation play a role in the occurrence of the wording effect, and how the mapping process for forbid/allow questions interacts with other contextual clues within the language environ-

---

[1] Most sections of the meta-analysis presented in this chapter (and in Chapter 3) were published in the *Journal of Quantitative Linguistics* (1999); and in *Taalgebruik ontrafeld, verslag van het 7e VIOT-congres* (1997).

ment and with respondents' accessible knowledge and attitudes. Such an understanding contributes to a further appreciation of whether a monocausal theory explaining the forbid/allow asymmetry can be developed, and which aspects of the communicative setting should be incorporated within that theory. Furthermore, it is interesting to see which other wording variables (i.e. other than forbid/allow) influence the asymmetry size, in order to decide which question variables should be varied systematically to obtain a good understanding of the cognitive processes underlying the forbid/allow asymmetry (Cook et al., 1992).

Many forbid/allow researchers have formulated explanations for the asymmetry. Some reasoned from theory and systematic hypothesis-testing (the indifferent respondent hypothesis), and some by formulating retrospective hypotheses explaining the nonoccurrence of an asymmetry for a specific forbid/allow question. Schuman & Presser (1981: 283), for instance, remark that "the forbid/allow effect can best be attributed to a subtle interaction between words and subject matter, with grammatical structure perhaps playing an additional role in creating an educational difference in some instances, but these interpretations are too much after the fact to be offered with great confidence [...]". Of course, all such explanations for variations in the asymmetry size could have been tested experimentally. Most explanations, however, were based on the results obtained for one question only. It is therefore more useful to first check whether these explanatory suggestions remain valid when analysing all previous forbid/allow questions at the same time.

A meta-analysis of existing forbid/allow research will be employed to discover which characteristics from the communicative setting affect the occurrence and size of the wording effect. It is possible to carry out such an analysis of existing research since the previous chapter demonstrated that forbid/allow questions measure similar attitudes. This finding allows the percentages obtained in split ballot experiments to be compared in meaningful ways.

Four categories of variables which may interact with the main effect of 'forbid' and 'allow' will be distinguished: respondent, or psychological, characteristics (attitude strength), linguistic characteristics (that focus on the effects of linguistic complexity), content-related characteristics (e.g. whether the issue addressed in the questions was forbidden or allowed at the time of administration), and experimental characteristics (e.g. the administration mode). The dependent variable is the difference between the percentage of 'not forbid' and 'yes allow' answers obtained, weighted for the number of respondents who answered each question (see Section 3.2). For each of the characteristics coded, three different effect types will be taken into account: the significance of the effect, the amount of variance being explained (within and between experiments), and the mean effect size. The size of each of these effects is important. First of all, the significance of the effect is a prerequisite upon which to base conclusions on any effect, although it is partly dependent on the occurrence of characteristics in this question set. For example, if only one question was linguistically complex in the question set, the effect of this variable is less likely to reach significance. Secondly, the percentage of variance explained is an indication of the explanatory power of a variable, but it can also be a manifestation of incidental variation in the presence or absence of a particular variable in this question set. Again, if there is little variation in linguistic complexity within this question set, this variable is unlikely to explain a great deal of variance in asymmetry sizes obtained. Thirdly, the effect size indicates whether the effect of an explanatory variable on the asymmetry size is large enough to be of importance and must therefore be taken into account in future research. Once again, the effect size can be computed by dividing the mean effect by the standard deviation of the asymmetry size (see Section 3.2). The effect size can then be judged using the criteria defined by Cohen (1977).

Meta-analytic techniques make it possible to generalize the effects of explanatory variables on the asymmetry size beyond the level of single questions. Before proceeding any further, it is worth giving an introductory account of the methodological status of meta-analysis.

A meta-analysis is not an experiment. Hence, it does not involve a systematic manipulation in which the answers obtained for a set of forbid/allow questions that are linguistically complex, for example, are compared to the answers obtained for a set of equivalent forbid/allow questions that are not linguistically complex. A systematic manipulation of this kind allows strong conclusions to be drawn about the interaction effect of linguistic complexity, as all other relevant question characteristics are held constant. In a meta-analysis, however, the answers obtained for a variety of linguistically complex forbid/allow questions are compared to the answers obtained for a variety of *other* forbid/allow questions that are not linguistically complex. Due to the absence of a systematic manipulation, there may be an overlap between relevant variables that was not taken into account: if many questions that are linguistically complex were also incidentally administered orally, the effects of each variable assessed separately may be overestimated or underestimated. For this reason, the effects of each characteristic are not only estimated individually, but also in combination with one another.

In order to interpret these overlaps, the analyses in the current chapter consist of three steps. In the first step, the individual effects of each characteristic on the asymmetry size are estimated. In the second, the change in the effects of each variable is analysed when a set of characteristics similar to each other (linguistic characteristics, for example) are estimated simultaneously. In the third step, the analysis focuses on changes in the effects of a characteristic when all characteristics are analysed jointly (Section 5.2.1). By employing these step-by-step analyses, it is possible to investigate the interplay between a variety of characteristics within the language-use situation and pinpoint the characteristics of relative importance (compared to the other characteristics) in explaining variations in the asymmetry size obtained.

Two additional notes on the limitations of meta-analytic techniques should be made, one on interaction effects and one on causality. In Section 2.2.1 it was argued that a variety of characteristics from the language-use situation may be expected to interact with one another, as respondents use many clues from the communication setting as a whole to infer the intended meaning and retrieve an attitude. This implies that both linguistic complexity and the administration mode could influence the asymmetry size and there could also be an interaction effect between those two characteristics. If this is the case, this means that their effects do not simply add up, but that one effect weakens or strengthens the other. The step-by-step analyses described above help to detect overestimations or underestimations of the effects of each characteristic, but are not able to determine interaction effects. Computing each interaction effect that may be theoretically relevant is problematic, however, because not all combinations of characteristics are present in the question set. With this in mind, only a few interaction effects will be analysed in the current chapter.

A last note to be made on the nature of meta-analytic techniques concerns the use of the term 'effects'. This chapter speaks about 'effects', whereas only relations are measured. Looking at the above discussion of the limitations of meta-analytic techniques, it is obvious that no causal conclusions can be drawn because no experimental manipulation was applied. However, as a certain causality is expected theoretically, the term 'effects' will be used when discussing the analyses.

In this chapter, an inventory of explanatory variables relevant to explaining variations in the asymmetry size will first be made. The way the variables are coded will also be discussed (Section 5.1). Section 5.2 presents the results of the analyses. The first step will be to analyse which of the four clusters of characteristics distinguished is most important in explaining variation in the asymmetry size. The results section will discuss the mean effects of each characteristic on the asymmetry size obtained and the significance of these effects. Each characteristic will be examined to see whether its estimated effect changes due to incidental overlaps in the question set, when taken in combination with the other characteristics (Section 5.2.1). It will be shown that characteristics related to attitude strength are especially important as explanations for the asymmetry size. Furthermore, the effect of one of the characteristics indicating linguistic complexity of the question (abstractness) will prove to be interesting. These characteristics will therefore form the basis for the analysis of the interaction effects (Section 5.2.2).

In particular, the interaction effect between abstractness and complexity will lead to a number of hypotheses concerning the explanation of the asymmetry (Section 5.3).

5.1 DEFINITION OF RELEVANT CHARACTERISTICS

In the literature on the forbid/allow asymmetry various question characteristics are mentioned that may affect the size and direction of the asymmetry. Occasionally this is accompanied by some sort of theoretical hypothesis, but often characteristics are not observed in a structured way. The literature on response effects or wording effects in general, can help in the detection of relevant question characteristics, as can general linguistic or cognitive literature. Many of these studies are not applicable to the set of forbid/allow questions, however, either because they refer to different text types or longer texts, or because certain characteristics do not occur in the question set or do not occur often enough, causing difficulties in measuring the effect of such a variable in this meta-analysis.

In this section, a variety of possibly relevant characteristics will be examined. For each of the four types of characteristics (characteristics from the experimental setting, psychological characteristics of respondents, linguistic characteristics and content-related characteristics) the selection and coding of variables will be discussed.

5.1.1 Characteristics from the experimental setting

A first characteristic of the experimental setting concerns the way the questions are administered. Several methods of administration have been used in forbid/allow research, oral methods (face-to-face or telephone), and written (mail survey or self-administered questionnaires in class). In the literature it is assumed that oral *administration modes* lead to larger response effects than written modes, because respondents have less time to think about the meaning of the question and the implications of their answers in oral administration modes (Ayidiya & McClendon, 1990; Bishop et al., 1988; Hippler & Schwarz, 1987). It could therefore be hypothesized that the time pressure associated with oral administration could lead to a larger asymmetry than written methods, because respondents might be more likely to miss the fact that 'not allowing' implies 'forbidding' and 'not forbidding' implies 'allowing'.

A second characteristic of the experimental setting involves the answering options used. Two factors may be important: the number of answering options, and the inclusion of explicit or implicit 'no opinion' or 'don't know' filters. In the two new forbid/allow experiments (Chapter 3) four-point answering scales (yes!/

yes/no/no!) were applied, whereas previous forbid/allow research used two-point answering scales (yes/no). The use of four-point scales might have affected the asymmetries obtained. The use of 'no opinion' or 'don't know' filters could be a relevant factor for variation in the asymmetry size as well, as these extra scale points offer the opportunity for respondents with weak attitudes to avoid giving a 'yes' or 'no' answer. Offering an explicit 'no opinion' or 'don't know' filter can affect the distribution of substantive answers (Ayidiya & McClendon, 1990). Unfortunately, variation with respect to this characteristic is not reported systematically in previous forbid/allow research. In some cases an explicit 'don't know' filter seems to have been offered, sometimes implicitly. Furthermore, the number of nonsubstantial answers for each question is only seldom reported. Sometimes valid percentages are provided, but sometimes the percentages for 'yes' and 'no' do not add up to 100%, leaving the impression that the answers not reported were spontaneous 'don't knows'. Due to this ambiguity, it was decided not to analyse the effect of this variable and not to analyse the influence of the number of answering options offered either. The effect of the latter characteristic will be investigated through experimental research (Chapter 6).

Thirdly, various respondent or interviewer characteristics could be viewed as being part of the experimental setting. Obviously, in this meta-analysis characteristics of individual respondents cannot be related to their answering behaviour, because these data are not provided. Nor can the influence of specific interviewer characteristics be investigated. However, one respondent characteristic can be approximated: *educational level*. Respondents with higher educational levels are supposed to feel more involved with a variety of issues and in the literature it is assumed that respondents who lack involvement in an issue are responsible for larger response effects. It is also assumed that respondents with higher educational levels are able to handle linguistic complexity more easily. So again, the asymmetry should be smaller for respondents with a higher educational level. For the current meta-analysis the characteristic educational level will be approximated by coding whether the forbid/allow questions were posed to a homogeneous sample of students or to a heterogeneous sample of respondents.

Various other characteristics from the experimental setting could influence variations in the asymmetry size. A *random sample* was drawn in most experiments, while in one experiment a quota sample was used. This variation in sampling methods is too small to reach conclusions with respect to this variable, but the effect of this variable will be computed in order to gain some indication. Another consideration is whether the meaning of the English verbs 'to forbid' and 'to allow' are full equivalents of the Dutch 'verbieden' and 'toelaten' or the German 'verbieten' and 'erlauben'. This is referred to in the literature as the issue of whether the forbid/allow asymmetry is cross-culturally stable. It is interesting to compute the effect of the variables country and language, although such an effect is difficult to interpret due to an overlap between these and other question characteristics.

In conclusion, this overview of experimental setting characteristics has made clear that various characteristics can be distinguished. In this meta-analysis, the effects of the *administration mode* (oral or written), the *type of sample drawn* and the *educational level* of respondents will be traced. A preliminary summarizing analysis will also estimate the countries (and languages) with the greatest chances of finding a large asymmetry. Another obvious characteristic is the way the answering options are presented to the respondents. This variable could not be examined in this meta-analysis, however, due to lack of reliable reports on these data. The effects of characteristics from the experimental setting on the asymmetry size mainly say something about the circumstances under which the asymmetry is most likely to occur, although some of the characteristics have cognitive implications as well.

5.1.2 Psychological characteristics

An important psychological factor is of course respondents' attitude strength. In previous forbid/allow research the indifferent respondent hypothesis was put forward. In response effects research in general, weak attitudes are seen as a factor that could cause respondents to be more susceptible to superficial characteristics of the question or the experimental setting.

As discussed in Section 2.1, Hippler & Schwarz (1986), Waterplas et al. (1988) and Krosnick & Schuman (1988) theorize that attitude strength is an important variable for the forbid/allow asymmetry. Hippler & Schwarz (1986) define attitude strength in terms of indifference and ambivalence. Others define attitude strength by using dimensions such as extremity, intensity, certainty, importance and knowledge (Krosnick & Abelson, 1992, see also Section 4.3). According to Krosnick and Abelson strong attitudes are extreme, intense, certain and important. Furthermore they are supported by knowledge about the attitude object. Attitude strength is usually viewed as a multidimensional construct, although some dimensions can be mutually dependent. For example, the importance and extremity of attitudes are related to each other because important attitudes are more often the subject of conscious thought processes (Wood, 1982), causing "important attitudes to be more extreme than unimportant attitudes" (Krosnick & Schuman, 1988:949).

Attitude strength is a respondent characteristic and not a question characteristic, and as such causes coding difficulties in a meta-analysis. It can be approximated by question characteristics, however. The attitude strength hypothesis and the dimensions of attitude strength can be used to derive the kind of questions that will probably lead to a larger group of respondents holding stronger attitudes. Two variables are coded for assessing the effect of psychological character-istics: the complexity of the issue in the question and the relevance of the issue. Relevant issues are important to the majority of the respondent group and atti-tudes towards those issues are supported with knowledge, making them more extreme. Less 'indifferents' will be found for relevant issues in the sample than for irrelevant issues. Similarly, the complexity can be judged retrospectively: complex issues are more difficult to evaluate and cause ambivalence and insecurity about one's own opinion. It follows, therefore, that more respondents holding weak attitudes will be found for questions about complex issues.

The relevance and complexity of an issue are both highly dependent on the degree to which the issues are 'hot topics' in public debate at the moment of administration and on the way in which they are discussed in the media. Rele-vance, as well as complexity, is dependent on respondents' individual attitude structures. Hence, the actual degree of relevance and complexity for individual respondents at the moment of question administration cannot be assessed after the fact. In order to obtain an indication, these variables were coded by asking a separate group of subjects to judge them.

First the *complexity of the issue* in the question was coded. The hypothesis concerning attitude strength states that respondents holding a weak, moderate or ambivalent opinion on the matter at stake, find agreeing to either answering option too extreme, because of the extreme connotations of 'forbid' and 'allow'. If the issue in the question is very complex, more respondents are likely to hold an ambivalent or weak opinion, so in that case the asymmetry should be larger. Which issues are felt to be complex and which are not, depends on individual respondents. In a way, each issue in this question set is complex: one can always think of arguments to forbid or allow an activity. But some issues can be judged to be more complex than others. Some possible criteria can be: How many steps does a respondent have to make before he realizes what the dilemma is? How compelling is the logic behind these steps? In order to code the complexity of each issue, 45 students were asked to judge the complexity of various issues in forbid/allow questions, using the criteria mentioned above. Sets of 9 questions were each rated by 15 students, who could choose between the judgement 'complex' or 'very complex'. This resulted in an interrater reliability of 0.8, implying that a mean complexity score of the judges per question can be constructed. The attitude strength hypothesis leads us to expect that questions about very complex issues lead to a larger asymmetry because more respondents will hold an ambivalent opinion on these issues.

Secondly, the *relevance of the issue* was coded. The same students that judged 9 questions on their degree of complexity, rated the issues in 9 other questions on their degree of relevance. They were asked to use the following criteria: how important do you find this issue? Have you thought a lot about this issue? Do you feel personally involved with this issue? Subjects could choose between 'relevant' and 'very relevant', resulting in an interrater reliability of 0.87.[2] The attitude strength hypothesis leads us to expect that the forbid/allow asymmetry will be smaller for questions on very relevant issues, because very relevant issues have been thought over more often and more intensely, causing people to hold more extreme opinions on these issues (Krosnick & Abelson, 1992). The scores for relevance and complexity were recoded as dummy variables, split around the mean: questions coded with a high mean complexity score obtained 1, questions with a low mean complexity score were scored with a zero.[3] The scores for relevance and complexity for each question, as well as the codes for the other characteristics discussed here, can be found in Appendix II.

5.1.3 Linguistic characteristics

Some literature (Schuman & Presser, 1981; Waterplas et al., 1988) hypothesizes that the asymmetry will be larger if the question is *linguistically complex* because it requires more working memory to process such questions during the interpretation stage. In turn, this would cause respondents not to realize at the answering stage that the answer 'no' to 'forbid' implies a 'yes' to 'allow'. Linguistic complexity was put forward as an important factor by Schuman & Presser (1981), because the cognitive load caused by linguistic complexity, particularly among the less educated, would cause subjects to miss the fact that 'not forbid' implies 'yes allow'. Schuman and Presser go on to mention the degree of question abstractness, but it is unclear whether they are referring to the complexity of the linguistic form or of the issue at stake. In the previous section the complexity of the issue was addressed. In the current section, abstractness (or vagueness) will be discussed as a linguistic feature.

In wording effect research, question length, readability, and the use of syntactic negations or passives in questions are sometimes seen as indicators of linguistic complexity. For example, Molenaar (1986) coded characteristics such as reading ease of the question (RE-formula, Douma, 1956) and abstraction of the question text (Günther & Groeben, 1978) in his meta-analysis. Both formulas

---

[2] One might object that the concepts complexity and relevance overlap and are in fact different labels for the same construct. A low correlation between the judgements of relevance and complexity was found, however, which suggests that this overlap is not the case in the present study.

[3] Throughout this chapter, questions about issues that were judged to be very relevant or very complex will be referred to as 'relevant' or 'complex', whereas questions about issues that were judged to be less complex or relevant, will be referred to as 'non-complex' or 'non-relevant'.

were developed for longer texts, however, and do not seem suitable for short questions (Molenaar, 1986:62). Molenaar also coded the number of sentences in the question and the presence of subordinate clauses.

In more general linguistic literature, linguistic complexity is often approached from a parsing perspective (e.g. Frazier, 1985). This line of research is not directly relevant to the linguistic complexity of forbid/allow questions, however. In an application of linguistic literature, Petrič (1992:30) mentions the following linguistic variables crucial to the readability of texts[4]: the difficulty of single words, sentence length and sentence complexity. Abstraction of words is also important but, according to Petrič, the degree of abstraction is difficult to determine. Sentence length only seems a useful variable if the text consists of more than one sentence and a mean sentence length can be computed. If texts consist of a small number of sentences, Petrič prefers a variable 'number of sentences', similar to the one Molenaar used. Sentence complexity is usually judged on the basis of the presence of subordinate clauses, passive constructions and embedded structures. Onrust et al. (1993) also mention the presence of nominalizations as an indicator of text complexity and abstraction.

For the current analyses, three indicators of linguistic complexity were coded: the number of sentences, the use of nominalization and the degree of abstractness[5]. First, the *number of sentences* was coded: most questions consist of one sentence only, if more sentences were used this variable was coded 1.[6] Longer texts are believed to place a heavier burden on working memory, and would therefore be more difficult (Angleitner et al., 1986:81). Hence, the prediction would be that the asymmetry size is larger for longer questions. This expectation should be modified beforehand, however, because a question can be longer due to the fact that an introduction on the subject is given in order to diminish the burden on working memory: an explanatory introduction to a question may make

---

[4] What is relevant for questions administered orally, is not necessarily important for written texts, and vice versa (Petrič, 1992: 3-5). This problem will be excluded from consideration in this research, at least during the coding stage.

[5] Next to the three indicators of linguistic complexity discussed here some other linguistic characteristics increasing the difficulty of the text can be distinguished. Those characteristics do not occur often enough, however, to allow an estimation of their effects. Examples of those variables are: the use of passives (which does not occur often, and is partly covered by the content variable 'presence of an actor in the question'), the use of negations (which hardly occurs), the use of difficult word orders or words with a low usage frequency (like 'Sichzurschaustellen' in Hippler & Schwarz's research), and the use of subordinate or conditional clauses.

[6] Question length could have been coded differently. For example by counting the number of words or clauses, in stead of the number of sentences. This did not differentiate sufficiently between questions in this question set, however.

it easier instead of more difficult to process the information given.

Second, the use of *nominalizations* was coded. Nominalizations are supposed to increase linguistic complexity because the degree of abstraction of the text is raised by leaving out the actor of the nominalized verb (Onrust et al., 1993). In this question set, however, almost every question contains a nominalized phrase[7]. For this analysis questions were coded according to whether they consist of nominalized phrases followed by predicates indicating the actor or the object of the verb (as in: 'Do you think the government should forbid *the showing of X-rated movies?*'). Although the use of predicates renders the question content less abstract, it also increases the linguistic complexity of the question. The expectation is that asymmetry will be larger for questions that contain such constructions.

Finally, the degree of *abstractness* or vagueness is usually measured as an indicator of linguistic complexity. Vagueness can refer to ambiguity of sentence structure[8] or word meanings, as well as to the degree of abstraction of words used in the question. Question ambiguity can be caused by words or clauses with various possible meanings, by double-edged relations between clauses, or by the lack of connection between the answering options and the question (Angleitner et al., 1986). Ambiguity can cause the respondent to interpret the question in a way not intended by the researcher. The use of abstract terms, however, does not necessarily cause the question to be interpreted wrongly, but it can cause difficulties for the respondent when comparing the abstract term to the more specific or concrete terms in his own memory. Specific information in the respondent's memory has to be integrated with inferences in order to compare it to the abstract term in the question. Furthermore, people often find it harder to retrieve abstract information from long-term memory than concrete information (Nisbett & Ross, 1980:47-51). A complication is that a word or phrase can be abstract or vague to one respondent, causing him to find the question as a whole difficult to answer, whereas another respondent may immediately find an adequate specification for an abstract phrase like 'public speeches against democracy'. In fact, only among those respondents who judge a phrase to be vague is there the expectation that the asymmetry is larger for questions coded as 'abstract'. Likewise, the coding of abstractness is reasonably subjective, although clearly 'smoking in public spaces, like restaurants' (from Bishop's research) is much less abstract and vague than 'exclusion of minority groups for certain jobs' or 'public speeches in favor of communism'.

---

[7] It is hardly surprising that many forbid/allow questions consist of nominalized phrases: 'forbid' and 'allow' are often followed by nominalized verbs indicating which action is the object of forbidding/allowing, in English, German as well as in Dutch.

[8] Syntactic ambiguity does occur in this question set, but not often enough to be worthwhile coding it and estimating its effects.

5.1.4 Content-related characteristics

The effects of several content-related characteristics were looked into. In the literature on response effects, content-related characteristics are only assumed to unintentionally affect the answers obtained if they are associated with respondent characteristics. Wording effects research suggests that a relevant characteristic is whether a motivation is included in the question for one of both answering options. Experiments by Schuman & Presser (1981) show that the addition of an argument always causes the option that was supported to be chosen more often, independent of the content of that argument. In the forbid/allow literature, Waterplas et al. (1988) mention the following content-related characteristics which may be relevant. Is the question about a moral or about a judicial prohibition? Who is the instigator of the prohibition: the government, the nation, the legislator or no one in particular?

Other characteristics may be relevant besides those mentioned in the literature. Parallel to the distinction between morality and judiciality, a distinction can be made between issues mainly dealing with prohibitions beforehand (permission that has to be asked and may be denied) and issues dealing with prohibitions that are more general and lead to some sort of punishment. It may also matter whether the question text explicitly states for whom something will be forbidden/allowed. In addition, it is worth considering whether the status quo at the moment of administration is a relevant factor: the forbid/allow effect may change if the issue is forbidden at the moment of administration, as opposed to a situation in which the issue is allowed at that time.

Hypotheses on the effects of content-related characteristics formulated in advance are not very strong. Furthermore, the way these characteristics should be defined and coded is not very clear-cut in each case. Once a characteristic has been shown to affect the asymmetry size, however, this may provide opportunities to start hypothesizing about the causes of that effect.

According to Waterplas et al., the issue of whether the question addresses a *moral versus a judicial prohibition* is relevant. One possible effect of this characteristic could be that questions on moral prohibitions are less concrete than those on judicial issues, causing a larger asymmetry for moral issues. A judicial prohibition is often more concrete, in the sense that the way in which the prohibition should be implemented is more obvious. For a moral prohibition, on the other hand, the emphasis is more on 'this should not be happening', without explicitly stating for whom something is forbidden and how. The issues coded as 'moral' are issues with high degrees of 'political correctness', like some questions on ethnic issues, questions on freedom of speech and questions on sex.

The effect of *status quo* could be that the active and changing connotation of 'forbid' weakens if the activity at stake is forbidden when the question is posed.

This would cause the asymmetry to diminish in size, because respondents may find it easier to say 'yes' to 'forbid' if forbidding refers to the actual state of affairs. At the same time, the connotation of 'allow' may become more active, thereby counteracting this effect: respondents may then think it too extreme to answer affirmatively to 'allow'. Intuitively one would say however, that the connotations of 'forbid' are more extreme than those of 'allow', and that the asymmetry will diminish when the status quo of the issue at stake is forbidden.

Five questions contain an argument in favour of forbidding the issue. This presence of a *motivation in the question* is a difficult variable to code, because some motivations are worded conditionally (forbid/allow the extraction of natural gas *'if* it affects the natural characteristics of this area'). The presence of an argument in favour of forbidding the issue would probably lead to a smaller asymmetry (Molenaar, 1982).

In some questions the actor of forbidding/allowing is 'one' ('Sollte *man* das Salzstreuen generel verbieten/erlauben') or is omitted altogether ('Do you think smoking [..] should be forbidden/allowed'). In other questions the actor is 'the government', 'the legislator', or 'parliament'. Although the *actor in the question*, if present, is still quite vague in most cases (who is 'the government'?), the inclusion of an actor could make the question more concrete compared to questions in which the actor is absent. Waterplas et al. (1988) therefore mention the presence of an actor and the type of actor as a relevant variable. For this meta-analysis, the matter of whether the actor is explicit or whether the actor is left implicit was coded. The expectations associated with the effects of the presence of an actor are unclear. For those questions in which the actor remains implicit, one would expect the question to be less concrete and therefore to lead to a larger asymmetry.

In some questions the actor of the behaviour or phenomenon that should be forbidden/allowed is explicitly mentioned ('the increase of railway fares *by the Netherlands Railways*'), whereas in others it is left implicit. For example, in the question on 'the showing on X-rated movies' it is unclear at which people such a prohibition is aimed. Similarly to the previous characteristic, the presence of an indirect object, indicating for *whom* something is forbidden or allowed, would probably lead to a smaller asymmetry.

Some questions are about behaviours that are prohibited beforehand: a permit must be obtained before it can be done (e.g. 'nightly calls for prayer from the mosque'). Other questions are about behaviours that can only be punished afterwards (e.g. 'the exclusion of ethnic groups for job vacancies'). In coding prohibition beforehand or *punishment* afterwards it was decided to code individual actions that cannot be coordinated by the government beforehand, but can be followed by punishment (e.g. racist public speeches). If the prohibition applies to this type of individual action, it is unclear to what extent this behaviour can be forbidden and what kind of punishment will follow. It may also be unclear to what extent the government is an adequate promulgator of that prohibition. More doubts can therefore be raised about the consequences of forbidding, which could cause a large asymmetry to occur.

To sum up, the effects of four types of relevant characteristics will be investigated: characteristics from the experimental setting, psychological characteristics, linguistic characteristics, and content-related characteristics. Results of the analyses will be discussed in the next section.

5.2 RESULTS

This section first reports which of the four clusters identified appear to be of particular importance in explaining variation in the asymmetry size. It will go on to discuss the mean effect of each characteristic on the asymmetry size obtained and the significance of these effects. For each characteristic it will be discussed whether the estimates of its effect change once it is estimated in combination with the other characteristics due to possible overlaps in the question set (Section 5.2.1).

As reported in Chapter 3 (Table 3.3), the mean difference between 'not forbid' versus 'allow' answers is 14.2%. The total variance, within as well as between experiments, proves to be large (97). The mean asymmetry of 14.2% found is important, because it indicates that the use of forbid/allow causes some general effect on the answers and that the wording effect is in fact considerable. The variance in the asymmetry size is also important however: apparently the wording effect does not occur under all circumstances. If variation in the asymmetry size can be explained, this provides insight into the factors that are relevant for the occurrence of the asymmetry. This offers additional tools with which to explain the asymmetry. It also provides possibilities for analysing which characteristics of the communicative situation as a whole play a role in the question-answering process and lead to a larger mapping difference in forbid/allow answers.

Before discussing the effects of each characteristic separately, a short overview of this results section is provided by looking at the proportion of variance explained by each of the four clusters of characteristics distinguished in the previous section. As shown in Table 5.1, psychological characteristics (relevance and complexity) explain 48% of the total variance in the asymmetry size and characteristics from the experimental setting explain 35%, whereas linguistic characteristics and content-related characteristics provide less of an explanation for the variation in the asymmetry size obtained. In total, 67% of the variance in the asymmetry size can be explained by the characteristics described in this chapter

(Table 5.4), which can be regarded as considerable.[9]

Type of cluster explanatory variables	% variance explained
Psychological characteristics	48 %
Characteristics from the experimental setting	35 %
Linguistic characteristics	14 %
Content-related characteristics	8 %

Table 5.1: *Percentage variance explained in the difference between 'not forbid' and 'yes, allow' per type of explanatory variable*

Linguistic and content-related characteristics contribute relatively little to the amount of explained variance. In itself, this is not very surprising. First of all, it is very difficult to predict the effects of linguistic complexity without taking the function or context of the question into account in the analysis. If the context and the specific issue of the question had been taken into account during the coding stage, it would have been obvious that the content could not have been made less complex: the complex question was worded as simply as possible (Verhagen, 1997). Coding the presence of nominalizations and question length provided the best possible indications of linguistic complexity in this analysis, but in view of this point they were not the most meaningful. What is more, it is not necessarily the case that all meanings, connotations and other linguistic characteristics related to each word in the question, always play a role in the representation of the utterance as a whole (Verhagen, 1997). One question, containing one nominalized phrase does not necessarily lead to a more complex text, whereas a question in a questionnaire that is awash with nominalizations is more likely to be experienced as complex.

The psychological characteristics coded for this meta-analysis explain most of the variation obtained in the asymmetry size across questions, whereas the other characteristics seem to be of relatively little importance. As was argued earlier (Section 5.0), however, the effect of each characteristic does not only depend of the variance it explains. Other effects that should be looked into are the significance of the effects and the mean effect sizes. For example, the characteristic of issue relevance may explain a relatively large part of the variance in the asymme-

---

[9] The percentages variance explained in this table were estimated for each cluster separately. The total percentage of explained variance by all characteristics is not computed by adding the four percentages given here, due to possible overlap between variables. The percentage of the variance in the asymmetry size that is explained by the combination of linguistic and psychological characteristics, for example, is 52%, and not 48% + 14%.

try size, and may therefore appear to be an important variable. However, this could be caused by the fact that the extent to which the issues were judged to be relevant varies greatly over questions in this particular question set. The effect size should therefore be taken into account as well: if the mean effect of relevance is small, it is not such an interesting variable in spite of the variance it incidentally explains. Hence, the time has come to examine the effect of each coded characteristic separately.

5.2.1 Individual and combined effects

This section discusses the effects of each characteristic coded, focusing on the three types of effect sizes that were distinguished in the introduction to this chapter: the significance of the effect, the percentage of variance explained and the mean effect size.

Similar to the analyses reported in Chapter 3, the total variance (97) is divided into variance between experiments (called Level II), which is 65, and variance within experiments (called Level I), which is 32 (see Table 3.3). This is the maximum amount of variation that can be explained. The categorization of experiments in this meta-analysis was done by definition. In addition, the fact that there are not many experiments in this question set which consist of more than one question creates difficulties interpreting the variance explained (especially within experiments) on a content level: variance explained within experiments can always be understood as variance between questions, but variance explained between experiments can either indicate variation between experimental groups (populations, countries, etc.), or variation between questions. Despite these limitations on providing a theoretical interpretation of the variances, the distinction in levels of variance does enable us to make a more precise distinction as to how a characteristic influences the asymmetry size. In accordance with this principle, the distinction in levels of variance will be made where relevant.

In the introduction to this chapter it was explained that overlap between variables should be pinpointed by looking at the individual effects of each characteristic, as well as by investigating whether these individual effects change once they are analysed in combination with several other characteristics, or in combination with all other characteristics (the 'total effects'). Basically, the analyses show that the estimates do not change drastically when the 'total effects' are taken into account: the estimates of individual characteristics only change substantially on some occasions, when analysed in combination with characteristics from the same cluster. Accordingly, the estimation of 'total effects' will only be used at the end of this section to summarize which characteristics from the communicative setting are relatively important in explaining variation in the asymmetry size. Five characteristics prove to be especially important: relevance, complexity, abstractness, educational level and the extent to which the issue in the question is about a moral or a judicial prohibition.

Characteristics from the experimental setting

In order to summarize the forbid/allow data, an analysis was carried out to identify the countries in which the asymmetry is largest when corrected for the number of respondents who answered each question. It turns out that Belgian and Dutch findings do not differ significantly from the other findings. An analysis per author reveals that Rugg's asymmetry is larger but not significantly different to the asymmetries found by other researchers. Bishop et al.'s findings are significantly small compared to the asymmetry sizes found by other authors, and Krosnick and Schuman's asymmetry is somewhat larger than the asymmetry sizes found by the others.

These results for the effects of country/language and authors are based on weighted data (based on the number of respondents), so they cannot be traced back directly in the question set. Furthermore, they are mainly provided for the purpose of summarizing some aspects of the forbid/allow findings. These effects do not provide any understanding of the general circumstances likely to influence the asymmetry size. The effects of the characteristics described below do this to a larger extent.

The characteristic 'educational level' was coded by assigning the value '1' if questions were posed to a homogeneous sample of students, and '0' if some other sample of respondents answered the forbid/allow question. The effect of educational level is given in Table 5.2 (under 'individual effects'). The asymmetry size is indeed significantly smaller when a question is posed to a homogeneous sample of respondents with higher educational levels: the asymmetry is 4% for questions posed to students and 16.65% for questions posed to others. In terms of effect sizes, a change of 12.64% in the asymmetry size is a large effect ($d=1.3$).

	individual effects		combined effects	comb. % variance explained.
	change in asymmetry size in percentages	% variance explained	change in asymmetry size in percentages	
education	(16.65) -12.64= 4.01	tot.:35%	(12.52) - 12.05= .47	tot: 35
oral	(13.12) + 1.57=14.69	tot.:29%	(12.52) +1.48= 14	II: 40.9
random	-14	-		

Table 5.2: *Individual and combined effects of three experimental characteristics*

The effect of 'administration mode' is in line with expectations as well. As questions posed within an oral administration mode were given the code '1', Table 5.2 shows that oral questions lead to a significantly larger asymmetry than questions posed in a written administration mode. Nevertheless, the effect size is relatively small (d=.16). For the effect of 'sampling method' no hypothesis was formulated beforehand. The effect is nonsignificant (p>.05), however. The effect size and the percentage variance explained by this variable are therefore irrelevant. The lack of significance is probably due to the fact that variation was small, as a quota sample was used in one experiment only.

As the effects of educational level and administration mode are both significant, the substantiality of these effects should be assessed. This can be evaluated by the effect sizes (which were discussed above) and by the amount of variance explained.

The variance explained by whether or not a homogeneous sample of students was used is relatively large: 35% of the total variance (97) in the asymmetry size can be attributed to variation in this characteristic. Of the variance in the asymmetry size between experiments (65), 43% is explained by this characteristic. It does not explain variance between questions within experiments[10]. The relatively large degree of variance between experiments explained by this characteristic can be attributed to the relatively coincidental structure of this set of forbid/allow questions, in which respondents' educational level was never varied within one and the same experiment.

The administration mode explains 29% of the total variance in the asymmetry size. Variation in asymmetry size obtained within experiments (between questions) is not explained by this characteristic, indicating that the four questions posed by Bishop et al. (the only experiment in which administration mode was alternated) do not vary due to variation in administration mode when weighted for the number of respondents.

By combining the three experimental characteristics investigated here, 35% of the 97 variance in the asymmetry size can be explained (see right-hand column, Table 5.2). The variance between experiments explained by these combined experimental characteristics is 40.9%, whereas the variance explained within experiments is so small as to be negligible.

The total variance explained by these three combined variables is 35%, whereas the variable of educational level on its own already explains 35% of this

---

[10] The proportion of variance explained within experiments depends on the explained variance between experiments. Due to the weighting given on the basis of the number of respondents, this is difficult to compute however. For the variable 'educational level' the variance explained within experiments is *not* 100%-42%=58% of 36%.

variance, while variation in the administration mode explains 29%. At first sight, this might seem a puzzling result: if educational level systematically affects the asymmetry size and administration mode does so as well, then why doesn't the percentage of variance explained amount to 64% (35%+29%)? This can of course be explained by accidental overlaps of characteristics in this question set (see Section 5.0): apparently many questions posed to students did not differ in the administration mode that was used. However, a combined estimate for the effects of the three experimental characteristics shows that the effects of administration mode and type of sample drawing do not change in terms of direction and hardly change in size (see Table 5.2, under 'combined effects').

When the effects of experimental characteristics are estimated jointly with all the other characteristics (see Table 5.5), the direction of the effects remains unaltered as well. Together with the effects of relevance, complexity, abstractness and an emphasis on morality, the effect of educational level is reasonably large compared to the effects of the other characteristics analysed in the current research. Accordingly, it can be concluded that homogeneous samples of students answer forbid/allow questions less asymmetrically than heterogeneous samples of respondents. This may be related to attitude strength, since it is assumed that more highly educated respondents feel involved with a larger variety of issues.

Psychological characteristics

The psychological characteristics coded were relevance of the issue and complexity of the issue: question characteristics derived from the attitude strength hypothesis that were coded on the basis of judgements derived from a separate experiment. For complexity the hypothesis is supported. The more *complex* the issue was judged to be, the larger the asymmetry obtained: as can be seen under 'individual effects' in Table 5.3, questions about non-complex issues show an asymmetry size of 10.75%, whereas questions about complex issues show an asymmetry size of 18.40%. If an issue is more complex, more respondents will hold an opinion that is less crystallized, so more of them will be sensitive to the forbid/allow asymmetry. An alternative explanation is that more respondents will have a very nuanced opinion, causing them to regard an affirmative answer to either question as too extreme. Complexity explains 36% of the variance between experiments, and 12% of the variance within experiments (not in the table).[11] First of all, this indicates that some issues were judged to be more complex than others within

---

[11] As noted earlier, due to the fact that the data were weighted for the number of respondents per question and for the number of questions in each experiment, the variances within and between experiments and the percentages of variance explained do not simply add up to a total variance.

experiments on the same subject. Secondly, it implies that variances in asymmetry sizes for questions answered by different respondents in different experiments can be explained to a considerable extent by the characteristic 'complexity', but that the same is true of questions answered by the same respondents within the same experimental setting.

The variable *relevance* also accounts for a good deal of the variance between and within experiments. For relevance however, the direction of the effect is more difficult to interpret, as it is in the opposite direction to what was expected: the more relevant the issue was judged to be, the larger the asymmetry obtained. As shown in Table 5.3, questions about non-relevant issues lead to a mean asymmetry size of 11.68%, whereas questions about relevant issues are related to mean asymmetry sizes of 17.29%.

In addition to these individual effects, it is important to assess whether the effects are influenced by overlaps in characteristics. As the cluster of psychological characteristics consists of two variables only, overlaps for these variables were investigated jointly with the variables from the cluster of linguistic characteristics. As can be seen (under 'combined effects') in Table 5.3, the effects of relevance and complexity do not change due to overlaps with other variables in this cluster.

In conclusion, the effect of *relevance* is consistent in a direction that was not expected. The prediction was that respondents should hold more salient attitudes towards issues that are relevant. According to the attitude strength hypothesis, attitudes that are salient are thought about more often. Thinking about issues leads to polarization, which should cause the asymmetry to be smaller instead of larger. For *complexity*, however, the effects are similar to those predicted: more complex issues should lead to more ambivalent attitudes and therefore to a larger problem in mapping the opinion onto the 'yes' or 'no' answering options. This is confirmed by the data. Relevance and complexity seem to be concepts that are quite closely related and are both associated with attitude strength. In the light of this discovery, the next section (Section 5.2.2) investigates whether there is an interaction between these two variables which may shed more light on the unexpected result for relevance.

Linguistic characteristics

Three linguistic characteristics were coded for the current analyses. Two of these are barely related to variation in the asymmetry size: the use of nominalizations and the number of sentences. The use of *nominalizations* (followed by predicates) was expected to increase the linguistic complexity of the question and therefore cause a larger asymmetry. This proved to be the case but the effect is very small and insignificant when estimated individually (see Table 5.3). The percentage of variance in the asymmetry size it explains is therefore irrelevant.

	individual effects		combined effects	com-bined % vari-ance expl.
	change in asymmetry size in percentages	% vari-ance expl.	change in asymmetry size in percentages	
relevance	(11.68) + *5.61* =17.29	tot.:38%	(8.09) + *8.98*=17.07	
complexity	(10.75) + *7.65* =18.40	tot.:45%	(8.09)+*10.20*=18.29	tot.:52%
abstractness	(13.61) + *1.08* =14.69	tot.:36%	(8.09) - *7.81*= .28	II:41%
no. of sent	(13.41) + *6.27* =19.68	tot.:1%[12]	(8.09) +*6.18*= 4.27	
nominaliz.	-14.03	-	(8.09) +*1.42*= 9.51	

Table 5.3: *The effects of linguistic and psychological characteristics*

Analysed jointly with the other variables from this cluster the effect is significant but still small. It can be concluded that the use of nominalized phrases does affect the asymmetry size to some extent but it is not an important variable for explaining variations in the asymmetry size. The *number of sentences* turns out to affect the asymmetry size in the expected direction as well. It was expected that the use of more than one sentence in a question could be an indication of a complex issue which requires an introduction. It was also suggested that questions containing more than one sentence may be more difficult, because they place a heavier burden on working memory. Estimated individually, as well as in combination,

---

[12] The variance explained by this variable is 1%, and the variance explained between experiments is estimated to be 0%. In fact that is not entirely correct. The analyses are conducted under the assumption of 'homoscedasticity', which means that the variance in asymmetry size for questions with one sentence (coded 0) is expected to be similar to the variance for questions containing more sentences (coded 1). For some characteristics this assumption does not hold. This is the case for 'number of sentences', for 'motivation', for 'status quo' and for 'punishment': variables that turn out to be 'heteroscedastic'. The variance for questions containing one sentence, for example, is larger (66.68) than for questions containing more sentences. This does not come as a complete surprise, due to characteristics of this set of forbid/allow questions: there are simply many more questions containing one sentence than questions containing several sentences in this data set, and the variance in asymmetry size is likely to be larger for a larger group of questions than for a smaller one. The assumption of homoscedasticity could not be relaxed for the analyses, however, as this would cause power problems. Fortunately, the total variance explained does not suffer from this complexity (because it is estimated as the squared correlation between observed and estimated scores).

the asymmetry size is larger for longer questions, as expected. Furthermore, Table 5.3 shows that the effect of number of sentences hardly changes when estimated together with other variables. An overlap between number of sentences and issue complexity does not seem to play an important role, thereby ruling out the first explanation. The focus should therefore be on the explanation associated with memory overload. The number of sentences hardly explains any variance, which, in this case, indicates that there is not much variation on this characteristic in the present question set. The variance it does explain is mostly within experiments, due to the fact that some questions containing more than one sentence were included in the new experiments reported in Chapter 3, as well as in the experiment by Waterplas et al.

The linguistic characteristic *abstractness* proves to be far more important. Estimated individually, abstractness leads to a larger asymmetry. The effect on the mean difference between answers to forbid/allow questions is small but significant, and it explains quite a large percentage of the variance in the asymmetry size obtained (mostly between experiments). As shown in Table 5.3, it explains 36% of the overall variance. It explains some variance between experiments (9%), whereas the variance within experiments explained by this variable is negligible. The fact that abstractness mostly explains variance between experiments and not within, in spite of being a question characteristic, can be accounted for by the way the experiments were defined: many experiments consisted of one question only. Most of these were experiments replicating the 'speeches against communism' question used by Rugg (which was coded to be abstract). This question usually led to a large asymmetry, whereas experiments containing more than one question on different subjects, usually showed smaller asymmetries.

An interesting phenomenon is the turnaround in the effect of abstractness when it is estimated in combination with the other linguistic and psychological characteristics. This suggests an overlap between this and another variable, possibly complexity, since many abstract questions were coded as dealing with complex issues as well. In estimating the individual effect of abstractness, the abstract (and often complex) questions are compared to the non-abstract (often non-complex) questions and the effect is in the expected direction. However, if abstractness is separated from complexity, abstractness apparently does not lead to a more difficult interpretation. Despite the use of abstract terms, respondents may find it easy to arrive at their own interpretation of the abstract term if it is about a non-complex issue. This preliminary hypothesis on the effect of abstractness is not affected by the estimation of total effects (Table 5.5): a possible overlap with variables other than those from the linguistic and psychological cluster, means the effect of abstractness does not change but merely increases slightly. The next section (Section 5.2.2) therefore explores the interaction between abstractness and complexity.

Content-related characteristics

Content-related characteristics only explain a small part of the total variance in the asymmetry size (8%). Generally speaking, this set of variables does not seem to have much of an influence on the differences in size or direction of the forbid/allow asymmetry. The total variance explained by this cluster (8%) is an estimation, however, obtained by taking the mean total variance explained by each characteristic individually. This was necessary because some difficulties arose when looking at the variance explained by the content-related characteristics as a whole: combined estimates cannot be made for this set of variables, as many combinations of variables do not occur. One of the cells for that combination does not exist for almost every possible combination of content-related characteristics, distorting the estimates of the asymmetry for the combined characteristics.[13]

Because of these measurement problems, Table 5.4 can only provide individual estimates for each of the variables in the cluster of content-related characteristics. Furthermore, in the total analysis of combined characteristics (Table 5.5), the effects of only two variables from this cluster could be estimated: the effect of 'moral' and of 'motivation'. In this total analysis, the effect of whether the issue is governed by a moral prohibition or a judicial prohibition is particularly large. The effect of whether or not an argument in favour of forbidding the issue was included in the question ('motivation') proves to be of intermediate size.

	individual effects	
	change in asymmetry size in percentages	% variance explained
moral	(8.00) + *8.45* = 16.45	tot.:40%
punishment	(20.37) - *6.88* = 13.50	tot.: 3%
motivation	(14.55) - *5.27* = 9.28	tot.: 2%
whom	(13.89) + *2.39* = 16.28	tot.: 1%
status quo	(13.55) + *8.62* = 22.17	tot.: 1%
actor	-7.34	-

Table 5.4: *The effects of the content-related characteristics*

Although content-related characteristics as a group explain much less of the total

---

[13] And there is yet another problem: the assumption of 'homoscedasticity' does not hold for a number of variables within this cluster of content variables. See previous footnote.

variance than the linguistic or psychological characteristics, there is one character-istic that has quite a large effect on the asymmetry size ('moral'), and one content characteristic that has a moderate effect ('motivation'). The prediction was that issues that have a high *moral* connotation lead to a larger asymmetry than issues with a more concrete, judicial content. This proves to be the case in the individual as well as in the total estimates. Furthermore, this variable goes a long way towards explaining variance between experiments (40%). This is partly due to the fact that there is a great deal of variation in the coding of 'morality': many ques-tions in the question set were coded as dealing with moral issues, and many others were coded as dealing with judicial issues. For the other content-related characteristics, not so many questions were coded as being associated with a certain characteristic, which limits the maximum amount of variance such a characteristic can explain. The explanation for the smaller asymmetry obtained for judicial issues could be that those issues cause less ambivalence about how the issue should be forbidden/allowed and by whom.

The fact that questions containing a *motivation* for forbidding the issue are related to smaller asymmetries could indicate support for previous findings in wording effect research that respondents are guided by arguments in the ques-tion. Giving an argument for 'forbidding' (and 'not allowing') the issue, probably prompts respondents to answer 'yes, forbid' and 'no, not allow' more easily, although a small asymmetry remains. However, individual estimates show that this variable hardly explains any variance, probably due to a lack of variation within the question set with respect to whether or not an argument in favour of forbidding (or not allowing) was included. The other content-related characteris-tics seem of less general importance, for the current question set at least. Given the limitations of meta-analytic techniques it is impossible to conclude otherwise.

For the *punishment* variable it was predicted that issues dealing with a prohibi-tion beforehand (a permit request for example) evoke less doubt than issues relating to punishment afterwards. Questions implying prohibition beforehand were coded as '1'. Table 5.4 shows that these kinds of issues do lead to a smaller asymmetry. This characteristic mainly explains variance between questions within experiments (7%). For this question set it implies that this variable only explains variance in asymmetry sizes found in the two experiments reported in Chapter 3.

The *status quo* variable shows a significant effect as well. This explains 18% of the variance between questions within experiments (not in Table 5.4), indicating that it explains differences in the asymmetry size for this data set within the experiment on environmental issues on the one hand, and the experiment on ethnic groups on the other (see Chapters 3 and 4). It was expected that the forbid/allow asymmetry would be smaller if the questions concern activities that are forbidden at the moment of administration, because 'to forbid' would be less subject to change and less extreme if something is forbidden already. Of course, it follows that 'to allow' would acquire a more active and extreme meaning instead, but since 'allowing' seems to be intrinsically less extreme than 'forbidding', the asymmetry was expected to become smaller. The opposite proved to be the case: the asymmetry size is larger for issues that were forbidden at the moment of administration. It is unclear how this unexpected result should be interpreted. Perhaps there is an overlap between the effect of 'status quo' and other characteristics, as the 'status quo' was varied in one experiment only, in which all the questions dealt with ethnic groups.

For the *whom* variable it was coded whether the person for whom something is forbidden or allowed is mentioned explicitly in the question text. The question is regarded as more concrete if it contains an explicit actor, which was expected to result in a smaller asymmetry. This turned out not to be the case, as the asymmetry is somewhat larger.

The *actor* variable shows the effect of the presence of an explicit promulgator of the act of forbidding/allowing in the question text. The presence of such a promulgator would make the question more concrete and the asymmetry size smaller. This content characteristic turns out not to affect the asymmetry size ($p > .05$). It may be the case that a reference to 'the government' is quite vague in itself, which means it does not to make a difference whether such a vague actor is mentioned or no actor at all.

Total effects

The total set of characteristics (see Table 5.5) explains 67% of the total variance in the asymmetry size. Of the variance between experiments, 53.8% is explained by the characteristics coded for this meta-analysis, along with 44.4% of the variance within experiments. The effects are ranked according to size. The 'size' indicates how the standardized effect size should be judged: an effect larger than one standard deviation (9.85) is very large, 0.8 standard deviation is large, medium effects are around 0.5 standard deviation and small effects are about 0.2 standard deviation (Cohen, 1977; see Section 3.2).

The data in Table 5.5 can be used to show what the mean forbid/allow asymmetry looks like for combinations of characteristics. If none of the characteristics indicated in the left column apply, the mean asymmetry size is 5.69%. For questions that deal with complex issues and are posed to a homogeneous sample of students, the mean difference between forbid/allow answers is 7.89%. For questions containing vague or abstract terms posed to students, the asymmetry is reversed: about 9% more 'yes, allow' than 'not forbid' answers are obtained.

characteristic	change in asymmetry size in percentages	p	effect size	total % variance explained
relevance	(5.69) + *10.79* = 16.48	<.001	very large	
complexity	(5.69) + *8.76* = 14.45	<.001	large	
abstractness	(5.69) - *8.41* = -2.72	<.001	large	
educational level	(5.69) - *6.56* = -.87	<.001	large	tot.: 67%
moral/judicial	(5.69) + *6.14* = 11.83	<.001	large	II : 53.8%
motivation	(5.69) - *4.21* = 1.48	<.001	mediate	I : 44.4%
no. of sentences	(5.69) + *1.53* = 7.22	<.001	small	
oral	(5.69) + *1.52* = 7.21	<.001	small	
nominalization	(5.69) + *.4* = 6.09	<.001	very small	
random	-5.69	n.s.	-	

Table 5.5: *Total effects of the characteristics, ranked by size*

Table 5.5 allows predictions to be generated concerning results of future forbid/allow experiments in which characteristics are combined that do not occur in that specific combination in the current question set. Furthermore, it indicates which characteristics from the communicative setting should at least be taken into account when designing experiments in order to detect general patterns caused by the use of forbid/allow: the psychological respondent characteristics 'relevance' and 'complexity', the linguistic characteristic 'abstractness' (or vagueness of the terms used in the question), the educational level (which might also be related to attitude strength) and the content characteristic 'morality'.

Before the theoretical implications of these findings are elaborated on in Section 5.3, some interaction effects will first be investigated. It would be interesting to examine the interactions between a number of variables. For example, there is some theoretical indication that the effect of linguistic characteristics will be different for questions posed orally than for written questionnaires (see Note 4). This cannot be checked using this question set, however, because there is not enough variation between and within experiments to interpret this interaction analysis. Another interesting phenomenon which merits investigation is the interaction between complexity and relevance of the issue. Relevance shows a large effect contrary to the direction expected: questions on relevant issues lead to a larger asymmetry, not to a smaller one. This is a reason to look more precisely at the effect of relevance and the interaction between relevance and complexity. Another interesting interaction is between complexity of the issue and the abstractness of the text, as questions on complex issues are more likely to be couched in abstract terms.

5.2.2 Two interaction effects

As discussed in the previous section, it may very well be expected that text characteristics, respondent characteristics (and other characteristics) interact or overlap in their occurrence, and are subject to certain threshold values before they begin to have any effect at all (Verhagen, 1997). The overlap was investigated by the combined analyses in the previous section. In the current section, two interaction effects will be estimated: the interaction between complexity and relevance, and the interaction between issue complexity and abstractness. This will yield some understanding of the threshold values that have to be reached and of the interplay between characteristics from the communicative setting that are more or less related to each other.[14] The first analysis will provide a tool for getting rid of the puzzling results of relevance, whereas the second analysis will lead to some interesting hypotheses concerning future forbid/allow research.

Relevance and complexity

The attitude strength hypothesis predicts that questions about relevant issues will show a smaller asymmetry size than questions on irrelevant issues and that questions about complex issues will lead to a larger asymmetry than questions about less complex issues. For complex issues the asymmetry will be larger because complexity leads to an increase in ambivalence: the issue is too complex to elicit an (extreme) affirmative answer from respondents and need to be modified to offer the respondent more than the choice between 'yes' and 'no' in answer to the forbid/allow questions. Irrelevant issues are expected to generate a larger asymmetry because irrelevant issues are thought about less often and it is thinking more about a subject which makes attitudes more polarized and extreme. Extreme attitudes are more easily mapped onto the answering options to forbid/

---

[14] The limitations of meta-analytic techniques also concern the estimation and interpretation of interaction effects. In a non-experimental design, an interaction effect can imply overlap between the variables or a real interaction effect. It can only be interpreted as an interaction effect if all 4 cells relevant to the estimation of an interaction effect between two variables are filled. For both of the interaction effects estimated here, there is room to interpret them as real interaction effects. There is a certain overlap in this question set, but all cells are filled, so the interaction can be estimated and can be interpreted as a 'traditional' interaction effect. The overlap for abstractness and issue complexity, for example, is as follows: many questions on non-complex issues are non-abstract (92% of the questions on non-complex issues) and most of the complex issues are abstract (90% of the complex issues), but the other cells are filled as well.

allow questions, which have fairly extreme connotations due to the connotations of forbid and allow.

This attitude strength hypothesis is not supported by the meta-analysis, as relevant issues have been shown to lead to larger asymmetries. However this is in line with Krosnick and Schuman's finding (1988) that larger opinion 'intensity' leads to a larger asymmetry: a result that, according to them, is also contrary to expectations based on the attitude strength literature. An analysis of the interaction between relevance and complexity might shed more light on this unexpected result: complexity is about the need to think about an issue, whereas relevance is about the degree to which this is likely to be done, the degree of willingness to think about the issue. An interaction effect between these two variables is therefore not implausible.

Table 5.6 shows that there is a significant interaction effect. Relevant questions lead to a larger asymmetry, complex questions lead to a larger asymmetry, but questions about an issue that is relevant as well as complex do not cause the asymmetry to be twice as large, as might be expected on the basis of both effects separately. The effects of relevance and complexity seem to slow each other down or reach a ceiling value at some point.

	change in asymmetry size in percentages	p	% variance explained
relevance	(9.46) + 5.96 = 15.42	<.001	tot.: 48%
complexity	(9.46) + 9.74 = 19.20	<.001	II : 35%
relevance x complexity	(9.46) + 5.96 + 9.74 - 6.15 =19.01	<.001	

Table 5.6: *The interaction effect between relevance and complexity*

The attitude strength hypothesis predicts that the asymmetry is due to the answering behaviour of 'indifferents'. This prediction is supported with regard to questions about issues that are complex and not relevant (an asymmetry of 19.20%). Complex and irrelevant issues require respondents to give the issue some thought but the lack of relevance means they are not very willing to do so. The analysis shows that the asymmetry will be largest in such cases: respondents are very sensitive to the connotations of forbid/allow and find an affirmative answer too extreme because the issue is too complex to allow an extreme judgement to be formed in such a short time. However, if the issue is not relevant and not complex, the attitude strength hypothesis does not hold, as the asymmetry is smallest in that case (9.46%), although the theory predicts that it will be the largest. A possible explanation is that the respondent is not willing to think about the issue, but the lack of complexity allows him to form an opinion on the issue on the spot, using a relatively small amount of effort.

The attitude strength hypothesis does not hold for issues that are relevant either. The asymmetry obtained for relevant issues should be smaller but this is not the case. The asymmetry is larger for relevant non-complex issues than for irrelevant non-complex ones (which leads to an asymmetry size of 9.46%). If an issue is non-complex and relevant, respondents are not required to think hard about the issue but at the same time they are willing to do so. In this case the asymmetry should be smallest, yet it is estimated to be 15.42%. This unexpected result might be explained in a similar way to the result for issues that are complex as well as relevant.

Relevance, or indifference, is a central variable in the attitude strength hypothesis, but does not show the expected effect on the asymmetry size. This may be due to the way relevance was coded for this meta-analysis: issues were coded on their degree of relevance by students not belonging to the original group of respondents, years after the original question was posed. In addition to this, a mean relevance score was used to predict a mean difference between forbid/allow answers, where it would have been preferable to relate relevance and asymmetry size on an individual level.

Apart from these measurement problems, which are all but impossible to avoid in a meta-analysis, a theoretical note should be made as well. Why does complexity of the issue have an effect; as predicted, and why does relevance lead to unexpected results? It is important to note that the line of reasoning from complexity to a prediction about the asymmetry size is much shorter than the line of reasoning from the concept of relevance. From complexity there is a direct line of reasoning through predictions about the ambivalence of the attitude to a larger asymmetry. From relevance, the line goes from predictions of thinking a lot about the issue, to polarization of the attitude, to a smaller asymmetry (cf. Wood, 1982, see Section 5.1.2). Based on the results in this meta-analysis, it may be concluded that thinking more about an issue does not necessarily lead to polarization but can also cause a more pronounced, but balanced attitude to be formed. Also, thinking more about an issue could lead to a specification of the issue into one or more subdomains, causing relevance to be an adequate indicator for the expected asymmetry size only if the question addresses the issue at the right level of specificity (cf. Fishbein & Ajzen, 1975). If smoking in public places is very relevant to someone because he is a smoker working in a public building, it does not necessarily mean that this respondent has an opinion on government action on smoking in public buildings or on smoking in general.

Basically, the interaction effect between relevance and complexity discussed here, implies that complexity is the most important variable, and the relevance of the issue is a less determinant characteristic. When an issue is complex as well as relevant, the interaction effect between the two apparently neutralizes the contribution of relevance to the asymmetry size.

Complexity and abstractness

In themselves, complexity and abstractness produced the following effects: the more complex the issue in the question is, the larger the asymmetry, as was predicted by the attitude strength hypothesis. For abstractness, the effect was more difficult to interpret: abstractness estimated individually led to a somewhat larger asymmetry, but in combination with other linguistic and psychological characteristics, the effect of abstraction was reversed. As discussed in Section 5.2.1, this could be due to an overlap or interaction with the effect of complexity.

As can be seen in Table 5.7, the results of an interaction analysis show that the size of the asymmetry is about 18% for questions on complex issues, regardless of whether these questions contain abstract terms or not. Once again, complexity leads to a ceiling effect: if the issue is complex, then other characteristics do not seem to play a role. An interesting change is also discernible: estimated separately, questions on abstract issues lead to a larger asymmetry than questions on non-abstract issues. It was hypothesized that because of the burden placed on working memory by abstractness, respondents would not realize that not forbidding implies allowing. However this analysis has shown that if complexity is taken into account, the degree of abstractness is only important for non-complex questions. Furthermore, abstractness leads to a smaller asymmetry, which contradicts both expectations and previous results.

	mean change in asymmetry size	p	% variance explained
abstractness	$(11.11) - 3.05 = 8.06$	<.001	tot.:44%
complexity	$(11.11) + 7.25 = 18.36$	<.001	II : 34%
abstractness x complexity	$(11.11) - 3.05 + 7.25 + 2.86 = 18.17$	<.001	

Table 5.7: *The interaction effect of complexity and abstractness*

This finding can only be explained by retrospective hypothesizing, to be tested in an experimental design. A possible explanation is that abstraction was coded as an indicator of linguistic complexity, which increases the processing effort needed at the interpretation and attitude localization stage. The considerable burden on memory leads to a larger asymmetry at the answering stage because respondents do not pay enough attention to the implications of a negative answer. This may indeed be the case for questions about complex issues, but issue complexity itself already causes a maximum asymmetry size. At the same time, when answering questions on non-complex issues containing abstract terms, respondents may use the room for interpretation offered by the abstract term to interpret the question in such a way as to be able to form or locate an extreme opinion and so be able to choose between the answering options offered, thereby decreasing the asymmetry size. When answering questions about non-complex issues containing abstract terms, therefore, respondents choose an interpretation for the abstract term that enables them to be extreme and fulfil the specific communicative task of answering yes or no to a forbid/allow question.

5.3 CONCLUSIONS AND DISCUSSION

In Chapter 3 it was established that the forbid/allow asymmetry does exist. Overall, the 'not forbid' answer is chosen 14% more often than 'yes, allow': a small difference in question wording therefore has major implications for the answers given. The forbid/allow asymmetry can only be explained if it can be understood which factors influence the size of the wording effect or make it non-existent. Apart from variation in the use of 'forbid' or 'allow' many other question characteristics are shown to influence the size of the wording effect. This indicates that research on the influence of question characteristics on the answering process remains essential and should not be limited to the effects of 'forbid' and 'allow' alone: the effect of the use of either verb seems to be diminished (abstraction) or facilitated (complexity) by several question or respondent characteristics.

Much of the total variance in the asymmetry size (67%) could be explained by the characteristics coded for this meta-analysis. The analysis indicates that some characteristics do not play a role, while others have a considerable effect on the mean asymmetry size. Based on this analysis, therefore, it is possible to summarize the circumstances under which a large wording effect is likely to occur and under which circumstances the asymmetry is likely to be smaller. This is of practical use for further research into the forbid/allow asymmetry, as well as for questionnaire designers with doubts about their question wording. Here, it is used as a starting point for theory building, however. The effects of characteristics on the asymmetry size obtained can be generalized beyond the level of specific questions because of the meta-analytic techniques employed. The analyses in this section therefore provide an important contribution to the additional hypotheses offered in previous forbid/allow research: whereas Bishop et al. (1988), for example, could not provide an adequate explanation for their contradictory findings concerning administration mode (see Section 2.1.4), summarizing techniques such as the ones employed here can provide a more general description of the facilitating factors for the occurrence of the asymmetry. The meta-analysis could therefore summarize and rank the circumstances within the communicative setting as a whole that are important for the occurrence of the asymmetry.

The analyses indicate that the wording effect is likely to be small if a forbid/allow question is posed to respondents who are more highly educated, if the question is about an abstract issue, if it is about an issue that is judged to be not complex, and if the question is about an issue that is relatively concrete, so that respondents do not have to think about the feasibility of prohibition.

Many characteristics coded for this analysis, several of which are linguistic and several content-related, do not affect the size of the forbid/allow asymmetry. This is good news for questionnaire designers concerned about wording effects. It does not seem necessary to bother much about linguistic aspects that may place a slightly larger burden on working memory but do not affect the comprehensibility of the question. Note that this last point may well be crucial. As discussed earlier in this chapter, it is difficult to assess the linguistic complexity without taking the content and context of the specific question into account: a question that is linguistically complex may well be worded as simply as possible. What is more, one question that is linguistically complex and needs a lot of processing time may not be a problem, but a questionnaire full of that kind of questions may cause some sort of 'threshold value' to be reached, giving rise to larger wording effects.

Due to the limitations of non-experimental techniques discussed in the introduction to this chapter, it may be possible that some effects facilitating the forbid/allow asymmetry were not distinguished in the analyses presented here. Future research could try and detect other relevant characteristics through experimental research instead of meta-analytic techniques. Experimental research could try to establish whether it is the forbid answers or the allow answers that are sensitive to change caused by background variables. As a criterion for the best question wording, preference could be given to those questions to which the answers fluctuate least due to background variables unrelated to the attitude to be measured.

What do the findings presented here add to the insight into the causes of the forbid/allow asymmetry and the question-answering process in general? The large amount of variance in the asymmetry size offers room for additional explanations, apart from the connotations of 'forbid' and 'allow'. A more cognitive interpretation of the meta-analytic findings presented here is given below, based on which some hypotheses will be generated to be tested in the next chapters.

The analyses conducted in the current chapter indicate that the answer to an attitude question seems to be multidimensional: the net result of a complex judgment formation and mapping procedure and a reaction to elements of the question wording and communicative setting. Analyses conducted for Chapter 4 show that the asymmetry stems from the mapping stage of the question-answering process. The input characteristic of using either 'forbid' or 'allow' affects the way similar attitudes are mapped onto the answering options. In addition, the analyses reported in the current chapter seem to imply that several other respondent and input characteristics from the communicative setting interact with this mapping process.

Important characteristics are the ones related to attitude strength: the complexity of the issue and the level of education, whereas most linguistic or content-related characteristics play a minor role in explaining variations in the asymmetry size. The results of this meta-analysis suggest that the linguistic form of the question does play a role in the early stages of the question-answering process, but is immediately interpreted and represented by using the attitudes related to the issue at stake. The respondent understands his task and knows that he has to react to the issue. This task sets in motion a complex cognitive process of localizing attitudes and evaluating them, too complex to leave room for linguistic surface characteristics or small content-related characteristics to reach a threshold value and exert an important influence on the outcomes of the question-answering process. The only content-related characteristic that was found to affect the asymmetry size substantially is related to the complexity of the issue: moral issues involve a more complex judgement than judicial issues. The only linguistic characteristic affecting the asymmetry size is related to the content of the attitude retrieved: the abstractness of the issue.

In the search for a monocausal theory explaining the forbid/allow asymmetry, the connotations hypothesis remains to be tested further. Is it true that agreeing to 'forbid' implies a real act of opposition and disagreeing with 'allow' merely implies withholding one's support? Is this what causes the preference for giving negative answers to both questions? In addition, the effect of complexity found in this meta-analysis seems to indicate that attitude strength should be incorporated as an explanatory dimension, whereas it could explain variations in the mapping process. Furthermore, a hypothesis on the communicative restriction imposed on respondents by offering only two answering options may be derived from the effect of the characteristic 'abstractness'. This is dealt with in greater detail below.

Important characteristics are the ones related to attitude strength: the complexity of the issue and the level of education of respondents. Previous forbid/allow research was right in focusing on this respondent characteristic after all. The complexity of the issue explains a good deal of variation in the asymmetry size obtained when estimated on its own (45%), and seems to lead to some sort of ceiling effect when estimated in combination with the relevance of the issue or together with abstractness, in the amount of variance it explains, as well as in its mean effect on the asymmetry size obtained.

This is in line with theories on the effect of attitude strength which assume that more respondents holding a weak or ambivalent opinion will be found the more complex the issue in the question is. Respondents who hold a weak or ambivalent opinion will probably map their evaluation onto 'no' to the forbid as well as to the allow question, feeling that agreeing to either question is too extreme. Based on the effect found for complexity in this meta-analysis, one may hypothesize that the 'no' answer in particular seems to represent a melting pot of several different opinions, such as 'no, I do not think it should be forbidden/allowed', 'no, I do not have an opinion on this, so I do not want to answer affirmatively', or 'no, I only moderately agree with forbidding/allowing, so I cannot answer yes'.

Based on the experiments reported in Chapter 4 it was concluded that the meanings of 'yes' and 'no' differ due to the use of 'forbid' and 'allow'. In the current chapter the attitude strength dimension 'complexity' was seen to have an effect on the degree of the mapping problem. However, the analysis did not reveal how the mapping changed. Did the asymmetry size change because of a change in the forbid answers (more 'no' to forbid), because of a change in the allow answers (more 'no' to allow), or because of a change in both? Reasoning from the connotation hypothesis it can be hypothesized that 'no' to forbid as well as allow questions represents a melting pot of meanings. Within the framework of this meta-analysis it was not possible to investigate whether this hypothesis holds. This should be established experimentally.

The effect of issue complexity can be investigated experimentally by relating 'complexity' to the concept of 'extremity'. Most of the attitude strength dimensions eventually lead to a prediction about the polarization of attitudes. The same is true for issue complexity, which is assumed to cause more respondents to be ambivalent or hold moderate opinions. The degree of issue relevance also leads to predictions about the polarization of attitudes. Accordingly, it is interesting to measure the extremity of the attitudes directly (instead of approximating it by issue complexity) and relate the extremity of respondents' opinions to the likeliness of them mapping their evaluation onto 'no' or 'yes' to forbid/allow questions. As the connotations hypothesis focuses on the extreme connotations of forbid/ allow questions, or rather of answers indicating agreement with such questions, it seems likely that some relation should be found between this particular dimension of attitude strength and the mapping problem respondents encounter. More specifically, the hypothesis would be that the answering option 'no' to both questions represents a mixture of meanings, whereas affirmative answers reflect extreme opinions. This will be investigated in Chapter 7.

From a theoretical perspective, a second interesting phenomenon arising from this meta-analysis is that the main effect of complexity is modified by an interaction with abstractness. In other words, the effect of complexity is not the same for all levels of abstractness. This interaction appears to be an important explanatory variable found in this meta-analysis, as it could indicate that the source of the asymmetry should be sought in characteristics from the communicative task as a whole. Despite the fact that the main effect of forbid/allow arises at the mapping stage of the question-answering process, the effect of abstractness could imply that linguistic input early in the process can affect the mapping process.

Reading the question seems to lead to a representation of the text that depends on the accessible attitudes. In this process, it may be the case that respondents look for the interpretation that offers the best possibilities for fulfilling the communicative task as a whole and answer 'yes' or 'no' to the question. The attitude is then retrieved or formed and the respondent formulates an evaluation that has to be mapped onto the answering options. Another possibility is that respondents interpret the question using the accessible attitudes, formulate an evaluation and try to map that onto the answering options, but go back to reading and interpreting the question if mapping problems occur and then try to interpret the vague or abstract terms used in the question in a way that allows them to map their evaluation onto 'yes' or 'no'.[15]

Hence, the interaction effect of abstractness and complexity could indicate that respondents realize during question-answering that the use of forbid/allow causes problems in mapping their answers. They still try to fulfil their communicative task, however. If the question leaves room for it, they interpret the abstract or vague words in the question in such a way that it is possible for them to answer affirmatively (i.e. extremely) rather than stretching the meaning of the answering option 'no'. Based on this cautious hypothesis and in the light of the connotations hypothesis in general, it is interesting to investigate experimentally whether the mapping problem caused by the use of forbid/allow disappears once the communicative restriction of having to choose between 'yes' or 'no' is relaxed by offering more answering options, thereby providing the opportunity to express less extreme opinions more easily. If the wording effect disappears once greater communicative freedom is offered, this would indicate that the wording effect is caused by a combination of the use of forbid/allow and the answering options yes/no, instead of solely by the use of forbid/allow. This will be tested in the next chapter. The experiments designed for this test will also provide the opportunity to investigate the exact differences in the mapping process underlying forbid/allow questions, as a follow-up to Chapter 4.

---

[15] Note that this explanation for the effect of abstractness does not mean that forbid/allow questions measure different attitudes: findings in this meta-analysis explain why a larger asymmetry may be found in one forbid/allow question compared to another, but do not suggest that the interpretation of the issue in an allow question would be different from the interpretation of the equivalent forbid question.

Chapter 6
COMMUNICATIVE RESTRICTIONS
AND THE ANSWERING SCALES[1]

6.0 INTRODUCTION

This chapter subjects two questions to further research. The first focuses on the issue of whether the forbid/allow asymmetry is solely the result of offering respondents a yes/no answering scale, instead of a scale with more answering options. This will be referred to as the *communicative restrictions hypothesis*. It raises the possibility that the asymmetry is due to the use of forbid/allow combined with the use of yes/no and will disappear if more answering options are provided, allowing respondents to express moderate opinions.

The second question focuses on differences between the answering scales to forbid/allow questions. The two experiments reported in Chapter 4 showed that forbid/allow questions are equally valid – if random measurement error is filtered out. They measure the same attitude but this attitude is expressed differently on the answering scales due to the use of 'forbid' or 'allow'. This confirmed the *different scales hypothesis*. However, the analyses did not indicate how the scales for forbid/allow questions differ from each other. This will be investigated in the current chapter.

The first research question in this chapter concentrates on the communicative restrictions imposed on the respondents by offering a yes/no answering scale. A larger number of negative responses is obtained to forbid questions than the number of positive responses obtained to allow questions. This may still be due by the extreme connotations of 'forbid' and 'allow', which create a tendency among respondents to map moderate or ambivalent opinions onto 'no'. The effect of linguistic abstractness (see Chapter 5), however, suggests that respondents try to interpret the question in a way that allows them to fulfil their communicative task and gives the answering options 'yes' and 'no' an equal chance of being chosen. This effect and the connotations hypothesis in general, suggest that it would be logical to formulate a hypothesis stating that the mapping problem may disappear once the communicative restriction of having to choose between a simple 'yes' or 'no' is removed. Hence, in addition to the connotations of 'forbid' and 'allow', the communicative task of having to choose between 'yes' and 'no' when answering forbid/allow questions is hypothesized to be an important cause of the asymmetry (see Box 6.1).

---

[1] Many of the results reported in this chapter were presented at the 7th Annual Meeting of the Society for Text and Discourse (1997) and at the VIOT Conference (1999).

> **The communicative restrictions hypothesis**
> As the asymmetry is caused by the extreme connotations of forbid/allow, affirmative answering options may also be regarded as extreme. The asymmetry will therefore disappear when more answering options are offered, allowing the expression of an intermediate position and more moderate positions on the answering scale.

Box 6.1: *The communicative restrictions hypothesis*

The experiments reported in the current chapter were designed in such a way that respondents answered the regular two-point-scale forbid/allow questions containing only a yes/no answering option, as well as equivalent forbid/allow questions accompanied by a seven-point scale (agree-disagree), which permits respondents to express more moderate opinions than the extreme 'yes' and 'no', as well as to choose the midpoint of the scale. By offering a seven-point scale it can be established whether the asymmetry is caused primarily by the combination of the use of extreme verbs and severely restricting the answering possibilities, or whether it is the result of a more general effect of these verbs independent of the yes/no answering scale.

The second research question in the current chapter focuses on the differences between the answering scales to forbid/allow questions. The two experiments reported in Chapter 4 showed that forbid/allow questions are congeneric. Different answers to these questions reflect the same attitude: a respondent who is moderately pro-abortion may answer 'no' to a forbid question, but may also map this same opinion onto 'no' when answering an equivalent allow question. Apparently different answers (e.g. 'not forbid' and 'not allow') can reflect the same attitude, despite the fact that they do not logically have the same meaning.

The issue of *how* different answers obtained to forbid/allow questions relate to a similar attitude remains to be investigated, as the results of Chapter 4 did not indicate exactly how respondents use the answering scales to express their attitudes.[2] This will be analysed by focusing on two characteristics of the answers to forbid/allow questions: in the current chapter the width of the answering scales will be investigated by examining differences in variances and in homogeneity, while the next chapter focuses on differences in the meanings of 'yes' and 'no' to

---

[2] In Chapter 4, the essential tau-equivalence in the first experiment indicated that the scales to forbid/allow questions are of equal width, but that the meaning of 'yes' (and/or 'no') to the forbid question differs from the meaning of 'no' (and/or 'yes') to the allow question. The congenericity found in the second experiment implied that there was not only a shift in the meaning of 'yes' and 'no', but also a difference in the width of the answering scales due to the use of forbid/allow. These equivocal results could not be interpreted fully, however, so Chapter 4 concluded that forbid/allow questions are at least congeneric.

forbid/allow questions. In order to unravel the mapping mechanisms causing the forbid/allow asymmetry, a grasp of both these characteristics has to be obtained. Based on this, recommendations on the preferability of either question wording and the interpretation of the answers can be formulated.

If the scales to forbid/allow questions differ in width, the forbid scale may be wider or narrower than the allow scale, indicating that the cognitive distance between 'yes' and 'no' on one scale differs from the other. This will be reflected by differences in the variances of forbid answers and allow answers, as well as by differences in homogeneity, which entails the proportion of error score variance and true score variance.

Forbid questions and allow questions are equally valid if random measurement error is filtered out: their true scores correlate unity. It is unclear, however, whether the answers to forbid questions consist of a true score component that is the same size as the true score component of allow questions. In other words, does a set of forbid questions elicit answers of equal reliability, that is homogeneity, to a set of allow questions about the same issue?

A comparison of the homogeneity of forbid/allow questions is revealing because of its theoretical as well as its practical implications. If a set of allow questions reflects the underlying attitude less homogeneously than a set of forbid questions, this implies that respondents are less likely to express their opinions consistently when answering a set of allow questions on a certain issue than when answering a set of forbid questions. Respondents who are pro-abortion, for example, express this opinion relatively consistently in their answers to a set of forbid questions about abortion, but switch relatively often between 'yes' and 'no' when answering an equivalent set of allow questions. Cognitively, this would imply that the width of the answering scale to allow questions is smaller than the width of the answering scale to forbid questions: the distance between the response options 'yes allow' and 'not allow' is relatively small compared to the distance between 'yes forbid' and 'not forbid'. In practical terms, a larger homogeneity of forbid questions would imply that forbid questions are better in reflecting differences between respondents as to the attitudes on abortion they hold. Opinion research is basically conducted to find out what people think about an issue and how people differ from each other with respect to their attitudes about this issue. If a set of forbid questions about abortion is answered more homogeneously, the answers to this cluster of questions provide better possibilities for distinguishing differences between respondents' general attitudes towards abortion. In that case, 'forbid' is the preferable question wording.

No clear-cut hypotheses can be derived from theory to suggest that forbid questions are more reliable than allow questions or vice versa. The analyses in this chapter merely set out to establish whether forbid/allow questions differ in their reliabilities. If the reliabilities to forbid/allow questions differ, then the next step will be to establish why they differ. If the cognitive distance between 'yes' and 'no' on the answering scale to forbid questions differs from this distance for allow questions, a deeper understanding of the mapping process can be obtained by analysing the meanings of the answers to forbid/allow questions: what does 'yes forbid' mean and how does this meaning differ from 'not allow'? This will be the focus of the next chapter.

To sum up, an important goal of the current chapter is to gain insight into the mapping decisions respondents make in order to communicate similar attitudes, and the differences between those mapping decisions for forbid questions and allow questions. Furthermore, it will be investigated whether differences in these mapping decisions disappear when respondents are not forced to chose between 'yes' and 'no'. This is a test of the communicative restrictions hypothesis.

Before discussing the results, Section 6.1 describes the design of the experiments, the materials used and provides some details about the analyses conducted for this chapter. The results section first establishes whether the asymmetry for two-point-scale questions is found again (Section 6.2.1): if this was not the case, it would be difficult to interpret a possible absence of any wording effect on the equivalent seven-point-scale questions. Secondly, in order to establish whether the asymmetry is mainly due to the communicative restriction of offering two answering options, it will be analysed whether a wording effect occurs when this restriction is removed (6.2.2). Thirdly, the exact differences between the mapping process for forbid/allow questions will be analysed. Variances in the answers to forbid/allow questions discussed in Sections 6.2.1 (for the two-point-scale questions) and 6.2.2 (for the seven-point-scale questions) will be interpreted by focusing on differences and similarities in the reliabilities of forbid/allow questions, as well as differences in the mapping mechanisms for forbid/allow questions (Section 6.3). These findings will be integrated in Section 6.4.

6.1 INSTRUMENTS AND DESIGN OF THE EXPERIMENTS

For the analyses in this chapter 10 forbid/allow experiments were set up, each containing about six forbid/allow questions to enhance the generalizability of the results. In order to take into account the possible effects of the characteristics investigated in the previous chapter, forbid/allow experiments were set up over a wide variety of issues and posed to respondents of various backgrounds. Each experiment had an identical split ballot design and dealt with an issue that was a hot topic in public opinion in the Netherlands at the time of administration (spring 1997), for example, new medical developments or road safety. Several different administration modes were applied in the experiments, although a written administration mode was the predominant method used. In several experiments the questions were posed during classes at secondary schools. In these cases, the questionnaires were about topics relevant to secondary school students. In some cases, respondents were university students, while in others a general sample of people was drawn (e.g. from supermarket customers and passengers on public transport). For each experiment, the global theme, and the number and type of respondents are given below (see Box 6.2). First the general set-up common to all 10 experiments is discussed.

Each questionnaire developed for the experiments consisted of about 30 questions and several seven-point-scale forbid/allow questions. Each questionnaire began with a text in which a number of research goals were stated, intended to obscure the real goal of the experiments. This was followed by various questions on the subject of the questionnaire (see Appendix III for the forbid/allow questions included in each experiment). The experiments consisted of a number of questions, in most cases 6, with a dichotomous answering scale, separated by a variety of filler questions about related issues. In all but one experiment, the use of forbid/allow was varied over questions. Each questionnaire consisted of a second section, containing the same forbid/allow questions posed in the first (in the same forbid or allow version) but accompanied by a seven-point scale. This second section was introduced to the respondents by stating that the researchers wanted to measure the opinions as accurately as possible and that some questions might therefore sound familiar. Respondents were not given the opportunity to refer to the two-point-scale questions while answering the seven-point-scale questions.

Approximately 100 respondents were included in each experiment. Questionnaire versions were randomly distributed among the respondents, resulting in about 50 respondents per version. This design provided the opportunity for a) comparing the answers to two-point-scale forbid/allow questions, b) comparing the answers to seven-point-scale forbid/allow questions and c) comparing the answers obtained for two-point-scale forbid/allow questions with the answers from the same respondents to seven-point-scale forbid/allow questions (Chapter 7). These comparisons were made for the entire sample of respondents (N=1054) and for 61 forbid/allow questions with a two-point scale and 61 equivalent forbid/allow questions with a seven-point scale, on 10 different issues.

• **Experiment 1**
Theme: youth culture. *Subjects*: 100 secondary school pupils (HAVO - higher vocational education /VWO - pre-university education) in 4 different classes. *Procedure*: written questionnaires administered during class, versions randomized over students (but students sitting next to each other received the same version). Part two was completed after filling

in part one of the questionnaire and turning it face down. *Total number of questions:* 32. *Number of forbid/allow questions:* 7.

• **Experiment 2**

Theme: medical choices. *Subjects:* 100 university students. *Procedure:* a written questionnaire administered in several university canteens. *Total number of questions:* 22. *Number of forbid/allow questions:* 6.

• **Experiment 3**

Theme: hooligans. *Subjects:* 100 secondary school pupils (HAVO - higher vocational education/VWO - pre-university education) in 4 different classes. *Procedure:* a written questionnaire administered during classes. *Total number of questions:* 32. *Number of forbid/allow questions:* 6.

• **Experiment 4**

Theme: supermarket policies. *Subjects:* 100 supermarket customers. *Procedure:* oral questionnaire administered to people entering a supermarket. *Total number of questions:* 35. *Number of forbid/allow questions:* 6.

• **Experiment 5**

Theme: euthanasia and organ donation. *Subjects:* 118 secondary school pupils (VWO - preuniversity education). *Procedure:* written questionnaires administered during class, versions randomized over students (but students sitting next to each other received the same version). *Total number of questions:* 27. *Number of forbid/allow questions:* 6.

• **Experiment 6**

Theme: road safety. *Subjects:* 100 subjects at a station. *Procedure:* a written questionnaire administered at Utrecht Central Station. *Total number of questions:* 36. *Number of forbid/allow questions:* 6.

• **Experiment 7**

Theme: young people and television. *Subjects*: 100 workers in a hospital. *Procedure*: the written questionnaire was filled in during lunchbreak in the staff canteen. Persons sharing a table received similar versions. *Total number of questions:* 34. *Number of forbid/allow questions:* 6.

• **Experiment 8**

Theme: commercials. *Subjects:* 100 students and teachers at a university. *Procedure:* a written questionnaire administered in university canteens. *Total number of questions:* 42. *Number of forbid/allow questions:* 6.

• **Experiment 9**

Theme: intake restrictions and restricted number quota [plaatsingsfixus] for university studies. *Subjects:* 118 pupils in the 5th and 6th grade of secondary school (VWO - preuniversity education). *Procedure:* written questionnaires administered during class, versions randomized over students (but students sitting next to each other received the same version). *Total number of questions:* 30. *Number of forbid/allow questions:* 6.

• **Experiment 10**

Theme: right-wing political parties. *Subjects*: 118 pupils from 5 secondary school classes. *Procedure*: written administration during class. *Total number of questions*: 30. *Number of forbid/allow questions:* 6.

Box 6.2: *Description of the 10 experiments*

The meta-analysis in Chapter 3 showed that the extent to which an asymmetry was found varied greatly over experiments and questions. In Chapter 5, variation in the asymmetry size was estimated separately for variation caused by experimental conditions (variance between studies) and for variation caused by question characteristics (variance between questions). This distinction between two levels of variance helped to interpret findings in that particular question set. However, as the structure of the data was such that many forbid/allow experiments consisted of one question only, the variances were difficult to interpret on a more conceptual level.

In order to allow a more conceptual distinction between the levels of variance, 10 different experiments were set up and are described in the current chapter, each containing about 6 forbid/allow questions. Using this design, yet another source of variation between the answers to forbid/allow questions can be distinguished: variation caused by respondent characteristics. In the meta-analysis conducted for Chapter 5, respondent characteristics were derived from question characteristics. If a question was coded as dealing with a relevant issue, it was predicted that many respondents who had answered that particular question were likely to hold polarized opinions towards that issue. The meta-analysis did not result in a better indication of respondent characteristics, because the respondents' individual answers were not available. The experiments set up for the current chapter therefore provide possibilities for distinguishing between the variance in the answers to forbid/allow questions caused by respondent characteristics and the variance caused by question characteristics.

The total variance can therefore be attributed to three levels: a variance between studies (due to different themes, different types of respondents and different administration modes), a variance within studies between respondents (due to the different attitudes held by respondents), and a variance between questions (due to specific subissues or linguistic characteristics of the questions). This creates the possibility of looking not only at the mean effects of the use of forbid/allow over 61 questions, but also of relating variation in the answers to forbid/allow questions to differences between experiments (administration mode, global theme), between persons (whether answers to forbid or allow questions better reflect the differences between persons' opinions), and between questions (whether a person gives the same answer to each forbid (or allow) question on the same theme), thereby creating the possibility of differentiating between the effects of experimental conditions and theme, the effects of different attitudes between persons and the effects of question characteristics on the variations in forbid and allow answers.

The next section will discuss the following analyses. First, a couple of analyses will be conducted in order to obtain a general impression of the data obtained, focusing on the randomization procedure of respondents across versions, on the mean answers to forbid/allow questions obtained for each experiment separately (and a global analysis of the differences between the experiments) and on the number of asymmetries found in each experiment (Section 6.2). The question of whether the forbid/allow asymmetry has been replicated will then be addressed by analysing whether the two-point-scale forbid/allow questions posed in the 10 experiments show an overall asymmetry (Section 6.2.1). The variances in forbid/allow answers will also be discussed. The same will be done for the seven-point-scale questions (Section 6.2.2) as a test of the communicative restrictions hypothesis. In the next section (Section 6.3) the variances will be interpreted by relating them to the concept 'reliability'. Three types of reliability will be dealt with: test-retest reliability, a kind of parallel-test reliability and homogeneity. This will reveal how the mapping mechanisms underlying the answers to forbid/allow questions works, as well as how two-point-scale and seven-point-scale questions differ.

6.2 Results

Before the data for all experiments were analysed simultaneously, a number of analyses were conducted for each experiment separately. These were performed to ensure that the randomization procedure assigning respondents to forbid/allow versions was adequate, to check the existence of the forbid/allow asymmetry via 'traditional' analysis and to obtain a general impression of the data obtained.

First, the randomization procedure of respondents over versions in each experiment was checked by comparing the answers to the filler questions that were kept the same in both questionnaire versions. It turned out that the groups of respondents did not differ in their answers to the filler questions, indicating that the differences found between forbid/allow answers could be interpreted as due to the manipulated question wording and not to differences in attitudes between the groups of respondents who answered the questions.

Secondly, chi square analyses (for each two-point-scale question) and t-tests (for each seven-point-scale question) were conducted in order to find out whether an asymmetry could be shown for the forbid/allow questions posed. In almost every experiment, 2 out of 6 dichotomous forbid/allow questions showed a significant wording effect.[3] This is comparable to the number of significant asymmetries in the experiments reported in Chapter 4. The seven-point-scale

---

[3] Seventeen out of 61 two-point-scale questions showed a significant wording effect ($p<.05$), as well as 17 out of 61 seven-point-scale questions. This finding of 17 wording effects out of 61 observations is significant ($p<.001$).

questions showed about the same proportion of questions leading to a significant wording effect. Equivalent questions that displayed a significant wording effect accompanied by one type of answering scale did not necessarily show a significant difference when accompanied by the other type of answering scale, however.

The fact that the proportion of questions leading to an asymmetry is similar to the proportion in the experiments reported in Chapter 4 is comforting. First of all, it indicates that the nonoccurrence of the asymmetry for several forbid/allow questions was not specific to the two experiments reported in Chapter 4[4]. Secondly, when designing experiments in which each respondent has to answer several manipulated questions, there is always the risk of respondents developing their own pattern when answering. The fact that the asymmetry did not occur consistently in the last question of each experiment, or in the first, is some indication that these question order effects were avoided. At the other extreme, however, it could indicate that respondents answered the forbid/allow questions randomly, choosing arbitrarily between a 'yes' or a 'no' for each question. This concern proves not to be justified either, as a discussion of the reliabilities of forbid/allow questions in Section 6.3 will show.

Thirdly, the differences for forbid/allow questions in each experiment were computed and the ways in which these differences compared across different studies were assessed. Figure 6.1 shows that the mean scores obtained for forbid questions and for allow questions differ across experiments, which indicates that the answers differ due to the different themes in each experiment.

The mean asymmetry sizes obtained in each experiment also vary. In Experiments 3, 7 and 8 there is a relatively large mean asymmetry for the two-point-scale forbid/allow questions, whereas in Experiment 6 a mean tendency towards more 'yes allow' than 'not forbid' is found (contrary to expectations). Experimental characteristics discussed in Chapter 5, such as time pressure (due to an oral versus a written administration mode) or the educational level of respondents do not seem to explain these variations. Experiment 8, for example, shows a relatively large asymmetry, although it was administered by means of a written questionnaire to university students. These are all characteristics that should be related to smaller asymmetry sizes, according to the results of Chapter 5.

---

[4] Although it does raise the question once more of whether the asymmetry exists over all 10 experiments and is therefore a phenomenon that should be taken into account when posing a question with the verb 'forbid' or 'allow'. Fortunately, as Section 6.2.1 shows, this does turn out to be the case.

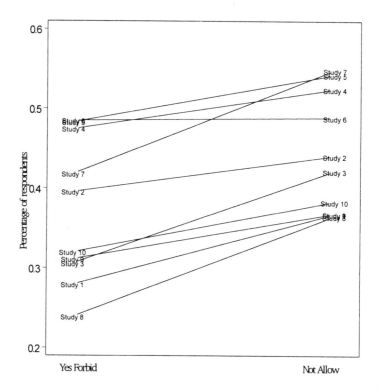

Figure 6.1: *Differences between experiments in asymmetries obtained*

6.2.1 The asymmetry for two-point-scale questions: a replication

A prerequisite for looking for explanations of the asymmetry is that the key phenomenon to be explained is present in the current data set. In other words, does the use of forbid/allow generally affect the answers obtained in the current data set? If the dichotomous forbid/allow questions are not answered asymmetrically in the current data set, the communicative restrictions hypothesis cannot be tested either.

An analysis of the asymmetries per experiment showed that some questions displayed an asymmetry, while others did not. This stresses the importance of finding out whether there is an overall effect of the use of forbid/allow, as well as taking into account the variation in asymmetry size (or occurrence and nonoccurrence of the asymmetry).

The mean answers to the two-point-scale forbid/allow questions of all 10 experiments show that there is a forbid/allow asymmetry[5]: overall 44% 'not allow' was answered, compared to 37% 'yes forbid' ($\chi^2=11.83$, df=1, p<.001). This means that the asymmetry was replicated. Overall, the number of respondents answering 'not allow' is larger than the number of respondents answering 'yes forbid'. Accordingly, 'not forbid' is answered more often than 'yes allow'.

How does the asymmetry vary across the different experiments? In Table 6.1 the variances of forbid and allow questions are provided for each level.

	forbid	allow	χ^2	p
mean percentage:	yes forbid: 37%	not allow: 44%	11.8	<.001
variances between studies	.008 (p<.001)	.005 (p<.001)	.81	n.s.
between persons	.027 (p<.001)	.023 (p<.001)	.59	n.s.
between questions	.197 (p<.001)	.217 (p<.001)	5.88	<.001

Note: χ^2 indicates the difference between the variance of 'forbid' and 'allow' at the different levels (df=1), and p the significance of this difference

Table 6.1: *Mean asymmetry size and variances of the two-point-scale forbid/allow questions*

In the first row, the *variances between studies* are provided. The variance of forbid questions (.008) is significant between studies, as is the variance of allow questions (.005). Hence, the mean score for forbid questions differs across studies, as does the mean score of allow questions. This has already been illustrated in Figure 6.1. This significant variance for the forbid/allow questions is not surprising: the answers to forbid as well as allow questions vary according to the different themes (from road safety to new medical techniques) that were addressed in each experiment, due to different respondents (from rail travellers at Utrecht Central Station to secondary school pupils) who took part in the different experiments, and due to differences in the administration modes for each experiment.

For this study it is more insightful to look at the differences in variances

---

[5] The dependent variable is dichotomous, which means the variance is known once the mean score is known ($s^2=(p*(1-p))$). For example, if the mean score to a question is 1, the variance is zero. A logit model was used [$\log(p/(1-p))$] in analysing these data but only the proportions (the percentages of yes/no answers obtained) will be reported.

between forbid/allow questions than at the variances of forbid and allow questions separately. These do not differ significantly between studies ($\chi^2 = .81$, n.s.). The differences in the mean answers to allow questions between studies are the same size as the differences in the mean answers to forbid questions between studies. A look at the correlations between forbid/allow across studies can also indicate whether the difference between forbid and allow questions is approximately the same size over studies. The correlation between forbid questions and allow questions with a two-point scale (.833, see Table 6.3) indicates whether a ranking of studies on the answers to forbid questions is similar to a ranking based on the scores obtained for allow questions for each study. If this correlation had been 1.0, the difference for forbid/allow questions would be the same size in each study. This is not the case, but the difference is small (the correlation coefficient is quite high), indicating that the asymmetry obtained in different studies is about the same: the wording effect does not differ much due to administration methods (oral versus written), types of respondents (e.g. secondary school pupils versus rail travellers) or the issues addressed (e.g. new medical technologies versus road safety). Hence, the differences in asymmetry sizes caused by experimental conditions (as depicted in Figure 6.1) cannot be shown statistically, which is probably partly due to the limited number of observations on the level of experiments.

As discussed earlier, differences in forbid/allow answers between persons over questions and differences within persons between questions can be distinguished within the differences in forbid/allow answers between studies. These are informative as well, because they indicate the extent to which forbid/allow answers vary due to respondent characteristics and due to question characteristics.

Table 6.1 shows that the *variance between persons* (within studies) is significant for forbid as well as allow questions. Due to differences between respondents, the answers to a set of forbid questions as well as to a set of allow questions differ from the mean answer to the forbid (or allow) questions for that experiment. This is not surprising, as one would expect the differences in attitudes respondents hold to be reflected in the answers they give.

The variance of forbid questions between persons does not differ significantly from the variance of allow questions, indicating that the differences between persons answering forbid questions are equal to the differences between persons who answered the same set of questions in an allow version. Assuming that respondents differ in their opinions, those differences are assessed equally well using forbid and allow questions.

The *variance between questions* (within persons and within studies) is significant for forbid as well as allow questions (Table 6.1). Due to differences in the specific subissues the questions address (and other characteristics specific to each question), the mean score of a specific forbid question differs from the mean of all forbid questions answered by a given respondent within an experiment and the same holds for allow questions. This variation for forbid as well as allow questions is not surprising either. It merely indicates that each question measures some specific issue or subissue compared to the other questions a respondent answered. It could indicate that the forbid/allow questions were not good representatives of the intended construct, i.e. that they did not measure one underlying construct or attitude, but it is rather premature to draw such conclusions at this point, as correlational analyses (Section 6.3) can shed more light on this subject.

It is important to note, however, that the variances of forbid questions differ significantly from the variances of allow questions (see Table 6.1). As variances can be interpreted as indicators of the reliability of forbid/allow questions, the larger variance for allow answers between questions could indicate that allow questions are less reliable (are answered less homogeneously) than forbid questions. However, it would be far too premature to draw conclusions on this aspect at this point, as this can only be done if it should emerge that forbid/allow questions measure a similar underlying construct. A comparison of reliabilities only makes sense once forbid/allow questions have been shown to measure similar attitudes. If they measure different attitudes, a comparison of whether forbid questions are better indicators of one underlying trait than allow questions are of another, is of little or no interest. Differences in homogeneity will be discussed further in Section 6.3.

For now, it is important to note that the variations due to respondent and question characteristics are much larger than the variations due to experimental characteristics, implying that the latter are relatively unimportant when it comes to explaining or generalizing the forbid/allow asymmetry. In other words, the asymmetry size does vary over experiments, but the mean asymmetry size shows the wording effect can be generalized across experiments. The next section reports on whether similar patterns were found for the seven-point-scale questions.

6.2.2 The asymmetry for seven-point-scale questions: communicative restrictions?

A comparison of the mean answers to the seven-point-scale forbid/allow questions across all 10 experiments shows that a wording effect is present[6]. For an

---

[6] Due to the fact that the analyses conducted here assume normality of the distributions, the distributions were normalized so as not to contradict model assumptions. In order to facilitate interpretation, the results were again transformed to a scale with the same mean and variance of observed scores.

asymmetry on the seven-point-scale questions, one would expect to find a tendency towards 'disagreeing' with forbid, rather than 'agreeing' with allow. This proved to be the case: the value '1' corresponds with 'disagree strongly' with forbid questions and 'agree strongly' with allow questions (and the value '7' with 'agree strongly' with forbid questions, and 'disagree strongly' with allow questions). The overall mean answer to the forbid questions is 3.59, whereas the overall mean answer to allow questions turns out to be 3.94 (χ^2=10.55, df=1, p<.001).

	forbid	allow	χ^2	p
mean score	3.59	3.94	10.55	<.001
variances between studies	.172 (n.s.)	.132 (p<.05)	.24	n.s.
between persons	.962 (p<.001)	.615 (p<.001)	5.84	<.001
between questions	4.305 (p<.001)	4.51 (p<.001)	1.29	n.s.

Note: χ^2 indicates the difference between the variance of forbid and allow at the different levels (df=1), and p the significance of this difference.

Table 6.2: Mean scores and variances of the seven-point-scale forbid/allow questions

More negative answers are given to seven-point-scale forbid questions than affirmative answers to allow questions of the same type. It can therefore be concluded that the wording effect is present for forbid/allow questions, even if answering scales that offer extended answering possibilities are used. This means that the communicative restrictions hypothesis should be abandoned.

The lack of support for the communicative restrictions hypothesis could be a reason to exclude the seven-point-scale questions from further analysis. However their inclusion may serve to provide an understanding of the mapping processes when answering forbid/allow questions. Despite the fact that the communicative restrictions hypothesis has to be rejected, the seven-point scales will be subject to further examination.

For this analysis, it is interesting to first look at the way the seven-point-scale questions differ between experiments. The variances of the seven-point-scale questions (Table 6.2) prove to be nonsignificant across experiments, a result that is contrary to that for the two-point-scale forbid/allow questions. This probably indicates that insufficient data (N is only 10) were available to show differences between experiments statistically, as the answers obtained for forbid as well as allow questions do vary over experiments due to the different issues dealt with by the questions.

Furthermore, Table 6.2 shows that the variance of forbid questions across experiments does not differ from the variance of allow questions across experiments. This result was also found for the two-point-scale forbid/allow questions. In addition, the correlation between forbid questions and allow questions accompanied by a seven-point scale across studies indicates whether a ranking of studies on the answers to forbid questions is similar to a ranking based on the scores obtained for allow questions for each study. As this correlation is .754 (see Table 6.3), it can be concluded that differences between the answers to seven-point-scale forbid/allow questions across experiments are not very large, implying that the asymmetry can be generalized across experiments successfully.

It might be interesting to know how the answers to forbid/allow questions differ across experiments, but from a conceptual point of view it seems more informative to look at the variances between persons and between questions. For the variances of forbid and allow questions separately, similar patterns are found for the seven-point-scale questions and the two-point-scale questions: the answers to forbid and allow questions differ significantly between respondents as well as between questions.

Looking at the differences between the variances of the seven-point-scale forbid and allow questions, a significant difference is found *between persons* within experiments, whereas no significant difference is found *between questions* (within persons). Furthermore, the variance of forbid questions between persons is larger than the variance of allow questions between persons. Differences between respondents who answered forbid questions are larger than the differences between respondents who answered equivalent allow questions. Note that this is contrary to results obtained for the two-point-scale questions. Not only is the variance for forbid questions larger than for allow questions (instead of the other way around), but the difference in variance is found between persons and not between questions.

Once again, the variances can be interpreted in terms of the homogeneity of forbid/allow questions. However, a comparison of homogeneity only makes sense if forbid/allow questions are shown to measure similar attitudes. The congenericity of forbid/allow questions was already demonstrated in Chapter 4, but results in the current data set should be in accordance with this before the homogeneity of forbid/allow questions can be compared. As discussed in the next section, the congenericity of forbid/allow can be approached by computing parallel-test reliabilities. A discussion of why the variance patterns for seven-point-scale questions differ from those of two-point-scale questions will therefore be postponed until the next section.

6.3 THE RELIABILITIES OF FORBID/ALLOW QUESTIONS

In the previous sections it was shown that a wording effect is found for two-point-scale as well as for seven-point-scale forbid/allow questions. This means that the asymmetry was replicated across 10 different experiments for the two-point-scale questions. The key phenomenon to be explained is present in the current question set, which means that the search for explanations for the asymmetry is warranted.

Finding a wording effect for the seven-point-scale questions means that the asymmetry is not simply caused by the combination of the use of forbid/allow and yes/no answering options, but can be generalized to less restricted communicative settings as well. The seven-point-scale questions remain in the analyses though, because an understanding of what happens during the answering of seven-point-scale questions can also provide greater insight into the processes underlying the answering of dichotomous questions.

Furthermore, the previous sections showed that the variance between dichotomous allow questions is larger than the variance between dichotomous forbid questions, and the variances of forbid/allow questions do not differ between persons. Yet, the variance between seven-point-scale questions did not differ and the variance between respondents was larger for forbid questions than for allow questions.

This difference will be explained at the end of this section (under 'homogeneity'). First it is necessary to have a look at two other indicators of the reliability of forbid/allow questions: parallel tests and test-retests, as these provide an insight into the issue of whether the forbid/allow questions posed measured any construct at all. The parallel tests are particularly important: the outcomes of these will give an indication of whether the congenericity of forbid/allow questions found in Chapter 4 is found again in the current experiments.

Three measures of reliability can be extracted from the data obtained in this study, two correlational measures and one measure based on the variances. First of all, the correlation between differently worded questions accompanied by the same answering scale will be computed (i.e. the relation between forbid-2p and allow-2p, as well as the relation between forbid-7p and allow-7p). This first measure can be regarded as a kind of parallel test, and indicating the extent of the convergent validity of forbid and allow questions. It can therefore be considered an indication of the congenericity of forbid/allow.

The second measure can be compared to a test-retest reliability, indicating the relation between similarly worded questions accompanied by different answering scales (i.e. the relation between forbid-2p and forbid-7p, and the relation between allow-2p and allow-7p). This can be interpreted as the convergent validity of two-point-scale and seven-point-scale questions, and therefore as an indication of congenericity of questions accompanied by different scales. These two correlational measures can be computed over studies (generalizing across persons), over persons (generalizing across questions), as well as over questions (generalizing across the scores obtained by different respondents).

The third measure of reliability is a measure of the homogeneity of forbid/allow questions. To what extent do forbid questions (and allow questions) form a homogenous test of someone's attitude towards an issue? How good are forbid and allow questions at making a distinction between the different attitudes of different persons? As in Chapter 4, this last type of reliability becomes important once it is clear whether the test-retest and parallel-test reliability of forbid/allow questions is high. Only if forbid/allow questions prove to measure similar attitudes in the current experiments, it is possible to interpret a difference in homogeneity (if found) and to interpret the differences in the variances for forbid/allow questions discussed in the previous sections. This allows more light to be shed on the issue of how the mapping problem causing the asymmetry works and the question wording which should be preferred.

6.3.1 Parallel tests of forbid/allow questions: congenericity

The correlation coefficient of differently worded questions accompanied by the same answering scale can be viewed as a kind of parallel test. It indicates whether forbid/allow questions are congeneric. The correlation coefficient is obtained at two levels: between studies and between persons. The correlations between questions are not available, because at no time did the same person answer two equivalent two-point-scale forbid questions (or allow questions).

	between studies		between persons	
	corr.	rel.	corr.	rel.
allow 2p-forbid2p	.833 (p<.001)	.91	.597 (p<.001)	.75
allow7p-forbid7p	.754 (p<.001)	.86	.596 (p<.001)	.75

Note: allow2p-forbid2p=the correlations (*corr.*) and reliabilities (*rel.*) between allow questions (2p) and forbid questions (2p).

Table 6.3*: Parallel-test reliabilities*

The correlation between forbid questions and allow questions with a two-point scale over studies (.833, see Table 6.3) and the correlation between forbid questions and allow questions with a seven-point scale over studies (.754, see Table 6.3) indicate whether a ranking of studies based on the answers to forbid questions is similar to a ranking based on the scores obtained for allow questions in each study. As was discussed earlier, these correlations indicate that the wording effect does not differ much due to administration methods, types of respondents or themes. Furthermore, the reliabilities[7] are relatively high: a reliability of .91 between forbid-2p and allow-2p indicates that differences between studies can be assessed very effectively using these questions.

Based on a comparison between the variances of two-point-scale questions it was hypothesized that allow questions may be a less reliable measure of the underlying attitude than forbid questions, because their variance between questions proved to be larger than the variance between forbid questions. It could also be the case, however, that the assumption that forbid/allow questions measure an underlying attitude does not hold. In that case the above interpretation of the larger variances for allow questions must also be rejected. This refers to the degree of construct validity, which can be brought to light by looking at the correlations between forbid questions accompanied by a two-point scale and allow questions accompanied by a two-point scale (Table 6.3). These correlations indicate whether the ranking of persons based on their answers to allow questions is similar to the ranking of persons based on their answers to forbid questions, and can therefore be viewed as an indication of the congenericity of forbid/allow as discussed (and found) in Chapter 4.

There is one complication, however. Unlike Chapter 4, the rankings obtained in the current chapter are influenced by the use of forbid/allow as well as by specific question content. If two respondents participated in the experiments, Respondent A answered Questions 1 and 3 in a forbid version and Questions 2 and 4 in an allow version, whereas Respondent B answered Questions 1 and 3 in an allow version and Questions 2 and 4 in a forbid version. Therefore, the correlation coefficient between allow-2p and forbid-2p indicates the correlation between the mean answers of Respondent A to Questions 1 and 3 and of Respondent B to Questions 2 and 4 (forbid questions), and between the mean answers of Respondent A to Questions 2 and 4 and of Respondent B to Questions 1 and 3 (allow questions).

Hence, a correlation coefficient of .597 between the two-point-scale forbid and allow questions can be regarded as quite high, as it indicates a reliability of .75. Under the assumption of parallel tests, this correlation is an indication of convergent validity, because this .75 indicates that questions on the same theme but on different subissues and in different forbid/allow versions do correlate quite highly, thereby suggesting that the forbid/allow questions could measure the

---

[7] The parallel-test reliability can be approximated by the Spearman Brown formula. Note, however, that this assumes parallelism of the various parts of the test. If this assumption is not fulfilled, an underestimation of the 'true' reliability is obtained (Lord & Novick, 1968).

same construct, comparable to the finding of congenericity found in Chapter 4. Based on this conclusion, it seems an adequate working hypothesis to state that the larger variance between two-point-scale allow questions should be attributed to a larger error score variance: a set of allow questions measures the underlying attitude less reliably than a set of forbid questions.

The parallel-test reliability of the seven-point-scale questions can be discussed along similar lines. Table 6.3 shows that the correlation between forbid-7p and allow-7p is .596, which is equal to the correlation between forbid-2p and allow-2p. This can be interpreted to indicate congenericity of forbid/allow questions: seven-point-scale questions measure similar underlying constructs irrespective of whether 'forbid' or 'allow' is used, which is similar to the result for two-point-scale questions.

6.3.2 Test-retests of forbid/allow questions accompanied by different answering scales

The test-retest reliability of forbid/allow questions is assessed by interpreting the correlations between forbid/allow questions accompanied by a two-point scale and questions accompanied by a seven-point answering scale. This measure indicates whether people respond differently when answering an equivalent question for the second time, in cases where the question only differs with respect to the type of answering scale that was offered.

Table 6.4 shows that the correlation between allow-7p and allow-2p (.867), and the correlation between forbid-7p and forbid-2p (.998) over studies is quite high. The number of answering categories does not lead to a different ranking of studies.

	between studies		between respondents		between questions	
	corr.	rel.	corr.	rel.	corr.	rel.
a2p-a7p	.867 (p<.001)	.93	.990 (p<.001)	.99	.673 (p<.001)	.81
f2p-f7p	.998 (p<.001)	1.0	.963 (p<.001)	.98	.620 (p<.001)	1.0

Note: a2p-a7p=the correlations (*corr.*) and test-retest reliabilities (*rel.*) between allow questions (2p) and allow questions (7p).

Table 6.4: *Test-retest reliabilites*

In Table 6.4 the correlation between persons gives an indication of the test-retest reliability of forbid/allow questions. First of all, there are the correlations between forbid-2p and forbid-7p, and between allow-2p and allow-7p, i.e. the correlations between similarly worded questions accompanied by a different answering scale. Both of those correlations are very high (.96 and .99, respectively). This indicates that the test-retest reliability of forbid/allow questions is quite high: respondents who answered a two-point question by circling 'yes', also answered affirmatively to the equivalent seven-point-scale question, resulting in an almost identical ranking of respondents based on their answers to seven-point-scale or two-point-scale questions. This shows that the answering behaviour of respondents was far from being random, which is some indication of the validity of both the forbid and the allow questions.

The last indication of test-retest reliability is provided by the correlations between questions, although these figures are harder to interpret. Each respondent was asked a dichotomous question and, after having answered a variety of filler questions, went on to answer a similar question accompanied by a seven-point scale in the same version (either 'forbid' or 'allow'). The correlations in Table 6.4 indicate the extent to which the deviance of question x (in the forbid-7p version) from other forbid-7p questions within persons corresponds with the deviance of question x (in the forbid-2p version) from other forbid-2p questions within persons. In other words, a set of forbid/allow questions within a study measures some sort of underlying attitude, but answers to a specific forbid/allow question can deviate from that attitude due to the content of the specific subissue being addressed in the questions. If these deviations are detected with a seven-point-scale question, can they also be detected with the two-point-scale question in the same version? The correlations computed between questions are conditional on the differences between persons' attitudes: all effects resulting from deviations caused by persons' specific attitudes are already accounted for in the correlations between two-point and seven-point questions between persons. The correlations of about .6 (in Table 6.4) can therefore be evaluated as quite high.

Tests-retests between differently worded questions accompanied by different answering scales can also be computed. These are not included in Table 6.4, as they are extremely difficult to interpret. The correlation over studies between forbid-2p and allow-7p (.622), and between allow-2p and forbid-7p (.862), indicates whether the number of answering categories as well as the use of forbid/allow influences the ranking of studies on their forbid/allow answers[8]. Secondly, there are two indicators of test-retest reliability which relate to persons who answered differently worded questions which were also accompanied by different answering scales: the correlations between persons between forbid-2p and allow-7p (.531), and between allow-2p and forbid-7p (.724), which reflect

---

[8] The correlation between forbid-2p and allow-7p is relatively low (.622), but does not differ significantly from 1.0.

differences in the answers due to the use of forbid/allow and due to the use of different answering scales (seven points/two points), as well as due to differences in specific subissues in each question. It is reassuring to know that these two correlations are positive, as negative correlations would have indicated a problem with reliabilities. Further evaluation of the strength of both correlation coefficients is problematic, however. One thing can be noted when observing these correlations, however: the correlation between forbid-2p and allow-7p between persons is relatively low, similar to the correlation between forbid-2p and allow-7p between studies. This correlation between persons is significantly lower ($\chi^2=6.54$, df=1) than the correlation between forbid-7p and allow-2p, which could indicate that the scaling problem surfaces primarily when mapping differences between the forbid-2p and allow-7p questions (see also Chapter 7).

6.3.3 Homogeneity: the variances of forbid/allow questions revisited

The parallel tests and test-retests of forbid/allow questions show that the correlation between forbid-2p and allow-2p and between forbid-7p and allow-7p is quite high (taking into account the fact that the questions were on different subissues), which indicates that forbid and allow questions measure the same underlying construct no matter what type of answering scale is used. This is in line with the finding of congenericity in Chapter 4. Furthermore, forbid and allow questions measure the attitudes with a reasonable degree of stability, even though the number of answering options differs. This is shown by high correlations between questions worded the same but accompanied by a different answering scale (correlations between forbid-2p and forbid-7p, and between allow-2p and allow-7p).

These results make it possible to interpret the differences in variances that were found for forbid and allow questions and for two-point-scale questions and seven-point-scale questions. Data indicate that, although forbid and allow questions measure the same underlying construct, a wording effect is found for the two-point-scale questions as well as for the seven-point-scale questions. Hence, similar attitudes are retrieved with forbid questions and with allow questions, as well as with two-point-scale questions and with seven-point-scale questions. However, the way the opinions are mapped onto the answering scales differs for forbid and allow questions, as testified by the wording effects found. Furthermore, the mapping mechanisms differ, as is shown by the differences in variances between forbid and allow questions, and by the differences in variances between two-point-scale questions and seven-point-scale questions. Two findings have to be explained in order to describe the mapping mechanisms underlying the wording effect. First of all, an explanation must be found for why the variance for seven-point-scale questions differs between persons, whereas the variance for two-point-scale questions differs between questions. Secondly, it has to be explained why the variance for seven-point-scale questions is larger for forbid questions, whereas the variance for two-point-scale questions is larger for allow questions.

In order to arrive at an explanation, one has to bear in mind that variances are scale dependent: the variance of seven-point-scale questions is inherently larger than the variance of two-point-scale questions. It is therefore necessary to look at the *proportions* of variance between persons for seven-point-scale questions and two-point-scale questions. An analysis should be carried out as to which proportion of the answer obtained for forbid/allow questions reflects differences between persons and which proportion of each answer reflects differences due to specific question characteristics[9].

A computation of this proportional measure shows that the proportion of variance explained between persons for forbid-2p is .124, and for allow-2p is .096. For forbid-7p it is .176, and for allow-7p .120. Accordingly, for two-point-scale questions as well as for seven-point-scale questions, the variance between persons is larger for forbid questions than for allow questions. This means that the variance between persons answering forbid questions from the mean forbid answers over persons, differs from the variance between persons who answered the same set of questions in an allow version. In other words, forbid questions are answered less homogonously across persons than allow questions. Assuming that respondents differ in their attitudes, these differences between persons' attitudes are not expressed equally well on forbid and allow questions.

If this computation is taken one step further, and the number of forbid (or allow) questions answered by each respondent is taken into account, a reliability measure that can be called 'homogeneity' emerges. How homogenous are forbid/allow questions, or in other words, how well do groups of forbid (and groups of allow) questions reflect an underlying attitude?[10]

In Table 6.5 it can be seen that neither forbid questions nor allow questions

---

[9] In other words, the proportion of true score variance and error score variance should be established. This proportional measure is obtained by dividing the variance explained by a question between persons by the same number added with the variance explained between questions.

[10] This is computed by dividing the variance between persons by the sum of the variance between persons and the variance between questions. When computing the homogeneity of the two-point-scale forbid questions the equation is: $.02778/(.02778+.31*.1967)=.31$. The numbers for these equations can be found in Tables 6.1 and 6.2 (variances for the two-point-scale and seven-point-scale questions), and the .31 by which the variance between questions is multiplied is used in order to take into account the number of forbid (or allow) questions (3) answered by each respondent in each study.

are very homogenous measures in this study: similar to Chapter 4, neither forbid nor allow questions provide a particularly reliable measure of the underlying attitude (towards road safety, for example). Note, however, that this reliability index depends on the number of questions that were part of the scale. In this research, each scale that was supposed to measure one underlying attitude consisted of three questions only. If 10 forbid questions had been posed to each respondent, the homogeneity would have gone up to .6, which is reasonable. However, instead of the similarities between forbid/allow questions, the differences between forbid and allow questions and between seven-point-scale and two-point-scale questions are more interesting for the current research.

	two-point-scale questions		seven-point-scale questions	
	forbid	allow	forbid	allow
homogeneity	.31	.26	.42	.31

Table 6.5: *The homogeneity of forbid/allow questions*

Table 6.5 shows that seven-point-scale questions measure the attitude more reliably than two-point-scale questions, both in the forbid and allow version. This was to be expected, because by using a seven-point scale variances increase. In addition it can also be seen that both for two-point-scale questions and for seven-point-scale questions, forbid questions measure more reliably than allow questions: in other words, forbid questions measure the underlying attitude more homogeneously than allow questions. So in terms of test-retests and parallel tests, forbid/allow questions are very reliable and tend to congenericity, indicating that they measure the same construct. But in terms of homogeneity, or cluster reliability, forbid questions lead to a more reliable measure of an underlying attitude than allow questions, both for seven-point-scale and two-point-scale questions.

The two differences between the variances of two-point and seven-point-scale forbid/allow questions can be explained by the two factors that were manipulated: the answering scale (seven-point versus two-point) and the question wording ('forbid' versus 'allow'). Both manipulations cause a mapping difference, as the use of forbid/allow does not cause different constructs to be measured (shown by a high correlation between forbid-2p and allow-2p and between forbid-7p and allow-7p), and the use of different scales does not cause different constructs to be measured either (shown by a high correlation between allow-2p and allow-7p and a high correlation between forbid-2p and forbid-7p).

The fact that the variance between forbid/allow questions differs between questions for the two-point-scale questions and differs between persons for the seven-point-scale questions, can be explained by the number of answering options offered. Respondents who hold moderate opinions do not experience many mapping problems when answering seven-point-scale questions: they can express subtle differences in their opinions towards subissues by answering 'fully agree' to one forbid question and answering 'slightly agree' to another (and similarly for allow questions). In other words, a respondent can vary in his opinion in relation to the specific subissue addressed in a question and still express a reasonably homogenous opinion towards the underlying attitude. Hence, the differences between questions are relatively small. On the two-point answering scale, however, the respondent is forced to answer either 'yes' or 'no'. The only way to express a moderate opinion on such questions is to answer 'yes' to one question and 'no' the next – in other words, to be less consistent in the answers he gives to a set of forbid questions and/or to allow questions. This is shown by a relatively large variance between two-point-scale questions both in the allow as well as in the forbid version.

The fact that the variance for seven-point-scale questions is larger for forbid questions than for allow questions (between respondents) might be explained by the connotations of 'forbid'. It could be the case that the connotations of 'forbid' are more extreme than the connotations of 'allow', causing respondents to map even moderate opinions more onto the extremes of the answering scale for forbid questions than they do when answering allow questions. This results in a larger variance between persons for forbid questions: small differences between persons are expressed more extremely in the answers to forbid questions than in the answers to allow questions (as expressed on the seven-point scale). If this explanation is borne out, the connotations hypothesis is wrong in assuming that both 'forbid' and 'allow' carry extreme connotations. In that case only 'forbid' would be extreme. This hypothesis will be examined in greater detail in the next chapter.

In any case, this possible difference in the extremity of the connotations of 'forbid' and 'allow' does not manifest itself as a difference in variances between persons, but in the variances between questions instead. This is due to the lack of opportunities for expressing degrees of extremity on a two-point scale. This causes a respondent to answer fairly homogeneously to forbid questions (but not necessarily meaning 'no' when answering 'no', and meaning 'yes' when answering 'yes'), whereas he switches more in his answers to allow questions about the same theme in order to express the moderateness of his attitude towards the theme (resulting in a larger variance between questions for the two-point-scale forbid/ allow questions).

The mapping problems respondents encounter when trying to translate their opinions into one of the answering options offered is therefore demonstrated by the similarity between seven-point-scale questions and two-point-scale questions when analysed proportionally, and the difference between them when analysed scale dependently. This indicates that in both the seven-point-scale and the two-point-scale forbid/allow questions the same question-answering problem occurs twice, but via different mechanisms due to the fact that a larger number of scale points are offered.

6.4 CONCLUSIONS

The analyses reported in this chapter allow us to reach several conclusions. One of the research questions concerned the *communicative restrictions hypothesis*. This hypothesis must be rejected. The mapping problem is inherent in the use of forbid/allow, which is shown by a mean overall wording effect found for the two-point-scale questions and for the seven-point-scale questions (combined with the confirmation of congenericity for both types of questions). The communicative restrictions hypothesis posited that the mapping problem would disappear once more communicative room was offered to express moderate opinions. The wording effect found for seven-point-scale questions shows this is not the case. In other words, the mapping problem is caused by the use of forbid/allow, regardless of the type of answering scale that is used.

As the focus of this study is to explain the forbid/allow asymmetry as obtained for forbid/allow questions accompanied by a two-point yes/no scale, the rejection of the communicative restrictions hypothesis could have been reason to omit the seven-point-scale forbid/allow questions from the analyses to be carried out after this stage. However, it was decided to include them, as the analyses of the differences between seven-point-scale forbid and seven-point-scale allow questions, as well as analyses of similarities and differences between two-point-scale and seven-point-scale questions provide opportunities to analyse the mapping processes underlying the asymmetry obtained for two-point-scale questions more thoroughly, and draw conclusions more confidently. It was therefore interesting to include the seven-point-scale answers in the further analyses. This led to the following results.

First of all, an overall forbid/allow asymmetry has been found for the two-point-scale questions. This is in accordance with the meta-analysis presented in Chapter 3. Although every forbid/allow question was not necessarily answered asymmetrically, an overall asymmetry was found. This also means that the key phenomenon was replicated and can be explained in greater depth thanks to the data obtained by this set of experiments.

Secondly, it has been shown that both forbid and allow questions are very stable measures of whatever they measure (shown by high test-retest correlations over forbid/allow questions accompanied by different answering scales). This is an interesting finding because it indicates that the answers obtained to forbid/allow questions were not given randomly by respondents. Accordingly, it makes sense to look for explanations for the asymmetry.

Thirdly, it has been demonstrated that forbid and allow questions accompanied by a two-point scale as well as a seven-point scale measure a similar underlying construct, and not just opinions towards forbidding or allowing (parallel tests show a high correlation between a set of forbid questions and a different set of allow questions both on the same theme). This is in accordance with the congenericity found in Chapter 4. The fact that forbid/allow questions on a two-point scale as well as forbid/allow questions accompanied by a seven-point scale lead to a wording effect, should once again be interpreted as a mapping problem. The same attitudes are localized and retrieved when answering forbid questions or allow questions, but the answers are expressed differently on the answering scales.

The relevance of these preceding results lies primarily in the fact that they provide replications of earlier findings on a larger and more heterogeneous question set. For the current chapter, however, they represent prerequisites for answering the research question posed, namely how do the scales to forbid/allow questions differ? In other words, how does the mapping process underlying the wording effect work?

By including the seven-point-scale questions in the analyses, it was found that although both seven-point-scale and two-point-scale forbid/allow questions cause mapping problems, the mapping process works through different mechanisms dependent on the number of answering options offered. Differences in the variances show that a respondent expresses his moderate opinion by switching between 'yes' and 'no' options when answering two-point-scale questions, whereas for seven-point-scale questions moderateness is expressed by circling a response option that lies somewhere between the extremes of the answering scale. The communicative restrictions hypothesis makes some sense after all, as the mapping process is shown to work differently if the communicative possibilities for expressing an answer are restricted to two options only.

Furthermore, the seven-point-scale questions were found to be more reliable measures than the two-point-scale questions. This can be explained by the fact that respondents switch more between 'yes' and 'no' when answering sets of two-point-scale questions about the same issue, whereas they can more easily vary the extremity of their answers on a seven-point scale.

The implication for research design is that one should prefer a seven-point-scale question over a dichotomous question where possible, because the answers to the former better assess the differences between persons than the answers to the latter. In other words, seven-point-scale questions were shown to be more reliable.[11]

Another important recommendation is not to use just one question to assess the attitude to be measured, but several. The homogeneity of both forbid and allow questions proved to be quite low for both the two-point-scale and the seven-point-scale questions in this research. However, this seems to be caused by characteristics of the questionnaires used in general and not by the use of for-bid/allow. The number of questions in each cluster (three) in this chapter is rather small. Analyses show that cluster reliability would have risen substantially if more questions had been posed on each theme. The low homogeneity seems basically caused by the small number of questions per theme and the lack of content theory used when constructing the clusters. Furthermore, the questions were not pretested on whether they were good indicators of an underlying construct, but only on their comprehensibility and answerability.

More important than the difference in reliability between seven-point-scale and two-point-scale forbid questions, is the finding that forbid questions measure the underlying attitude more reliably than allow questions. This was not only found for the two-point-scale questions, but for the seven-point-scale questions as well. This provides additional evidence that forbid questions are more reliable: allow questions accompanied by a two-point-scale show more question specific variance. Whereas the findings in Chapter 4 were not unequivocal concerning the differences in reliabilities of forbid/allow questions, the current analyses, conducted over a larger variety of questions and experiments, show that forbid questions are more reliable than allow questions.

The practical implication for research design following from this finding is that forbid questions should be preferred, as the answers obtained to forbid questions provide a better indication of the differences between respondents' attitudes.

However, the preferability of forbid questions due to their larger reliability, requires further investigation. The knowledge that forbid questions measure the underlying attitude more reliably, allows the mapping process underlying the asymmetry to be unravelled further. In other words, this means that the cognitive difference between 'yes' and 'no' to allow questions is probably smaller than the cognitive difference between 'yes' and 'no' to forbid questions. Respondents are offered more scope to switch between 'yes' and 'no' when answering a set of allow questions on a given issue than when answering a set of forbid questions. However, this does not explain the exact working of the mapping process. What causes

---

[11] On the other hand, the high correlation between seven-point-scale and two-point-scale questions indicates that the two-point-scale questions do not perform so very badly. Furthermore it should be noted that despite of the larger reliability of seven-points-scale questions,the exact meanings of the answers as expressed on the seven-points-scale are unclear, similar to the meanings of the answers expressed on the two-point-scale options.

the difference in reliability? In other words, why do respondents switch more between 'yes' and 'no' when answering allow questions? It fails to provide insight into the ways the answers obtained to forbid/allow questions should be translated back to the similar attitude forbid/allow questions measure. Nor does it identify the exact cause of the asymmetry. Why do more respondents answer 'not forbid' than 'yes allow' (or 'not allow' than 'yes forbid')?

These issues will be examined in the next chapter, by focusing on the meanings of the answers 'yes' and 'no' to the two-point-scale forbid/allow questions. The answers respondents gave to two-point-scale forbid/allow questions will be related to the answers they gave to equivalent seven-point-scale forbid/allow questions. The result is a retrospective 4-group design, in which the meanings of 'yes forbid', 'not forbid', 'yes allow' and 'not allow' can be analysed, as well as the variations in these meanings over different questions or for different respondents.

Had the communicative restrictions hypothesis be proven to hold in the current chapter and no wording effect had been found for the seven-point-scale questions, the following analysis would have focused on the absolute meanings of the answers to forbid/allow questions. Now that the communicative restrictions hypothesis has been rejected, the analyses in the next chapter are only concerned with the *relative* meanings of forbid/allow answers, since the answers to seven-point-scale questions are expressed on unequal interval scales. This is one reason why some of the analyses in the next chapter are called 'explorations'. The second reason why the analyses in the next chapter are referred to as exploratory, is because no hard hypotheses concerning the meanings of yes/no to forbid/allow questions are available. Further insight into the meanings of 'yes' and 'no' and the mapping process for forbid/allow questions will have to be principally obtained from careful data analysis. The only hypothesis available to guide the analysis and interpretation to some extent, is the connotations hypothesis, which should be integrated with the attitude strength dimension of extremity, according to Chapter 5, in order to arrive at a monocausal theory explaining the forbid/allow asymmetry. This will be elaborated on in the next chapter.

7.0 INTRODUCTION

The previous chapter showed that forbid questions are more reliable measures of an underlying attitude than allow questions. This provides some insight into the mechanisms underlying the mapping process for forbid/allow questions. The mapping process can be unravelled further by analysing what meaning respondents assign to their 'yes' or 'no' answers to forbid/allow questions. In other words, what do respondents mean when they answer 'yes forbid', 'not forbid', 'yes allow', or 'not allow'? And what causes the difference in reliability between forbid and allow questions?

In the current research, it is not possible to give conclusive answers to questions like these. However, it is possible to analyse what respondents did when answering forbid/allow questions which offer them more communicative scope to express their opinions. In other words, to gain insight into the meanings of 'yes' and 'no' to forbid/allow questions, the answers respondents gave to the two-point-scale questions can be compared to the answers they gave to equivalent seven-point-scale questions. This will be done in the current chapter.

There are a number of hypotheses that can be used as a starting point or guideline in order to establish the meanings of 'yes' and 'no' to forbid/allow questions and to further unravel the question-answering process. These are outlined below. This description will show, however, that the hypotheses do not lead to unequivocal and strong criteria that can be subsequently tested. Instead, descriptive analyses of the meanings of 'yes' and 'no' will be carried out. These analyses will form the foundation for developing a theory of those meanings. The hypotheses are only a guideline for the data analyses to be conducted. The analyses presented in this chapter are therefore exploratory in nature and mainly consist of careful reasoning on the basis of the data.

The previous chapter showed that the variances between persons for the seven-point-scale forbid questions are relatively large, which indicates that differences between respondents' opinions are expressed more pronouncedly on the seven-point forbid scale compared to the seven-points allow scale. This suggests that respondents choose a more extreme option on the answering scales when answering seven-point-scale forbid questions than when answering seven-point-scale

---

[1] Many of the findings reported in this chapter were presented at the 7th Annual Meeting of the Society for Text and Discourse (1997) and the VIOT Conference (1999).

allow questions. Based on this observation, the previous chapter hypothesized that the verb 'forbid' may carry more extreme connotations than 'allow'. This could imply that a 'yes forbid' denotes a more extreme position (to the relatively small group of people who choose that option) than the answer 'not forbid': people who answer a two-point-scale forbid question affirmatively do so because they wish to express the meaning of a definite 'yes', whereas respondents who don't know or who have more moderate feelings about the issue will answer 'no'. Similarly, it could mean that the answer 'not forbid' carries a more extreme meaning than 'yes allow'.

The previous chapter also showed that the variance between the two-point-scale allow questions is larger than the variance between two-point-scale forbid questions. Respondents switch more between 'yes' and 'no' in their answers to a set of allow questions about a given issue than they do in their answers to a set of forbid questions. The question of which respondents switch when answering allow questions remains. Do all respondents switch or just the respondents who don't know or are ambivalent in their opinions? Is it mainly the respondents who answer 'no' who switch to 'yes' once in a while, or the respondents who say 'yes' who switch to 'no', or both? In other words, are 'yes allow' and 'not allow' equally moderate in their meanings or does one of the two answers represent a large variety of meanings and therefore express ambiguity?

In addition to this view, there is still the *connotations hypothesis* (Schuman & Presser, 1981). This states that "the verb 'forbid' sounds harsher and may therefore be more difficult to endorse, whereas 'allow' in some contexts might seem to encourage a deviant behaviour and therefore may invite opposition." Or, in the words of Clark & Schober (1992): "[...] to agree to forbid implies a real act of opposition, but to disagree with allow means merely to abstain from support." This could imply that the meaning of 'not forbid' is more moderate than the meaning of 'yes forbid', and that the meaning of 'not allow' is more moderate than the meaning of 'yes allow'. At the same time, it could imply the general pattern that 'not forbid' is chosen by more respondents than 'yes allow' because 'not forbid' is more moderate than 'yes allow'. By the same token, 'not allow' would be more moderate than 'yes forbid', causing more respondents to map their opinion onto the former response option.

The connotations hypothesis therefore makes general predictions about the answering behaviour of respondents and the meanings of the answers to forbid/allow questions. The hypothesis has been extended by various forbid/allow researchers (Hippler & Schwarz, 1986; Waterplas et al., 1988), who focused on a subgroup of respondents: those with weak attitudes. In previous chapters this has been called the *indifferent respondents hypothesis*. It states that respondents with strong attitudes should not be bothered by the extreme connotations of forbid/allow, whereas respondents with weak attitudes find affirmative answers too extreme, and avoid them by choosing the 'no' option when answering both types of question. In terms of the meanings of forbid/allow questions, this could imply that 'not forbid' is chosen by respondents who have a strong opinion that the issue should not be forbidden, as well as by respondents who are moderately in favour of forbidding but find 'yes forbid' too extreme, and by respondents with no real opinion on the issue. Likewise, the answer 'not allow' could reflect the opinions of respondents who are really against allowing the issue as well as opinions of those moderately in favour of allowing and those with very weak or indifferent opinions towards the issue.

The way in which attitude strength should be measured has been subject to quite some discussion (see Chapters 2 and 5). In the current study, exploratory analyses focusing on the role of attitude strength suggest that forbid/allow questions measure the same attitudes not only for the group of respondents as a whole, but also for the subgroup of respondents holding moderate, weak or no opinions. In Chapter 5, puzzling conclusions were reached on the effects of two indicators of attitude strength, the complexity and the relevance of the issue addressed in the question. Both the complexity and the relevance of the issue were related to larger asymmetries (Section 5.2.1). Both indicators are linked to the polarization or extremity of respondents' attitudes. It was predicted that a complex issue would produce an ambivalent attitude and would therefore lead to a larger asymmetry. For a relevant issue, meanwhile, it was predicted that the respondent had already given the issue a great deal of thought, leading to polarization of the attitude, and therefore to a smaller asymmetry. In Section 5.2.2 it was argued that the unexpected results for the effect of relevance might be caused by the fact that this characteristic is not related as directly to the concept of extremity as was assumed. Furthermore, the interaction effect between complexity and relevance suggested that the attitude strength dimension complexity is more important for the explanation of variation in the asymmetry size than relevance and is related more directly to the extremity of the attitudes held. It was argued that future experimental research should focus directly on the attitude strength dimension 'extremity'. The literature on attitude strength in general, suggests that attitude strength is a multidimensional concept, made up of dimensions such as personal relevance, intensity, importance, extremity and certainty. It seems that many (but not all) attitude strength dimensions can be incorporated if the degree of attitude strength is defined solely in terms of extremity of opinions. This also offers opportunities for integrating the connotations hypothesis and various aspects of the attitude strength hypothesis, as the connotations hypothesis also focuses on the extreme connotations of forbid/allow or the affirmative answers to these questions.

Therefore, in the experiments set up for the current and the previous chapter, not only forbid/allow questions accompanied by a yes/no answering scale were posed, but equivalent forbid/allow questions accompanied by a seven-point-scale were administered to the same respondents as well. The only type of attitude strength not detected by such a scale, is that of respondents who really don't know, that is to say respondents who are certain that they do not have an opinion on the issue. This could have been solved by offering an explicit 'don't know' option in addition to the seven-point scale. On the other hand, the explicit inclusion of such an option is known to attract many respondents who actually do have an opinion, so it was decided not to include one. Apart from this point of respondents really 'not knowing', the connotations hypothesis and parts of the attitude strength hypothesis can be integrated (see Box 7.1).

The connotations hypothesis and extremity

People answering 'yes' to either forbid or allow questions will hold extreme positive attitudes towards forbidding or allowing the issue addressed in the questions, while respondents holding moderate attitudes (as expressed in their answer to the seven-point-scale forbid/allow questions) will answer 'no' to the two-point-scale forbid/allow questions.

Box 7.1: *The connotations hypothesis and extremity*

A comparison of the answers respondents give on the two-point-scale forbid/allow questions to the answers the same respondents give to equivalent seven-point-scale forbid/allow questions therefore provides an understanding of the meanings of 'yes forbid', 'not forbid', 'yes allow' and 'not allow' and of the way this meaning varies over different questions or for different respondents.

In a way, this approach is comparable to the experiment conducted by Hippler & Schwarz (1986), who asked respondents (N=54) to rate the extremity of another fictitious person's opinion on allowing/forbidding peep shows (see Chapter 2 for a more detailed discussion). This study seemed to indicate that 'yes forbid' was seen as more extreme than 'not allow', but it only compared 'forbid' with 'allow' and did not indicate whether the answer 'not forbid' encompasses a larger variety of meanings than 'yes forbid', which the connotations hypothesis also predicts. Moreover, it is more interesting to let respondents rate the extremity of their own opinions instead of somebody else's in order to visualize the mapping process of respondents when answering forbid/allow questions and to really find out how the answers 'yes' and 'no' to forbid/allow questions should be interpreted.

For the current experiments, the connotations hypothesis predicts that people answering 'yes' will hold strong (i.e. extreme) positive attitudes towards forbidding or allowing the issue addressed in the questions, while respondents holding moderate attitudes, as expressed in their answer to the seven-point-scale forbid/allow questions, will answer 'no' to the two-point-scale forbid/allow questions. Accordingly, it is predicted that the affirmative answers to forbid/allow questions will correspond with 'agree' answers towards forbidding/allowing as expressed on the seven-point-scale questions, while the negative answers to forbid/allow questions are expected to correspond with 'disagree' answers as expressed on the seven-point scales, as well as with moderate answers. In addition to predictions about the mean meanings of the two-point-scale answering options, various predictions can be made about the variances in those meanings. These are too many to list in advance. For example, if 'yes' is extreme, it should show a smaller variation in meanings than 'no', since 'no' can mean 'no!' but can also reflect very moderate opinions. Predictions such as these will be explored in the current chapter.

7.1 ANALYSES

The mapping process for forbid/allow questions and the mechanisms underlying the asymmetry will be analysed by focusing on the meanings of the answering options to forbid/allow questions. The 10 experiments that provide the data for the analyses were described in the previous chapter (Section 6.1). Here, a note should be made on the design used and the analyses to be conducted in the current chapter.

A posthoc four-group design was constructed on the basis of the respondents' answers: respondents who answered 'yes forbid', respondents who answered 'not forbid', respondents who answered 'yes allow', and respondents who answered 'not allow'. The meanings of 'yes' and 'no' can be interpreted in terms of the seven-point-scale answers obtained, because the design of the experiments was such that each respondent answered several seven-point-scale questions equivalent to the two-point-scale questions. In other words, the seven-point-scale questions only differed from the two-point-scale questions in the number of scale points offered. Furthermore, analyses conducted in the previous chapter showed that the test-retest reliability of forbid-2p and forbid-7p (as well as of allow-2p and allow-7p) was very high, indicating that respondents answered the questions far from randomly and that the questions measure the same attitude.

Hence, a comparison of respondents' answers to the two-point-scale questions with their answers to equivalent seven-point-scale questions can provide an indication of what a 'yes' or 'no' to two-point-scale forbid/allow questions means. It indicates how the answering scales to forbid/allow questions differ, what causes forbid questions to be more reliable than allow questions and how to interpret the answers to forbid/allow questions.

Unfortunately, a straightforward comparison is not possible, due to the fact that the communicative restrictions hypothesis was only supported to a very limited extent: the mapping problem did not disappear when a seven-point scale was offered. The wording effect found for the seven-point-scale forbid/allow questions shows that similar attitudes are mapped differently onto the seven-point agree-disagree scales due to the use of forbid/allow. The agree-disagree scale to forbid questions differs from the agree-disagree scale to allow questions.

A prerequisite for obtaining insight into the absolute meanings of 'yes' and 'no' to the two-point-scale questions is that the seven-point answering scales to forbid/allow questions are equivalent to each other. This proves not to be the case. Hence, an average meaning score of '5' for 'yes allow', as expressed on the seven-point allow scale, cannot be compared to an average meaning score of '2' obtained for 'not forbid' as expressed on the different seven-point forbid scale. It would have been possible to compare these meanings in a straightforward manner using a different experimental set-up, in which the two-point-scale forbid/allow questions are followed by an equivalent seven-point scale in which the verbs 'forbid' and 'allow' did not occur. Since such a neutral scale was not available in this instance, some other way of obtaining comparable scales has to be found. Hence, the seven-point answering scales will have to be standardized.

Such a standardization can be obtained by transforming the observed scores to each seven-point-scale forbid/allow question to a standardized score[2]. The answering scales to forbid/allow questions resulting from this standardization procedure can be compared because the midpoints of the scales become similar to each other. These midpoints will be referred to as 'zero-points', but in fact they reflect the mean opinion of respondents who answered forbid questions as well as the mean opinion of respondents who answered allow questions. As the forbid/allow questions were administered to two random subgroups of a random sample, and because forbid/allow questions were shown to measure similar attitudes (in Chapter 4 as well as in the previous chapter), the mean opinion of respondents who answered allow questions can be assumed to be equal to the mean opinion of respondents who answered forbid questions. Hence, standardization of the answering scales provides the opportunity to compare the relative distances of the meanings of 'yes' and 'no' from the mean opinion expressed about the issues addressed in the questions posed in the current research. However, standardization of the answering scales does have some consequences for the

---

[2] This transformation is acquired by subtracting the mean answer to each forbid question from each forbid question's score, and dividing the result by the standard deviation obtained for that forbid question. This is done for each forbid and for each allow question. The result of this computation is that each answer to a seven-point-scale forbid question and each answer to a seven-point-scale allow question can be expressed in terms of its standard deviation from a fixed scale midpoint.

variances around the mean scores for the meanings. For this reason, the analyses concerning the *variations* in meanings are referred to as 'an exploration'.

The remainder of this chapter presents the analyses of the meanings of yes/no to forbid/allow questions. First, the mean score for the meanings of the answers to forbid/allow questions will be discussed. This will serve as a basis for explaining the asymmetry. But the mean scores for the meanings do not provide a full understanding of the mapping process underlying the asymmetry. Accordingly, Section 7.2 goes on to investigate the variation in the mean scores for the meanings. In Section 7.3, the mean meanings and the variation in meanings will be interpreted, in an attempt to describe the mapping process underlying forbid/allow answers. In Section 7.4, the interpretations will be summarized and integrated.

7.2 RESULTS

What did respondents who answered 'no' to a forbid question answer on the equivalent forbid question accompanied by a seven-point scale? In the next subsection the mean meanings of 'yes' and 'no' to forbid/allow questions will be described. This will indicate how the answers to forbid/allow questions should be interpreted. In addition, it is important to analyse how those meanings vary across studies, respondents and questions, as this provides the opportunity to obtain a further understanding of the mapping process. The following section presents the variation in the meanings of 'yes' and 'no'.

7.2.1 The mean meanings of yes and no

The mean scores for the meanings of the answers to forbid/allow questions are provided in Table 7.1.

answer on 2-p	not forbid	yes allow	not allow	yes forbid
distance from 7-p midpoint	-.41 (2.635)	-.49 (2.761)	.63 (5.361)	.72 (5.255)

Note: Estimated mean scores for the meanings of the two-point-scale answering options in terms of the answers on the seven-point-scale are given between brackets.

Table 7.1: *Distance of each answering option's meaning from the midpoint of the scale in standard deviations*

This table shows that respondents answering 'not forbid' on the two-point scale answered also gave an answer indicating a considerable degree of disagreement to the seven-point-scale question ('1' on this scale meant 'disagree with forbid'). The same holds for respondents who answered 'yes allow', as they gave answers indicating a considerable measure of agreement to the allow question on the seven-point scale.

Respondents who answer 'not forbid' or answer 'yes allow' express a mean opinion on the seven-point scale that also shows them to have a reasonably favourable attitude towards the issue in the question (i.e. against forbidding/in favour of allowing). A similar pattern is true for respondents who answered 'not allow' and 'yes forbid'. They also express an opinion denoting considerable opposition to the issue in the question on the seven-point scale. This consistency in the answers given to similar questions accompanied by different answering scales was already shown by the correlations (test-retests) between the two-point-scale questions and seven-point-scale questions in the previous chapter.

For the current chapter, it is interesting to establish whether the mean meanings of the four answering categories differ from each other. As already stated in the previous section, the observed meanings of the answering options to forbid/allow questions cannot be interpreted due to the wording effect found on the seven-point-scale forbid/allow questions. For this it is necessary to look at the standardized scales.

Table 7.1 shows that respondents who answered 'not forbid' to two-point-scale forbid questions obtain a mean score on the seven-point-scale forbid question which is -.41 standard deviations away (i.e. to the left on the scale) from the mean answer to the seven-point-scale forbid questions. Respondents who answered 'yes allow' to a two-point-scale allow question also express an answer on the seven-point scale that is positioned to the left of the mean answer to seven-point-scale allow questions. However, compared to the meaning of 'not forbid', the meaning of 'yes allow' is positioned further to the left on the scale (-.49). Figure 7.1 presents this data in the form of a graph.

Statistical tests show that the meaning of 'yes allow' is more extreme than the meaning of 'not forbid', and that the meaning of 'yes forbid' is more extreme than the meaning of 'not allow' ($p < .05$). On a more conceptual level, this means that affirmative answers reflect more extreme opinions than negative answers to questions with the opposite wording: 'yes allow' is more extreme than 'not forbid', and 'yes forbid' is more extreme than 'not allow'. This difference in the relative mean scores for the meanings is in line with the connotations hypothesis, which states that forbidding and allowing both carry extreme connotations. From this hypothesis it could follow that affirmative answers to either question are more extreme than negative answers to the opposite question: 'not forbid' is less extreme than 'yes allow', and 'not allow' is less extreme than 'yes forbid'.

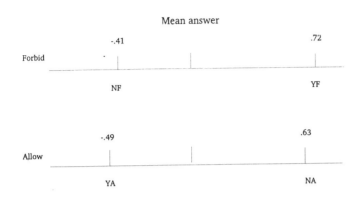

Figure 7.1: *The extremity of the answering options for forbid/allow questions*

For now, it is important to note that these differences in the extremity of 'not forbid' versus 'yes allow' and of 'not allow' versus 'yes forbid' explain the forbid/allow asymmetry. Due to the standardization of the seven-point-scale answers into z-scores, the answers to the seven-point-scale questions can be related directly to proportions (using a z-table). This makes it clear that the 'no' answers, which are less extreme than the 'yes' answers to the opposite versions, are likely to be chosen by more respondents: under the assumption of normal distributions, the mean opinion in the population and opinions close to that mean are likely to be held by more respondents than opinions further away from that mean (i.e. the midpoint of the scale). So, between versions, the number of respondents likely to choose 'not forbid' and 'not allow' is larger than the number of respondents likely to choose 'yes allow' or 'yes forbid', respectively. This is directly related to the key phenomenon to be explained in this study: the asymmetry in the percentages 'yes' and 'no' obtained to forbid/allow questions.

The difference in extremity of 'not forbid' compared to 'yes allow' and of 'not allow' compared to 'yes forbid' explains the higher percentage of respondents choosing that option, at least to some extent. It does not describe how the question-answering mechanism works within versions. If a respondent has to answer one question in either version, the respondent has to choose between 'yes' or 'no' and does not have the opportunity to compare forbid versions with allow versions. In order to obtain an insight into the question-answering process, the meanings of the answering options have to be compared *within* versions, instead of making a comparison of meanings between versions.

The connotations hypothesis describes forbidding and allowing as both carrying extreme connotations, causing moderate respondents to map their opinions onto 'no'. Within versions, it would therefore be interesting to know whether 'not forbid' is less extreme than 'yes forbid' and whether 'not allow' is less extreme in its meaning than 'yes allow'. The standardized meanings presented in Table 7.1 show that 'yes forbid' is indeed further away from the midpoint of the scale than 'not forbid' (p<.05). At the same time, however, 'not allow' is more extreme in its meaning than 'yes allow' (p<.05). Within versions, therefore, the mean meanings of the answering options to forbid questions do support the idea that a negative answer reflects more moderate opinions than the affirmative answer, but at the same time the mean meanings of the answering options to allow questions do not support this hypothesis.

Another comparison within versions to gain insight into the question-answering process could follow from a hypothesis raised in the previous chapter. There, it was put forward that forbid questions are more extreme than allow questions. Between persons, the variance for seven-point-scale forbid questions proved to be larger than the variance for seven-point-scale allow questions. This implies that subtle differences between persons' opinions are expressed more pronouncedly on the seven-point forbid scale than on the seven-point allow scale. It would therefore be interesting to further investigate these differences in scale width and find out whether the distance between the mean scores for the meanings of 'not forbid' and 'yes forbid' differs from the distance between the mean scores for the meanings of 'yes allow' and 'not allow'. Unfortunately, this cannot be analysed using the present data.[3]

For the present, it is important to note that, between versions, 'not forbid' is less extreme than 'yes allow', and 'not allow' is less extreme than 'yes forbid' (see Figure 7.1). This difference in the mean scores of meanings between versions can be related directly to the forbid/allow asymmetry. Furthermore, 'yes forbid' shows a mean score for meaning that is further away from the midpoint of the answering scale than 'not forbid', whereas 'not allow' is more extreme than 'yes allow'. The former pattern was to be expected, based on the connotations hypothesis. It

---

[3] The distances between 'yes' and 'no' cannot be compared on the observed scales because it is not known how the scales to the seven-point-scale forbid/allow questions differ from each other. Nor can the comparison be made on the standardized scales, because standardization changes the length of the scales, causing the larger scale (which was the 7p-forbid scale) to become smaller and the smaller scale (the 7p-allow scale) to become larger than it was originally. As a result there is no difference between the standardized distance between 'yes forbid' and 'not forbid' and the standardized distance between 'yes allow' and 'not allow'.

is contrary to expectations, however, that a different pattern emerges for allow questions.

One would expect the degree of extremity to be related to the amount of variance around the meaning: more extreme options are likely to vary less in their meanings, whereas a larger variance in meanings is expected to cause the less extreme meanings. The next section presents the variances in meanings of the answering options, which provides the opportunity to analyse whether this is the case.

7.2.2 The variation in meanings of yes and no

Looking at the variation in meanings that respondents attribute to their forbid/allow answers provides a further understanding of the mapping process. Whereas the mean scores for the meanings show how the answer should be interpreted, the extent to which those meanings vary shows how well-defined these meanings are. The variances around the means will therefore be analysed, similar to the analyses conducted in the previous chapter (Section 6.3). They give insight into the extent to which the meanings of 'yes' and 'no' vary over studies between persons, and within persons between questions.

The variances between studies prove to be insignificant[4], so without loss of fit these can be fixed at zero. This means that the variance of the mean answer on forbid-7p that was given by respondents who answered 'yes' to forbid-2p does not differ significantly between studies. The same holds for the mean answer expressed to forbid-7p that was given by respondents who answered 'no' to forbid-2p, and similarly for the allow questions. Hence, only the variances between persons and between questions need to be discussed.

Table 7.2 provides the variances around the mean meanings as expressed on the standardized scales.[5] As can be seen in this table, the variances between persons are significant, showing that the mean meaning of 'not forbid' for a set of ques-

---

[4] This insignificance is, as noted in Section 6.3.2, due to power problems: 10 observations on the level of experiments offer a small a priori chance of showing differences between experiments. Furthermore, the differences between persons and questions are theoretically much more interesting than the differences between studies.

[5] The standardized variances differ from the observed variances due to the fact that standardization equals the variances of the forbid seven-point scale to the variances of the seven-point-scale allow questions (both becoming 1.0), although the observed variances were shown to be different from each other in the previous chapter. As the focus in this section is on an interpretation of the differences in meanings of the answering options to forbid/allow questions between versions, the differences in standardized variances can be better interpreted than the differences in observed variances in this exploration.

tions answered by one respondent differs from the mean meaning of 'not forbid' given by all respondents within a given experiment. The same holds for the mean meanings of the other three answering options compared to the mean meaning score for that answering option. This indicates that the meaning of a given answering option to a two-point-scale forbid/allow question is person dependent: for one person 'not forbid' may correspond with a mean score for '3' on the seven-point-scale forbid questions, for another person it may correspond with a mean score of '2' on the seven-point-scale questions.

answer 2-p	not forbid	yes allow	not allow	yes forbid
variance between persons	.19 (p<.001)	.14 (p<.001)	.14 (p<.001)	.18 (p<.001)
variance between questions	.45 (p<.001)	.51 (p<.001)	.55 (p<.001)	.60 (p<.001)

Table 7.2: *The variances between persons and questions (and their significance) in the meanings of the answers to the two-point-scale questions as expressed on the standardized seven-point scales.*

The differences between variances (between persons) proved to be insignificant. The meanings of the two-point-scale answering options differ between persons, but the extent to which they differ is not related to the answering option: the meaning of 'yes allow' does not vary more between persons than the meaning of 'not forbid' or 'not allow'.

The variances between questions within persons are significant for each of the answering options as well. This indicates that the meaning of a 'not forbid' answer to a specific question differs from the mean meaning of all questions to which a given respondent within an experiment answered 'not forbid'. So the variances show that the meaning of each of the answering options to two-point-scale forbid/allow questions is partly dependent of the specific subissue addressed in a question.

Does the extent to which the meanings of the answering options to forbid/allow questions vary within persons over questions, differ systematically for one answering option compared to the other? The variance in meaning of 'not allow' between questions (.55) proves to be similar to the variance in meaning of 'yes allow' (.51), but the variance in meaning of 'yes forbid' between questions (.60) is larger than the variance in meaning of 'not forbid' (.45, p<.05). Between versions, the variance of 'not allow' (.55) equals the variance in meaning of 'yes forbid' (.60) between questions, but the variance in meaning of 'yes allow' (.51) is larger than the variance in meaning of 'not forbid' (.45, p<.05).

In the next sections these patterns in means and variances will be explained and a theory for the question-answering process for forbid/allow questions will be developed. The asymmetry will not only be explained in terms of the likeliness of moderate opinions based on z-scores and normality assumptions (Section 7.2.1), but also in terms of the cognitive processes underlying the wording effect.

7.3 INTERPRETATION OF THE MEANINGS AND THEIR VARIATIONS

First, the guideline hypotheses presented in the introduction to this chapter will be used as a starting point to interpret the figures and describe the mapping process underlying the forbid/allow asymmetry.

In the discussion of the mean scores for the meanings of the answering options to forbid/allow questions, the higher percentage for 'not forbid' compared to 'yes allow' (and for 'not allow' compared to 'yes forbid') was explained by the greater extremity of the meanings of 'yes'. The meanings of 'not forbid' and 'not allow' are more moderate than the meaning of 'yes allow' and 'yes forbid' respectively and those answering options are therefore likely to be chosen more often.

The next question is whether the relative moderateness of 'no' is caused by a larger variance in meaning of the two negative answering options, as the combined connotations/extremity hypothesis predicts. A comparison *between* versions shows that this is not the case, as the variance of 'not forbid' (.45) is smaller than the variance of 'yes allow' (.51), and the variance in meanings of 'not allow' (.55) does not differ from the variance in meanings of 'yes forbid' (.6). It can therefore be said that between versions, differences in the extremity of the answering options cannot be explained by a larger variation in meanings of 'not forbid' compared to 'yes allow' and of 'not allow' compared to 'yes forbid'.

A similar pattern is shown when the variances *within* versions are compared. The combined connotations/extremity hypothesis would predict that respondents holding moderate opinions prefer 'not forbid' to 'yes forbid' because forbidding is seen to be relatively harsh. Likewise, moderate respondents would prefer 'not allow' to 'yes allow', because allowing carries an extreme connotation of support for a behaviour. This leads to the prediction that the negative answers to either version not only have a more moderate mean meaning than the affirmative answers to the same question version, but also that the variance in meanings of 'no' will be larger than the variance in meanings of 'yes' to the same version. Two kinds of respondents will answer 'no': those who really mean 'no!' (not forbid/not allow), and those who merely want to express 'not yes' (forbid/allow).

Within versions the differences in extremity cannot be explained by differences in the variances, however: for forbid questions, the mean meaning of 'not forbid' is less extreme than the mean meaning of 'yes forbid', but the variance in meanings of 'yes forbid' is larger. For allow questions, the mean meaning of 'yes allow' is more moderate, but the variances in meaning of 'yes allow' and 'not allow' do not differ. Straightforward predictions based on the connotations hypothesis do not seem to explain the patterns in the variances found for the meanings of yes/no to forbid/allow questions. Another line of reasoning therefore needs to be established to explain why one of the less extreme answering options in terms of mean meaning (i.e. 'not forbid') also shows the smallest variation in meaning. If this question can be answered properly, it might lead to a further unravelling of the mapping process underlying the answering of forbid/allow questions. At the same time, this explanation should be able to account for why the answering options to forbid questions show a pattern in variances and means that differs markedly from the patterns found for allow questions: for allow questions as opposed to forbid questions, the mean meaning of 'yes (allow)' is less extreme than the meaning of 'no (not allow)', and the variance in meanings of 'yes allow' equals the variance in meanings of 'not allow'. The interpretation will proceed by reasoning from the data.[6] It will be argued that the concept of extremity can be used to explain these patterns in variances, but that it must be applied differently than in the connotations hypothesis.

7.3.1 Extremity as an explanatory factor

The larger variance in the more extreme answering options (as opposed to options that are moderate in their mean meaning scores) may be explained by the fact that if respondents map their opinion onto an answering option with an extreme meaning, they might feel a need to modify this extremity by choosing a moderate answering option on the seven-point scale. The extremity of the answering option 'yes forbid' is accordingly modified on the seven-point scale, causing a large variance in the meanings of 'yes forbid'. Respondents mapping their opinion onto the more moderate 'not forbid' do not need to modify their answer, because it is already relatively moderate. This could also explain the difference in variances between versions: 'yes allow' is more extreme than 'not forbid', so if respondents mapped their opinion onto 'not forbid', they feel less need to modify this moderateness when given the chance on a seven-point scale than respondents who mapped their opinion onto the relatively extreme 'yes allow'.

---

[6] This process of theory building is called 'an exploration'. Using the standardized means and variances of the answering options, the scales to forbid/allow questions can be compared, but only relative to each other. Forbid answers can be compared to allow answers and vice versa, but an objective point of reference is not available.

This gives rise to the question of whether the small variance in meanings of 'not forbid' compared to 'yes allow' should be interpreted as a positive or as a negative feature of forbid questions. The negative interpretation would be that respondents who map their opinion onto 'not forbid' assign a larger variety of meanings to the relatively small part of the seven-point scale they map their opinion onto than is reflected by the relatively homogeneous answers they give. In other words, respondents answering 'not forbid' may answer '2' relatively homogeneously on the seven-point-scale forbid question, but this score of '2' may in fact reflect a variety of moderate and more extreme opinions against forbidding. In this interpretation, the seven-point forbid answering scale is less able to show subtle variation in opinions and differences between respondents, than the allow answering scale. In contrast to this negative interpretation for forbid questions, the positive interpretation would be that extremity in the meaning of a yes/no answering option is not in fact preferable, because respondents modify the extreme answering option 'yes allow' once they get the chance when offered an answering scale containing more scale points. This would imply that the more moderate option 'not forbid' reflects respondents' true opinions more consistently than the extreme 'yes allow', which reflects a variety of moderate and extreme opinions in favour of allowing.

The wording effect found for the seven-point-scale questions means there is no way to decide whether the negative or positive interpretation for forbid questions is true. However, there are a number of reasons for preferring the positive interpretation for forbid questions.

The first of these is that analyses concerning the homogeneity of forbid/allow questions showed that forbid questions (accompanied by a two-point scale as well as by a seven-point scale) measure differences in opinions between respondents more reliably than allow questions. In this exploration it would therefore be reasonable to give forbid questions the benefit of the doubt over allow questions. This decision also seems reasonable from a cognitive point of view. It would be in line with the finding that respondents switch more between yes and no in their answers to sets of two-point-scale allow questions about the same issue (as opposed to two-point-scale forbid questions) to assume that respondents vary more in the meanings they attach to the answering options to allow questions than in the meanings they attach to the forbid answering options. The smaller reliability of allow questions is reflected by the larger variation between questions in meanings of 'yes allow' (compared to 'not forbid').

Secondly, the test of the communicative restrictions hypothesis in the previous chapter showed that respondents use more scale points when answering seven-point-scale forbid/allow questions than when answering two-point-scale questions. It does not seem very plausible to assume that this is the case for all respondents, except for those who answered 'not forbid' on the two-point-scale questions. There is no reason to assume that those respondents should all of a sudden choose a relatively small number of scale points on the seven-point scale to express an equally large amount of variation in true opinions.

Following this line of reasoning, the interpretation that favours forbid questions should be preferred: the answering option 'not forbid' reflects respondents' true attitudes more consistently than the answering option 'yes allow'. For the cognitive processes underlying the answering of forbid/allow questions, this means that the connotations hypothesis is correct in stating that 'forbid' and 'allow' carry extreme connotations, causing 'yes forbid' to be more extreme than 'not allow', and 'yes allow' to be more extreme than 'not forbid' (which, in turn, means that the former answering options are chosen by more respondents than the latter). Within versions, however, an additional cognitive mechanism seems to be at work, which is also related to extremity.

For forbid questions, the answering option 'yes forbid' is relatively extreme, causing the meaning of 'not forbid' to be more moderate and better defined, as it is not necessary to modify a moderate answer. For allow questions, the question-answering process works according to a similar mechanism, but operates differently due to a difference in the extremity of the answering options to forbid and allow questions.

An explanation of the relative extremity of 'yes forbid' may be derived from the semantic properties of 'forbid' and 'allow'. The answering option 'yes forbid' is extreme, as it unambiguously refers to an act of inserting a barrier, to a restrictive action[7]. The answering option 'not allow' refers to a similar action. Therefore, 'not allow' is extreme, and needs to be modified on the seven-point answering scale (which is indicated by a large variance). The answering option 'yes allow' is more ambiguous in its meaning than 'yes forbid', however. It can refer to an action of removing a barrier, which might in some contexts seem to imply that deviant behaviour is encouraged, according to Schuman and Presser, but it can also refer to the non-action of not inserting a barrier (similar to the meaning of 'not forbid'). The large variance in meanings of 'yes allow' might therefore reflect a tendency of respondents to modify extreme answering behaviour ('yes allow' in its meaning of remove a barrier), as well as an ambiguity in meanings of 'yes allow' (which also reflects the more moderate not inserting a barrier).

The variance in meanings of 'not allow' equals the variance in meanings of 'yes allow', due to the ambiguity of 'yes allow'. The ambiguity in one of the answering options to allow questions makes the other answering option ambiguous as well: 'not allow' is extreme for it refers to inserting a barrier, and therefore requires modification but at the same time 'not allow' can imply not remove a barrier. The

---

[7] The analysis here is based on Talmy's (1988) framework of force dynamics. This will be elaborated on in the next section.

fact that 'yes allow' is not very well-defined in its meaning means that 'not allow' is not very well-defined either, as shown by equal variances in meanings of 'yes allow' and 'not allow'. The meanings of both answering options to allow questions therefore seem less well-defined than the meanings of the answering options to forbid questions, which may also explain the fact that respondents switch more in their answers to allow questions, thereby causing the smaller reliability of allow questions.

In terms of the mapping process in general, this analysis could indicate that respondents find allow questions easier to answer, as they may encounter less of a mapping problem. They switch between 'yes' and 'no' when answering sets of allow questions about the same issue and switch in the meaning they attach to 'yes allow', more than in the meaning they attach to 'not forbid'. When answering allow questions they do not seem to feel very restricted by the meanings of allow, nor by the meaning of the answer 'yes allow'. When answering forbid questions their mapping problem becomes more evident, as the meaning of 'yes forbid' is relatively extreme and therefore well-defined. Respondents modify this extremity by moderating their answers on the seven-point scale. The fact that the meaning of 'yes forbid' is better defined than all of the other answering options, implies that the meaning of 'not forbid' is also well-defined. Because of its reference to a non-action its meaning seems to be rather moderate, which might cause the 'disagree to forbid'-side of the seven-point forbid scale to entail a rather moderate meaning as well. Respondents probably tend not to distinguish many subtleties within this moderate area on the seven-point scale, resulting in a relatively homogeneous moderate meaning of 'not forbid'.[8]

With respect to the connotations hypothesis, this exploration shows that the asymmetry in the answers to forbid/allow questions is related to the extreme connotations of both verbs, causing the affirmative answering options to be chosen by a smaller number of respondents than the negative options. This does not mean, however, that the connotations hypothesis (combined with the attitude strength hypothesis) is fully supported. If that were the case, the variances in meanings of the negative answering options would have been larger than the variation in meaning of the affirmative options: 'not forbid' would have shown a larger variance than 'yes forbid', and 'not allow' would have shown a larger variance than 'yes allow'. To describe the cognitive mechanisms in the question-

---

[8] Note that this is a modification of the hypothesis formulated in the introduction to this chapter, which assumed that the connotations of 'forbid' might be more extreme than the connotations of 'allow'. The findings discussed here suggest that 'yes forbid' is more extreme than all of the other answering options. If the connotations of forbidding in general are more extreme, one would expect the extremity of 'not forbid' to be more pronounced as well.

answering process for forbid/allow questions, the connotations hypothesis should be extended by focusing on the extremity as well as on the extent to which the meanings of the answering options are well-defined. The resultant description of the question-answering process will be recapitulated in the next section. The next section also contains a more detailed discussion of the implications of this analysis for the answering behaviour of 'indifferent' or moderate respondents.

7.4 INTEGRATION AND DISCUSSION

Forbid/allow questions cause similar attitudes to be retrieved, but those attitudes are expressed differently on the answering scales due to the use of these verbs. This chapter, as well as the previous one, is concerned with an analysis of how exactly the scales to forbid/allow questions differ or, in cognitive terms, how the mapping process underlying the answering process for forbid/allow questions works. An exploratory analysis focusing on the meanings of the answering options to forbid/allow questions enabled us to develop a more comprehensive theory concerning the question-answering process for forbid/allow questions, using the combined *connotations/extremity hypothesis* as a guideline. In the current chapter, the focus was not on the assumed extremity of the connotations of 'forbid' and 'allow', but on the relative meanings of the answering options to forbid/allow questions. Is 'yes forbid' more extreme in its meaning than 'not allow'? Do the meanings of 'not allow' and 'not forbid' show larger variations than 'yes allow' and 'yes forbid', respectively, due to the assumption that the former options are repositories of various meanings?

The analyses presented in this chapter provide the means to explain the forbid/allow asymmetry by comparing the relative extremity of the answering options to forbid/allow questions. Analyses show that the meaning of 'not forbid' is less extreme than the meaning of 'yes allow'. Similarly, the meaning of 'not allow' is less extreme than the meaning of 'yes forbid' (see Figure 7.1).

This could be in line with the connotations hypothesis as expressed by Schuman and Presser. They stated that both 'forbid' and 'allow' carry extreme connotations, which could imply that 'yes forbid' and 'yes allow' carry more extreme connotations than 'not allow' and 'not forbid', respectively. This finding also confirms the results of the small-scale experiment conducted by Hippler & Schwarz (1986), which showed that respondents rated another person's fictitious opinion as more extreme if it was 'yes forbid' than if it was 'not allow'. In the current experiments, respondents rated the extremity of their own opinions and a comparison was made using standardized scores. The differences in extremity can therefore be related directly to the higher percentage of respondents choosing 'not forbid' over 'yes allow' (and choosing 'not allow' over 'yes forbid'). Under the assumption of normal distributions, the number of respondents holding moderate opinions (relatively close to the midpoint of the scale) is larger than the number of respondents holding extreme opinions (further away from the midpoint of the answering scale). As 'not forbid' is more moderate than 'yes allow', and 'not allow' more moderate in its mean meaning than 'yes forbid', the former options are likely to be chosen more often, and the forbid/allow asymmetry is the result. Hence, as long as comparisons between versions are made in order to explain the forbid/allow asymmetry (the phenomenon that more respondents will answer 'not forbid' than 'yes allow', and more respondents will answer 'not allow' than 'yes forbid'), the connotations hypothesis holds and can be referred to as the 'connotations explanation' in the future. The extent to which the connotations hypothesis explains the forbid/allow asymmetry is summarized in Box 7.2.

Connotations explanation

'Not forbid' is perceived as less extreme than 'yes allow', and 'not allow' is perceived as less extreme than 'yes forbid'. Since any random group will be likely to consist of more respondents holding moderate opinions than of respondents holding extreme opinions, the former answering options are likely to be chosen more often than the latter. This smaller degree of extremity in the meaning of 'no' to both question wordings is caused by a collective assignment of moderate meanings and not by a relatively large variance in the meanings of moderate answers.

Box 7.2*: The explanation for the asymmetry: why 'not forbid' is chosen by more respondents than 'yes allow', and 'not allow' is chosen by more respondents than 'yes forbid'*

This 'connotations explanation' does not describe, however, why the mapping process works like this and exactly how it works for a given respondent. How do respondents translate their opinions into one of the answering options offered when responding to one or more forbid questions, or one or more allow questions? In other words, how should the answers to forbid/allow questions be interpreted? Furthermore, the causes of smaller reliability of allow questions have to be determined. We have yet to discover what causes respondents to switch more between 'yes' and 'no' in their answers to allow questions. The combined connotations/extremity hypothesis predicts that moderate respondents will map their evaluations onto 'no' for either question. If this is true, one would expect this to be reflected in a larger variance of meanings of 'no' but this is not the case. It seems, therefore, that the combined connotations/extremity hypothesis must be replaced by another theory describing the cognitive mechanisms by which respondents answer a forbid question or an allow question.

As discussed in the previous sections, these cognitive issues can only be explored. The wording effect found on the seven-point-scale forbid/allow questions means that no stable point of reference was available in order to analyse the meanings of yes/no to forbid/allow questions. The lack of a neutral scale, meant that a theory on the question-answering process can only be developed by reasoning and careful comparison. In the previous sections, this was done by treating the data as a point of departure and working 'bottom-up' towards a theory. In the following section a top-down presentation will be given: the theory will first be described, followed by a discussion of the evidence supporting it. The analysis of the question-answering process for forbid/allow questions is presented explicitly as a theory here. It should be tested and developed further in future research, using a neutral scale on which to express the meanings of the answering options. A discussion of the theory developed in this chapter will be preceded by a recapitulation of the need to replace the existing theory (i.e. the combined connotations/extremity hypothesis) with a theory that provides a more accurate description of the mapping process underlying forbid/allow answers.

7.4.1 The connotations hypothesis

In exploring the cognitive processes that cause similar attitudes to be mapped differently onto the answering options to forbid/allow questions, a further investigation of the plausibility of the connotations hypothesis was first required. The connotations hypothesis correctly predicted the direct cause of the asymmetry, outlined in Box 7.2. But although the difference in extremity between versions (between 'yes forbid' and 'not allow' and between 'yes allow' and 'not forbid') explains the difference in the percentages obtained for these answering options, it does not describe the cognitive mechanisms at work when a respondent is answering a forbid or an allow question. Do respondents regard 'yes forbid' as more extreme than 'not forbid', and 'yes allow' as more extreme than 'not allow'? And do all moderate respondents prefer to map their opinions onto 'not forbid' rather than onto 'yes forbid' (and onto 'not allow' rather than onto 'yes allow'), even those respondents who are moderately in favour of forbidding or allowing?

Schuman & Presser (1981) stated that "the verb 'forbid' sounds harsher and may therefore be more difficult to endorse, whereas 'allow' in some contexts might seem to encourage a deviant behaviour and therefore may invite opposition". Hippler & Schwarz (1986), Waterplas et al. (1988) and Krosnick & Schuman (1988) extended this connotations hypothesis by incorporating various dimensions of attitude strength: the extreme connotations of forbid/allow would cause respondents holding weak or moderate opinions to map their opinion onto 'not forbid' or 'not allow' instead of onto 'yes forbid' or 'yes allow', respectively.

One would assume from the connotations hypothesis that 'not forbid' is less extreme in its meaning than 'yes forbid', and that 'not allow' is less extreme than 'yes allow'. This pattern was not confirmed by the data, however: a comparison within versions showed that the affirmative answers were not consistently more extreme than the negative ones. Although 'not forbid' is less extreme than 'yes forbid', the opposite seemed to be the case for allow questions, with 'yes allow' being less extreme than 'not allow'.

The extension of the connotations hypothesis by Hippler & Schwarz (1986) and others, focusing on the answering behaviour of moderate or indifferent respondents, predicts the answer 'no' to be a repository of various meanings. Accordingly, 'not forbid' should vary more in its meaning than 'yes forbid', and 'not allow' should vary more in its meaning than 'yes allow', due to the fact that indifferent or moderate respondents map their opinion onto 'no', and not just those respondents who really mean 'no!'. The exploration in this chapter also failed to confirm this prediction, because the variance in meanings of 'not allow' was found not to differ from the variance in meanings of 'yes allow', while the variance of 'yes forbid' was even larger than the variance of 'not forbid'.

The asymmetry may be related to the extremity of opinions, but not in accordance with the hypothesis expressed throughout this book and at the beginning of this chapter. 'No' was not shown to hold a repository of various meanings and the mean meaning of 'yes allow' was not found to be more extreme than the meaning of 'not allow'. Hence, the connotations hypothesis combined with the attitude strength hypothesis cannot help to describe the cognitive processes, apart from explaining the asymmetry in terms of the moderateness of 'not forbid' and 'not allow' relative to 'yes allow' and 'yes forbid', respectively. The cognitive processes can be described, however, by reasoning from the larger reliability found for forbid questions (as reflected by the larger number of respondents switching in their answers to allow questions), and a comparison of the extremity of the meanings of each of the answering options to forbid/allow questions. This process is detailed below.

7.4.2 The meanings of yes and no and the mapping process

The previous chapter concluded with an important difference between forbid questions and allow questions. It emerged that allow questions measure the underlying attitude less reliably than forbid questions. Based on the analysis of the difference in mapping processes for seven-point-scale questions versus two-point-scale questions, it was hypothesized that mapping an answer for two-point-scale forbid questions was less of a problem than the mapping stage when answering allow questions. The verb 'forbid' was shown to create a preference for using the extremes of the seven-point scale anyway, so offering only the extremes in the form of a two-point-scale forbid question does not seem to severely restrict the possibilities for expressing moderate opinions. When answering the two-point-scale allow questions, however, the respondent is given greater freedom. Within this structure, the respondent can express moderateness by switching between 'yes' and 'no' when answering several questions about the same theme.

This hypothesis was developed further in the current chapter. This did not take the form of a comparison between the forbid answering scale and the allow answering scale, but was achieved by comparing the meanings (and the variations in those meanings) for each of the four answering options to forbid/allow questions. This led to a modification of the hypothesis formulated in the introduction to the current chapter: it is not the extremity of 'forbid' in general that leads to an extreme positioning on the seven-point answering scale, but the answering option 'yes forbid' that is especially extreme and related to the large variance on the seven-point-scale forbid questions, whereas disagreeing to forbid implies a relatively homogeneous and moderate standpoint. In addition to this, it may be the case that switching between 'yes allow' and 'not allow' is a way of expressing moderateness, but that this tendency is also related to the ill-defined meaning of both the answering options 'yes allow' and 'not allow'. This modification is based on two lines of reasoning: on the idea that respondents tend to modify extreme positions and on an analysis of the well-definedness of meanings of the answering options.

Firstly, the modification is based on the idea that respondents find it difficult to map their opinions onto an extreme answering option. Some might prefer to agree to the question, but they do not like to take a position that is out on a limb, and therefore tend to modify that position when given a chance to do so on a seven-point answering scale. This idea is supported by the finding that 'yes forbid', which was found to be extreme in its mean meaning, has a large variance in meanings as well. Its variance is larger than the variance in the moderate 'not forbid', since disagreeing to forbid seems to be so moderate that there does not seem a necessity to distinguish between several kinds of moderateness on the seven-point scale.

Secondly, the modification is based on an analysis of the meanings of 'yes forbid', 'not forbid', 'yes allow' and 'not allow', in accordance with the framework of force dynamics (Talmy, 1988). This analysis shows that the meanings of the answering options to forbid/allow questions are not equally well-defined. The answering option 'yes allow' is particularly ambiguous, which makes 'not allow' relatively ill-defined as well. This explains the variance patterns for forbid/allow questions, as well as the respondents' tendency to switch more between 'yes' and 'no' when answering allow questions.

Force dynamics is a semantic category identified by Talmy (1988), and is "a generalization over the traditional linguistic notion of the 'causative'" (Talmy 1988: 40), which includes concepts such as the exertion of force, resistance to such exertion, blockage of a force and the removal of such a blockage. There are a number of reasons which invite analysis of the meanings of the answering options to forbid/allow questions in terms of this theory. Talmy uses it to analyse the meanings of several verbs comparable to 'forbid' and 'allow', such as 'helping', 'letting', 'hindering' and 'causing'. For example, the sentence 'John does not go out of the house' provides a relatively objective description of a situation, whereas in the sentence 'John cannot go out of the house' a force dynamic pattern is discernable in which John wants to go outside, but there is a force or barrier restricting his behaviour. By distinguishing this semantic category of 'force', it can be described how forbidding and allowing can both be 'actions' and both be extreme, but can differ in the extent to which they exert a force and to which they cause or allow something to happen. This difference in causation or force is already hinted at by Schuman and Presser's connotations hypothesis, when they state that "allow in some contexts might seem to encourage a deviant behaviour". This suggests that it does not do this in other contexts, and in those contexts it is perhaps less 'encouraging' in nature.

Force dynamics distinguishes between causing and letting, and various sub-types of those actions. Furthermore, force dynamics can distinguish between stronger antagonist types (the affecting entities 'cause' or 'let') and weaker antagonist types (the affecting entities 'hinder', 'help', 'leave alone' or 'try').[9] The basic idea is that a force can have a tendency either towards motion or towards rest. How can these notions of force be applied to the verbs 'forbid' and 'allow'?

In almost every forbid/allow question, the government, 'the United States' or some other authority is the affecting entity (the antagonist) that does the forbidding or allowing. In most cases, one can assume that if this authority 'forbids' or 'does not allow' something, this will cause the actual behaviour under discussion to cease. In other words, the antagonist can be assumed to be fairly strong in most forbid/allow situations. What does all of this imply for the meaning of 'yes forbid'? This seems to represent the subtype of causing in which the antagonist's

---

[9] It is difficult to determine who the agonist and the antagonist are in forbid/allow questions. In the question 'Do you think the government should forbid the sale of soft drugs? yes/no', the government could be the affecting entity (antagonist), while persons who buy or sell soft drugs are the implicit agonists. But in the question-answering situation, there is someone else involved, the respondent, and it is not clear whether he considers himself an affecting entity (e.g. by identifying with the government), or the affected entity (e.g. by identifying with the persons buying or selling soft drugs) when answering forbid/allow questions. Fortunately, as the focus is on *differences* in 'force' between forbid/allow questions, this theoretical problem does not seem to affect the analysis.

force influences the agonist (the affected entity) and wins: the force of the antagonist is stronger than a potential force of the agonist. More specifically, it probably comes closer to the subtype of causing referred to by Talmy as 'the onset causing of rest' (as in 'The water's dripping on it made the fire die down', 1988: 57): a barrier is inserted by the antagonist causing the behaviour of the agonist (who is often left implicit in forbid/allow questions) to be blocked and stop.[10] Accordingly, 'yes forbid' seems to be relatively unambiguous in its reference to causing, to an act of inserting a barrier, and to a force dynamic pattern which brings about a change.

The meaning of 'yes allow' seems to be more ambiguous, as it may imply causing (removing a barrier) as well as letting (not inserting a barrier). The letting pattern may be specified as the pattern of the 'secondary steady state', in which the agonist keeps on doing what he was doing because the antagonist (the authorities) does not do anything (comparable to 'The plug's staying loose let the water drain from the tank' (1988: 59) and to the Dutch *gedogen* or *oogluikend toestaan*, which means something like 'tolerate'). Compared to 'yes forbid', the antagonist in 'yes allow' seems to exert a weaker force: the antagonist is of a weaker antagonist type, as the 'allowing' by an antagonist seems to be less the result of reasoning, and more of letting things be and doing nothing. The meaning of 'yes allow' could even be analysed as a situation in which the antagonist exerts a certain force upon the agonist, but in which the antagonist is so weak that his force does not influence the agonist (the subtype of the 'weaker antagonist', in which the antagonist might hinder the agonist's behaviour but does not block it). At the same time, 'yes allow' can mean causing or removing a barrier. In that case, 'yes allow' could be a 'shifting force-dynamic pattern', as in 'The plug's coming loose let the water flow from the tank' (1988: 57), in which the non-moving agonist that intrinsically moves (shows a controversial behaviour), is no longer blocked in his intrinsic movement by the antagonist (the authorities). In this case, the antagonist type is stronger.

The meaning of 'not allow' is comparable to the meaning of 'yes forbid', as it refers to a pattern in which the antagonist's force influences the agonist and wins. More specifically, it is closer to the subtype of 'the onset causing of rest': a barrier is inserted by the antagonist causing the behaviour of the agonist (who is often left implicit in forbid/allow questions) to stop. The answering option 'not allow' could also mean the 'onset causing of action', especially when it is referring to the 'sociodynamic' act of actually telling agonists the behaviour is not allowed, or the

---

[10] The answering option 'yes forbid' could also mean the onset causing of action (as in 'The ball's hitting it made the lamp topple from the table', 1988: 57), especially when it refers to the sociodynamic act of actually telling agonists the behaviour is forbidden, or the actual pressure the antagonist (the authorities) can impose on the agonist.

actual pressure the antagonist (the authorities) can impose on the agonist. But 'not allow' seems to refer to a weaker antagonist type than 'yes forbid', as it focuses less on the consequences of 'not allowing'. Similarly to 'yes forbid', 'not allow' seems to refer to causing, to inserting a barrier and to a pattern in which a change is caused. The meaning of 'not allow' is therefore the opposite of the 'shifting force-dynamic pattern' which can be encompassed by 'yes allow'. The meaning of 'not allow' also seems to be the opposite of the more moderate meanings of 'yes allow': 'not allow' may imply 'do not remove a barrier'. Due to the fact that 'yes allow' is not very well-defined in its meaning, the meaning of 'not allow' seems to be ambiguous as well. However, 'not allow' does not seem to be opposite to all other possible meanings of 'yes allow', as a weaker antagonist does not seem to fit the act of 'not allowing'.

The meaning of 'not forbid' seems to be letting (do not insert a barrier). It could be specified as a pattern in which the agonist keeps on doing what he was doing because the antagonist (the authorities) do not do anything. In comparison to 'yes allow', 'not forbid' seems to imply a stronger force: the antagonist is of a stronger antagonist type, as the 'not forbidding' by an antagonist seems to be more the result of reasoning and less of letting things be and doing nothing.

Based on the force dynamics analysis of the answering options to forbid/allow questions, it can be predicted that the meaning of 'yes forbid' is the most extreme and well-defined in its meaning compared to the other three answering options: its force is strongest, and its meaning is unambiguously one of causing and blockage. This was supported by the data (see Figure 7.1). Based on the idea that respondents tend to avoid taking extreme standpoints, one would also expect the variance in meanings of 'yes forbid' to be largest. Once respondents have chosen to map their opinion onto the extreme 'yes forbid', they tend to modify this extremity when given the chance to do so on the seven-point forbid scale. This tendency to modify extremity was also supported by the data.

'Not forbid' is more moderate in its meaning than 'yes forbid' and 'yes allow', as 'not forbid' only refers to letting. Its moderateness compared to 'yes allow' explains the higher percentage of respondents who map their answer onto 'not forbid' compared to 'yes allow', as has already been discussed (see Box 7.2). For the cognitive account of the question-answering process, the focus should be on differences within versions. In that case, the moderateness of the meaning of 'not forbid' compared to 'yes forbid' leads to the prediction that the moderate opinion reflected by 'not forbid' does not need to be modified on the seven-point scale. Disagreeing to the well-defined forbid question might be so moderate that no modifications are necessary on the disagree-side of the seven-point forbid scale: respondents probably choose a scale point that is somewhere in the middle of the moderate disagree-area. The answering option 'not forbid' thus reflects moderate opinions against forbidding, and does so fairly homogeneously. This is confirmed by the data: the variance in meanings of 'not forbid' is small compared to the variance in meanings of the other answering options.

For allow questions, a force dynamic analysis shows that the meaning of 'yes allow' is ambiguous, as it refers to causing as well as to letting. It is relatively extreme in its causal meaning (i.e. of removing a barrier), which could be modified on the seven-point allow scale. It is relatively moderate in its meaning of letting, of not inserting a barrier, which should be reflected by moderate answers on the seven-point allow scale as well. The meaning of 'not allow' is also ambiguous, as it can refer to inserting a barrier (comparable to 'yes forbid'). In this meaning, 'not allow' encompasses a weaker antagonist than 'yes forbid', causing it to be more moderate in its mean meaning than 'yes forbid'. This is indeed shown by the data and is directly related to the asymmetry between forbid and allow questions. Furthermore, in terms of the question-answering process for allow questions, 'not allow' is more extreme than 'yes allow' in its reference to causing and to inserting a barrier. Due to this relative extremity, one would expect it to be modified on the seven-point allow scale. The data testify to this: 'not allow' is more extreme than 'yes allow'. Furthermore, one would expect the variance in meanings of 'not allow' to be about the same size as 'yes allow' due to the extreme meanings it encompasses and its ambivalence in meaning. This is also borne out by the data. The variances in meanings of 'not allow' and 'yes allow' are equally large: 'yes allow' because it is ambiguous in its meanings and extreme in some of its meanings, 'not allow' because it is extreme and has to be modified and because it is ambiguous due to the ambiguity of 'yes allow'.

The theory to emerge is that the asymmetry is caused by the well-defined nature and extremity of 'yes forbid' compared to the moderateness of 'not allow', as well as by the moderateness of 'not forbid' compared to the extremity of 'yes allow'. This explains the higher number of respondents mapping their opinions onto 'no' (see Box 7.2) between versions.

Another cause of the asymmetry is the extremity of 'yes forbid' and the ambiguity of 'yes allow'. Due to the ambiguity of 'allow' in its reference to not inserting a barrier or removing a barrier (or in doing nothing with respect to an issue, as opposed to encouraging it), the answering option 'yes allow' is not very well-defined compared to 'not forbid' (which only refers to not inserting a barrier). This ill-defined meaning of 'yes allow' also has a negative influence on the definition of 'not allow': its mean meaning is extreme, as it refers to an act of inserting a barrier, but its variance in meanings is large, as it also refers to an act of not removing a barrier. This ambiguity may also be related to the fact that respondents can switch between 'yes' and 'no' when answering allow questions. The answering option 'yes forbid' is more well-defined, causing 'not forbid' to be well-defined as well. The latter is also more moderate, as it refers to not inserting a barrier.

Reasoning from this, it seems that respondents who hold moderate opinions against inserting a barrier will choose 'not forbid' and will do this with reasonable consistency for each question in a set of forbid questions addressing an issue. Respondents holding similar opinions who answer a set of allow questions will tend to choose 'yes allow', but, due to the ambiguity of this answering option, they will also switch between 'yes allow' and 'not allow', influenced by the possible implication that 'yes allow' means the issue should be encouraged. Respondents moderately in favour of inserting a barrier, will probably answer 'not allow', but respondents in favour of not doing anything will find 'not allow' rather extreme, causing them to modify that answer if given the chance. Respondents who are moderately in favour of inserting a barrier might have difficulties in choosing between 'not forbid' and 'yes forbid' when answering forbid questions. They may tend to prefer 'not forbid' since it is more moderate than 'yes forbid', but whatever their choice, they will tend to stick to it when answering a set of forbid questions.

Basically, the smaller reliability of allow questions compared to forbid questions is caused by the fact that 'yes allow' is not very well-defined in its meaning, which gives 'not allow' a measure of ambiguity as well. This causes respondents to switch between 'yes allow' and 'not allow' when answering a set of two-point-scale allow questions, thereby reflecting the variation in the meanings of 'yes/no allow' (and possibly a general indifference). Forbid questions leave less scope for doing this, as the meanings of 'yes forbid' and 'not forbid' are quite well-defined. This might cause respondents to encounter more of a mapping problem when answering forbid questions, but it also causes the answers to forbid questions to reflect the underlying attitude more consistently. In addition, it makes the answering option 'not forbid' relatively easy to interpret. In the light of this information, the main problem for forbid/allow questions is the ill-defined nature of 'yes allow', which also reflects on 'not allow'. Couched in more positive terms, 'yes forbid' is relatively well-defined, causing 'not forbid' to be well-defined as well. All of this is summarized as the 'Well-defined meaning hypothesis', in Box 7.3.

The well-defined meaning hypothesis

Allow questions are less reliable measures of an underlying attitude than forbid questions, due to less well-defined meanings of 'yes allow' and 'not allow' (compared to 'yes forbid' and 'not forbid'). The answering option 'yes allow' can refer to causing as well as to letting. In other words, it refers to not inserting a barrier as well as removing a barrier. 'Yes forbid', on the other hand, only refers to causing, to inserting a barrier.

Due to the ill-defined meaning of 'yes allow', 'not allow' is also ambiguous in its meaning. This gives respondents more reason, as well as more scope for switching between 'yes' and 'no' when answering a set of allow questions. The meaning of 'yes forbid' and 'not forbid' is also well-defined, causing respondents to be relatively consistent in mapping their attitudes onto the answering scales when answering a set of forbid questions.

Box 7.3: *The causes of the smaller reliability of allow questions*

The practical implication for research designers is that forbid questions should be preferred to allow questions. This is not only because of the greater reliability of forbid questions but also because the answers to forbid questions can be interpreted more easily and homogeneously. The answering options 'yes' and 'no' to forbid questions do not necessarily always reflect the opinions 'yes forbid' and 'not forbid' respectively, as their variances in meanings are fairly large. At the same time, the variance in the meaning of 'not forbid' is the smallest of all four answering options. The meaning of 'not forbid' can therefore be interpreted most easily: the group of respondents answering 'not forbid' expresses a relatively moderate opinion by choosing that answer, but is fairly homogeneous in its moderateness. What is more, respondents choosing 'not forbid' are relatively consistent when answering several forbid questions about the same issue, which accounts for the greater reliability of forbid questions.

Chapter 8

ON COGNITIVE MECHANISMS
UNDERLYING WORDING EFFECTS

8.0 INTRODUCTION

Surveys are widely used in the social sciences and very often form a basis for governmental and commercial planning or evaluating. In a broad range of areas decisions are based or jusitfied on survey data. Surveys provide the opportunity to collect data on a large number of persons relatively quickly, and find out about facts and behaviours as well as 'inner variables', such as attitudes, opinions or emotions.

Asking survey questions is a way of constructing data, and not of 'fact finding' (Bateson, 1984). This is demonstrated by the many variables that unintentionally influence the answers, variables which relate not only to the actual attitude or behaviour under study, but also to characteristics of the survey questions themselves. This goes against the hypotheses implicitly held by survey researchers, who basically assume a direct as well as a steady relation between true values within respondents' minds and the answers respondents give. As long as it is unclear how the answers given to survey questions are related to the true value of the variables the researcher is interested in, these 'response effects' are a serious threat to the validity of survey research.

Previous research has shown that a wide variety of characteristics influence survey responses. Question wording is not the only important factor. The characteristics of the respondent, the interviewer, and the task all play their part, as does the question form. Not surprisingly, there are similarities between this list of characteristics which influence responses and the components of basic communication models. The starting point of the current study was therefore to view the answering of survey questions not as a mechanical process in which the respondent translates his inner variables directly into a survey answer. Instead, it was conceptualized as a communication process in which the respondent makes inferences about the sender (or interviewer) and the intentions and research goals by interpreting characteristics of the question wording and the task.

A communicative model for the answering process of attitude questions is offered by Tourangeau and Rasinski's description of the question-answering process (Tourangeau & Rasinski, 1988), which is already being used in response effects research focusing on the effects of question order. This model basically consists of four steps: question interpretation, retrieval of the attitude, rendering a judgement and reporting an answer.

Response effects, then, can arise at the interpretation or retrieval stage. During this stage, the respondent has to infer the meaning of the question, aiming at an interpretation that is meaningful but that does not require unjustifiable effort: he uses the content and the immediate context of the question, as well as knowledge of the goals of the research and attitudes or beliefs that are readily accessible. In this case, the question text or context can change the nature of the object or issue being judged, or can change the considerations and beliefs that enter into the judgment. Response effects can also arise during the final stage, because the question text and context can change the standards or norms that are applied in making the judgment, or can change the way the judgment is reported.

It is not sure whether survey research benefits from refinement into tiny subprocesses, nor whether it would be possible to find measurement instruments that are able to distinguish between these activities. Therefore, in the present study, the question-answering process is basically conceptualized as consisting of two steps: interpreting the question and retrieving an attitude or set of relevant attitudes, versus mapping the evaluation onto one of the precoded answering options. This division into two stages is relevant to the validity of survey questions. Measuring what one intends to measure depends first of all on whether the attitude one intends to measure is retrieved and secondly, whether the answer obtained can be translated into the attitude that was retrieved.

The threat to validity caused by response effects is most serious in cases when the true value held by respondents is difficult to retrieve in other ways than by asking survey questions, as is the case when the true values concern attitudes, opinions or emotions. Furthermore, in 1974 Bradburn and Sudman concluded from their meta-analysis of response effects that so called 'task variables', such as the order of questions and of response options and the question wording, cause the largest 'distortions' in the answers. Recent studies using cognitive approaches to describe and explain the mechanisms behind response effects tend to focus on question order effects. Question wording effects, perhaps the most subtle type of response effects, have been somewhat neglected within this approach.

The forbid/allow asymmetry is a good example of this. This wording effect has been the subject of quite some experiments in the wording effect literature, is discussed in many reviews of survey literature, and is very often used in practitioners' handbooks in order to illustrate how subtle wording differences in attitude questions can have a dramatic influence on responses. An example of the forbid/allow asymmetry is usually taken from Rugg (1941), the earliest experiment concerning this wording effect reported in the literature.

The forbid/allow asymmetry is intriguing, because it demonstrates that questions using words that are each other's linguistic counterparts are not answered accordingly. The relatively large amount of research into the forbid/allow asymmetry gave rise to quite a few hypotheses explaining this wording effect, but not to a thorough understanding of the causes of the actual phenomenon. The differences in the answers to forbid/allow questions reported in the literature are relatively large and consistent compared to other wording effects. In short, the forbid/allow asymmetry is a rather extreme example of a wording effect that has been investigated relatively often but for which no reliable explanation exists. It is important to obtain such an explanation, however, as an understanding of the use of forbid/allow and of contrastive questions in general is required in order to develop balanced questionnaires. For these reasons, this wording effect was selected for further investigation in the present study.

The cognitive communicative framework employed in this study, combined with a variety of research designs, succeeds in providing an explanation for the forbid/allow asymmetry. Furthermore, this explanation offers a springboard for describing more general mechanisms behind wording effects and sets an agenda for future research. These aspects will be elaborated on in the current chapter. Section 8.1 briefly summarizes the steps taken in this study. Section 8.2 outlines the general explanation for the forbid/allow asymmetry. This results in the proposition of the Yes/No$^+$ Theory, which explains why the use of 'forbid' and 'allow' generally causes a wording effect to occur. It does not explain, however, why the wording effect varies greatly across questions. The mechanisms causing this variation are discussed in Section 8.3. Together, Section 8.2 and Section 8.3 present a theoretical integration of research outcomes with regard to the forbid/allow asymmetry presented in each separate chapter of this book. Section 8.4 goes on to discuss the extent to which the cognitive mechanisms found to underlie the forbid/allow asymmetry can be generalized to other response effects. It is proposed that the Yes/No$^+$ Theory not only holds for forbid/allow questions, but for any attitude question in which a qualifying dimension is used. In Section 8.5 the practical implications of this study are discussed for each stage of survey research: development of the questionnaire, administration of the survey and interpretation of the data. The final section of the book reflects on a number of points arising from this study that deserve attention in future research.

8.1 RECAPITULATION

The first chapter of this book provides an overview of the goals of this study. It discusses how response effects go against the implicit assumptions held by researchers using surveys to collect their data. Various approaches to survey research are discussed: the split ballot design, which is often employed in order to determine the existence of a response effect and explanatory approaches, which make use of cognitive or communication theories. It is argued that a cognitive approach would help to unravel the causes of the forbid/allow asymmetry in a way that is relevant to theory as well as to practice.

The second chapter contains a more thorough discussion and analysis of research on the forbid/allow asymmetry reported in the literature. It emerges that the asymmetry varies in size in the experiments, and that replications are less systematic than they seemed at first sight. Various explanations for the asymmetry are discussed. The two most important are the connotations hypothesis (Schuman & Presser, 1981) and the attitude strength hypothesis (Hippler & Schwarz, 1986). The *connotations hypothesis* states that 'forbid' sounds harsh and may therefore be difficult to endorse, whereas 'allow' in some contexts might seem to encourage a deviant behaviour and may therefore invite opposition, thus causing respondents to opt for the answer 'no' to both questions. The *attitude strength hypothesis* predicts that the asymmetry, like many other response effects, is caused by respondents holding weak or ambivalent opinions: the extreme connotations of 'forbid' and 'allow', combined with the tendency of all human beings to focus on the implications of 'doing' instead of 'not doing', creates a tendency among 'indifferent respondents' to answer 'no' to both forbid and allow questions.

Chapters 3 to 7 give an account of the core of this study: 12 experiments and two meta-analyses of forbid/allow experiments. In Chapter 3, a meta-analysis of forbid/allow research is reported, together with a meta-analysis of two new experiments. The asymmetry size was shown to vary considerably between questions but the use of 'forbid' and 'allow' generally affects the answers beyond the level of questions and experiments. The effect is in fact considerable. The variation in asymmetry size was not unexpected, as it had already been established by eyeball analyses. Furthermore, communication theories also describe that a linguistic element does not necessarily affect each and every reader in each and every context. With this in mind, further research was geared towards either explaining the wording effect whilst taking the differences between respondent characteristics and question text and context into account (Chapters 4, 6 and 7), or at pinpointing the communication contexts in which the wording effect tends to be larger (Chapter 5).

The fourth chapter gives an account of the two core experiments and focuses on identifying the stage in the question-answering process from which the asymmetry originates. Combining the model of the question-answering process formulated by Tourangeau and Rasinski with the connotations hypothesis from Schuman and Presser, resulted in the formulation of two competing hypotheses. The fact that more respondents answer 'not forbid' than 'yes, allow' was seen as originating either from the stage in which the question is interpreted and the attitude is retrieved (the *different attitudes hypothesis*), or from the stage at which the evaluation is mapped onto the response options (the *different scales hypothesis*). The results of both experiments supported the second hypothesis, both for respondents who hold strong attitudes and those holding weaker ones. This suggests that there is a psychological interval scale underlying the yes/no options.

The decisions respondents make when mapping their opinions onto this scale differ for forbid and allow questions. However, because the experiments in Chapter 4 were basically designed to investigate whether or not forbid/allow questions measure different attitudes, no consistent patterns could be found in the differences between the answering scales. Chapters 6 and 7 report on experiments that were specifically designed to establish the exact nature of the differences between these mapping decisions by analysing across questions, question contexts and respondents.

Before this, Chapter 5 seeks to identify the question or respondent characteristics that cause variations in the asymmetry size, and therefore cause variations in the process of mapping the opinions onto the answering scales. A meta-analysis of all forbid/allow experiments is reported in this chapter, which offers the opportunity to explore and summarize several hypotheses on the causes of the wording effect. Several linguistic characteristics (e.g. the use of nominalized phrases) and content characteristics (e.g. the status quo with regard to the issue addressed) of the questions were shown to have hardly any effect on the asymmetry size. Instead, characteristics relating to attitude strength, such as the complexity of the issue, were shown to have rather a large effect and to explain a great deal of the variance. A relation was also found between the asymmetry size and the linguistic characteristic of abstractness (or vagueness). This explanatory meta-analysis led to the formulation of two hypotheses. The effects of complexity and relevance were shown to contradict each other, while complexity seemed to produce some sort of 'ceiling effect'. Reasoning from this, it was hypothesized that perhaps 'extremity' is the most relevant attitude strength dimension for the forbid/allow asymmetry (the *combined connotations/extremity hypothesis*). For non-complex issues, the presence of abstractness seemed to diminish the asymmetry size, contrary to expectations. This led to the belief that respondents try to interpret the question in such a way that the mapping task is made easier. Despite the fact that the asymmetry stems from the mapping stage, processes at earlier stages of question-answering seem to influence the size of the wording effect. Based on this conclusion, the *communicative restrictions hypothesis* was formulated, suggesting that the wording effect may not only be due to the use of the words 'forbid' and 'allow', but also to the communicative restriction of having to choose between a simple 'yes' or 'no'. It was posited that if respondents were given more scope to express their opinions, the wording effect might disappear.

Chapter 6 reports on 10 experiments which investigated whether systematic patterns exist in the mapping process for forbid/allow questions and tested the communicative restrictions hypothesis. In these experiments, questions on a large variety of issues were posed to a large variety of respondents, thereby taking account of the question and respondent characteristics that were shown to affect the asymmetry size in Chapter 5. The results of these experiments led to the rejection of the communicative restriction hypothesis: the wording effect was shown to be caused by the combination of forbid/allow and *any* agree/disagree dimension. The finding that forbid/allow questions measure similar attitudes (Chapter 4) was supported, strengthening the theory that the differences in the answers arise during the mapping stage and not during the initial stages of the question-answering process. This is independent of the number of scale points used, as similar patterns were found for questions with four-point, two-point and seven-point scales. Furthermore, an important difference between forbid and allow questions was found: although forbid/allow questions are in principle equally valid, they differ in reliability. Forbid questions were shown to be a more reliable measure of the underlying attitude than allow questions. In other words, respondents switch more between 'yes' and 'no' in their answers to sets of allow questions designed to measure the same attitude than they do in their answers to similar sets of forbid questions.

Chapter 7 details the differences between forbid and allow answering scales by examining the relative meanings of 'yes' and 'no' to forbid/allow questions, using a combined extremity/connotations hypothesis as a guideline for the analyses. The larger reliability of forbid questions was explained by the extremity of 'yes forbid' and the well-defined moderateness of 'not forbid', and by the relative ambiguity in meanings of the answering options to allow questions. Due to the ill-defined meaning of the answering options to allow questions, respondents switch more often between 'yes' and 'no' when answering a set of allow questions about the same issue. The cause of the asymmetry was also found to be related to the differing degrees of extremity of the meanings of the answering options. The meaning of the answering option 'not forbid' is more moderate than the meaning of 'yes, allow', and 'not allow' is more moderate than 'yes forbid'. Since more respondents are likely to hold moderate opinions (i.e. closer to the mean opinion in the population), these moderate answering options are likely to attract a higher number of respondents. This is a partial confirmation of the connotations hypothesis and a direct explanation of the forbid/allow asymmetry. However, no confirmation was found for the attitude strength hypothesis. When answering forbid questions, respondents holding moderate opinions may map their opinions onto 'not forbid', but they do so homogeneously and consistently. When answering allow questions, respondents do not seem particularly inclined to map their opinions onto 'not allow'. Instead, they solve their mapping problem for allow questions by interpreting the ambiguous meanings of the answering options in such a way that they can switch between 'yes' and 'no'. This also explains the smaller reliability of those questions.

In the next section, a comprehensive theory explaining the forbid/allow asymmetry will be presented: the *Yes/No⁺ Theory*, in which relations between the research outcomes presented separately in each chapter will be made more explicit.

8.2 EXPLAINING THE ASYMMETRY: THE YES/NO⁺ THEORY

Despite the fact that 'forbid' and 'allow', as well as the answering options 'yes' and 'no', are each other's opposites, the number of negative answers obtained to survey questions containing the verb 'forbid' is larger than the number of positive answers obtained for questions containing the verb 'allow'. In terms of relational semantics, the verbs 'forbid' and 'allow', as well as the answering options 'no' and 'yes' are *contradictories* (see Chaffin & Herrmann, 1984): 'not allowing' directly entails 'forbidding' and vice versa, just like 'not no' means 'yes'. It is impossible to apply scales to both word pairs, yes/no and forbid/allow. This can be done in the case of *contraries* such as 'good-bad'. Something can be 'reasonably good', or 'very bad', but it cannot be 'slightly forbidden', or 'very allowed'.

If this contradictory relation between 'forbid' and 'allow' does not explain the difference in the answers obtained to forbid/allow questions, then what cognitive mechanisms during question-answering cause the differences? It could be the case that forbidding and allowing, although logically each others' opposites, carry connotations which are so extreme, that respondents activate attitudes towards forbidding or allowing things in general, resulting in the retrieval of an attitude towards the issue in question (e.g. 'abortion') and towards 'forbidding'. The extreme connotations of forbidding (and allowing) might inspire negative attitudes among the respondents, causing them to exhibit a preference opposed to both forbidding and allowing. In terms of the basic stages of the question-answering process for attitude questions, this implies that the asymmetry arises during question interpretation and location of the relevant attitudes or beliefs, that is to say fairly early on in the question-answering process.

An alternative explanation would be that forbid/allow questions cause similar attitudes to be retrieved, but that the use of either 'forbid' or 'allow' causes respondents to map their evaluation of an issue such as abortion differently onto the yes/no answering scale. Forbidding and allowing contradict each other but the attitude towards something that should be forbidden or allowed may well be of a contrary nature, yielding a gradual evaluation from being very much in favour of abortion through moderate attitudes towards abortions to being very much against abortion. This 'contrary' evaluation then has to be translated into one of the contradictory answering options 'yes' or 'no' to forbid/allow questions. In that case, the connotations hypothesis would predict that a moderate pro-abortion opinion will be mapped onto 'no' when answering a forbid question as well as when answering an allow question, because the extreme connotations of both verbs make respondents reject a positive answer, thereby causing the asymmetry in the answers.

Two experiments conducted in this study demonstrated that differences in attitudes could be detected, but only with regard to attitude change over time (over a four week period) and not in relation to attitude differences due to the question wording. The second hypothesis was therefore supported. Respondents retrieve similar attitudes when answering forbid/allow questions and the asymmetry reflects differences during the mapping stage in the question-answering process due to the use of 'forbid' and 'allow'.

Similar attitudes towards a subject like abortion are translated differently into the answering options yes/no due to the use of forbid/allow. In other words, 'yes, allow' does not mean the same as 'not forbid', and 'not allow' does not mean the same as 'yes forbid'. This was found to apply both to respondents with strong attitudes and respondents with weak attitudes. This is an important finding, as the attitude strength hypothesis predicts that respondents with weaker attitudes, or respondents who know or care little about the issue, might be more susceptible to superficial cues in the presentation (e.g. the use of forbid/allow) during the stage of attitude construction. The analyses, however, did not confirm this version of the attitude strength hypothesis. The mapping stage in the question-answering process is the stage at which the asymmetry arises for the group of respondents as a whole. The general process does not differ for indifferent respondents and others. This result forms the core of the theory emerging from the present research, which will be called the Yes/No$^+$ Theory (see Box 8.1).

The Yes/No$^+$ Theory

The answering options 'yes' and 'no' to forbid/allow questions are not perceived by the respondents as being a simple 'yes' or 'no', but are given meaning relative to the meaning and perceived extremity of the evaluative verbs used in the question, and should be interpreted accordingly. The answers 'yes' and 'no' do not reflect nominal categories but should be viewed as the extremes of an interval scale which differs due to the use of the specific evaluative term used in the question: in this case, 'forbid' and 'allow'.

Box 8.1: *The Yes/No$^+$ Theory, the core finding emerging from this study*

Note that the Yes/No$^+$ Theory can be read as a description of the question-answering process to forbid/allow questions, as well as a psychometric theory. As a theory of the question-answering process, it focuses on the cognitive processes respondents go through between reading the question and giving an answer, and shows that the differences between forbid/allow answers are due to the mapping process. As a psychometric theory, the Yes/No$^+$ Theory focuses on the characteristics of the answering scales to forbid/allow questions. It shows that the differences between forbid and allow answers are not due to differences in the true scores, but that there is a difference in the response scales. Answers to forbid/allow questions should not be viewed as nominal categories (a 'yes, for' and 'no, against') but as interval scales that differ from each other. 'Yes' and 'no' have relative meanings and those relative meanings differ due to the use of 'forbid' and 'allow'. In other words, 'yes' to forbid questions means 'yes forbid', and 'no' to allow questions means 'no not allow'.

Now that the core of the Yes/No[+] Theory has been presented, we can turn our attention to *how* the answering scales to forbid/allow questions differ. The results obtained in the experiments on nature and environmental issues and on ethnic issues are not unequivocal. The research reported in Chapter 4 was specifically designed to test the different attitudes hypothesis, so it could not be used to fully investigate differences between the forbid/allow scales. Additional experiments were therefore conducted for the express purpose of analysing the differences between the answering scales for forbid and allow questions. These experiments enabled some differences between forbid and allow scales to be tested, while other differences had to be explored. Here, findings based on tests will be referred to as 'theory' or 'explanation', whereas findings based on explorative analyses will be referred to as 'hypotheses'.

8.2.1 The relative meanings of yes and no to forbid/allow

In earlier forbid/allow research, various hypotheses about the causes of the asymmetry were formulated. The most important of these was the connotations hypothesis offered by Schuman & Presser (1981): "the verb 'forbid' sounds harsher and may therefore be more difficult to endorse, whereas 'allow' in some contexts might seem to encourage a deviant behaviour and therefore may invite opposition" (1981:280). This hypothesis is vague as to whether different attitudes are being retrieved, or whether the evaluations are mapped differently onto the answering scales due to the use of forbid/allow. The Yes/No[+] Theory gives the opportunity to refine the hypothesis on this point. The modified connotations hypothesis reads as follows: "To answer 'no' to forbid does not mean the same as 'yes' to allow: to agree to forbid implies a real act of opposition, but to disagree with allow means merely to abstain from support" (Clark & Schober, 1992). The Yes/No[+] Theory accepts the premise that "to answer 'no' to forbid does not mean the same as 'yes' to allow" but the issue of how the meanings of the answering options to forbid/allow questions differ exactly, is more complicated than suggested by the explanations offered by Schuman and Presser or indeed by Clark and Schober.

The analyses conducted in the present study show that 'yes forbid' is relatively extreme in its meaning, more extreme than 'not allow'. Meanwhile, 'yes allow' was found to be more extreme in its mean meaning than 'not forbid'. This difference in relative extremity between the answering options to forbid and allow questions emerging from the data is directly related to the cause of the asymmetry. It can be assumed that a random population consists of more respondents holding moderate opinions close to the mean opinion in the population, than of respondents holding extreme opinions further away from the mean. Accordingly, the number of respondents choosing the moderate 'not forbid' is likely to be larger than the number of respondents likely to choose the relatively extreme 'yes allow'. A similar line of reasoning holds for the number of respondents likely to choose 'not forbid' compared to 'yes allow'.

Note that the theory explaining the forbid/allow asymmetry (summarized in Box 8.2) is not decisive as to whether Schuman and Presser are right in assuming that respondents who hold more moderate opinions prefer to map their answers onto 'no' instead of 'yes'. Similarly, this theory does not imply that Clark and Schober are right in assuming that "to say no to allow merely implies to abstain from support", or "to say 'yes' to forbid implies a real act of opposition". These are predictions about the question-answering process of respondents who answer either a forbid or an allow question. As such, these predictions could only be explored by comparing the meanings of 'yes' and 'no' within versions.

The relative extremity theory

The answering option 'yes forbid' is more extreme in its mean meaning than 'not allow', and 'yes allow' is more extreme in its mean meaning than 'not forbid'. In any random population, the number of persons holding moderate opinions, close to the mean opinion, is likely to be greater than the number of persons holding extreme opinions, further removed from the mean. Accordingly, the answering options 'not allow' and 'not forbid' are likely to be chosen by more respondents than the answering options 'yes forbid' and 'yes allow', respectively.

Box 8.2*: Differences in the relative extremity of the meanings of the answering options are directly related to the number of respondents choosing an answering option*

The hypotheses formulated by Schuman and Presser, as well as by Clark and Schober, suggest that the answer 'no' for many respondents basically means 'not yes'. In other words, respondents who hold moderate opinions, even moderate opinions in favour forbidding or allowing, might prefer to map their answers onto 'no', due to the extreme connotations of 'forbid' and 'allow'. This expectation is stated even more explicitly in the extension of the connotations hypothesis offered by Hippler & Schwarz (1986), which focuses on the cognitive processes of respondents who have weaker attitudes. According Hippler and Schwarz, it is the group of respondents who have moderate or ambivalent opinions, or those who don't care about the issue at all, who focus on the implications of the behaviour under consideration (forbidding, allowing), and who do not consider the implications of the absence of the behaviour, thereby clouding the idea that 'not forbid' implies allowing, and 'not allow' implies forbidding. One possible interpretation of this hypothesis is that the use of forbid/allow measures different attitudes for indifferent respondents or respondents with weak attitudes, that is to say an attitude towards the issue in the question, as well as an attitude towards forbidding or allowing. The experiments reported in Chapter 4 suggest this was not the case. The Yes/No$^+$ Theory allows for another interpretation of this theory, however, namely that indifferent respondents or respondents with weaker attitudes tend to map their evaluation onto 'no' when answering forbid/allow questions. This was explored in Chapter 6, in which 'weakness of attitudes' was defined as 'moderateness'. Reasoning from these hypotheses, one would expect the relative moderateness of the meanings of 'not forbid' and 'not allow' to be related to a larger variance in meanings of those answering options. The meaning of 'not forbid' could range from a firm 'no, not forbid!' to a very moderate 'yes forbid', whereas the variance in meanings of 'yes forbid' would be much smaller.

This prediction was not confirmed by the data. Between versions, the variance in meanings of 'not allow' equalled the variance in meanings of 'yes forbid', and the variance in meanings of 'not forbid' was smaller than the variance in meanings of 'yes allow'. Within versions, the variance in meanings of 'not forbid' was smaller than the variance in meanings of 'yes forbid', and the variance in meanings of 'not allow' did not differ from the variance in meanings of 'yes allow'. The mapping process underlying the asymmetry cannot therefore be explained using straightforward predictions based on the extremity of 'forbid' and 'allow'.

It can be explained, however, by analysing differences in the extremity of the answering options 'yes forbid', 'not forbid', 'yes allow' and 'not forbid' but along a different line of reasoning than that suggested by the connotations hypothesis. It is also important to take into account the extent to which the meaning of each answering option can be described as well-defined.

Analyses show that 'yes forbid' is perceived to be very extreme in terms of its mean meaning. This was confirmed by an analysis of the meaning of this answering option based on force dynamics (Talmy, 1988): 'yes forbid' is relatively unambiguous in referring to the insertion of a barrier. This does not mean, however that respondents who answered 'yes forbid' choose an extreme answering option on the seven-point scale. Respondents who map their opinion onto 'yes forbid' seem to feel this implies a strong position and tend to modify this extremity when given a chance on an answering scale which has more scale points. This accounts for a large variance in the meanings of 'yes forbid'. The meaning of the answering option 'not forbid' is unambiguous and more moderate. The disagree-area on the seven-point scale seems to be moderate also, causing respondents to rather homogeneously choose a scalepoint somewhere in the middle of this moderate area, resulting in a relatively small variance in meaning of 'not forbid'.

The answering options to allow questions are relatively ill-defined in their meanings compared to the answering options to forbid questions. The option 'yes allow' can entail removing a barrier (which is in some contexts rather extreme, and might "seem to encourage a deviant behaviour") or the more moderate non-insertion of a barrier. In the case of the extreme answering options, respondents may feel the need to modify their position on a scale with more points, causing a larger variance in meanings. However, the larger variance in meanings is also a reflection of the fact that 'yes allow' is ambiguous in its meaning. The relatively ill-defined meaning of 'yes allow', makes the answering option 'not allow' ill-defined by default. It is extreme in its reference to inserting a barrier (needing modification), but it can also refer to not removing a barrier. What is more, it incorporates a weaker antagonist than 'yes forbid'.

The ambiguity of 'yes allow' and 'not allow' causes the variances in meanings of the answering options not to differ from each other. More importantly, it provides an explanation of why allow questions measure the underlying attitude less reliably than forbid questions. Due to the relatively ill-defined meaning of the answering options to allow questions, respondents switch relatively often between 'yes allow' and 'not allow' when answering a set of questions on the same issue. They feel able to do this because the meanings of the answering options to allow questions vary, but also because the moderateness in the meanings of those answering options offers them the freedom to switch between 'yes allow' and 'not allow', thereby expressing moderateness or ambivalence in their attitudes. This is summarized in Box 8.3.

The relatively well-defined meaning hypothesis

The answering options 'yes allow' and 'not allow' are relatively ambivalent in their meanings, and moderate in some cases. This means that the answering scale to allow questions is narrower than the answering scale to forbid questions. This, in turn, causes allow questions to measure the underlying attitude less reliably.

Box 8.3: *Relative differences in well-defined meaning and extremity of meaning in the answering options cause the width of the answering scale to differ and result in differences in reliabilities*

The main result of this research is that forbid/allow questions do measure similar attitudes, but that these attitudes are expressed differently on the answering scales due to the use of 'forbid' or 'allow'. The suggestion is that these differences are caused by the extremity and clarity of meaning of the various answering options to forbid/allow questions: 'yes allow' is relatively ill-defined and moderate in some of its meanings, causing 'not allow' to be ill-defined as well. It is suggested that this narrows the scale for allow questions, causing respondents to switch more between 'yes allow' and 'not allow'. On the one hand they switch more in order to express moderateness, while on the other, the ambiguity of the meanings of the answering options to allow questions means that the options refer to different actions in different questions. In contrast, the meanings of the answering options to forbid questions are better defined. The option 'yes forbid' is relatively extreme and well-defined, causing 'not forbid' to be moderate and well-defined. Forbid questions are therefore answered quite consistently and reflect the underlying attitude comparatively well. For the effect of attitude strength, this hypothesis means that a 'nay-saying effect' as predicted by earlier theory, cannot be confirmed. Instead, it would seem that indifferent or moderate respondents express moderateness by switching between 'yes' and 'no' when answering a set of allow questions. When answering forbid questions they might experience more of a mapping problem, but they will tend to choose either 'yes forbid' or 'not forbid' and stick to one of these options when answering a set of questions.[1]

The next section discusses how variations in the asymmetry size can be accounted for within the general framework describing the question-answering process to forbid/allow questions. At this point, the meta-analytic findings are integrated into the framework. It also elaborates on the implications the theory presented here has for general text interpretation processes: how is it possible that characteristics which form early input during text interpretation do not influence the cognitive activities early on in the process (retrieving an attitude), but do have an impact on processes that occur much later (mapping an answer)?

8.3 INPUT CHARACTERISTICS INFLUENCING THE MAPPING PROCESS

The Yes/No[+] Theory describes the forbid/allow asymmetry as arising in the mapping stage of the question-answering process. This mapping process can be

---

[1] Note that in this description of the cognitive processes underlying the forbid/allow asymmetry, the reference to *connotations* is abandoned and extremity is discussed in terms of *meanings*. Throughout this book, Schuman and Presser's connotations hypothesis was used as a guideline hypothesis. There does not seem to be a theoretical reason, however, to define extremity as a concept that should be distinguished from a word's meaning.

described in terms of extremity and clarity of meaning, which is a description of the process, or of the differences in meanings of the answering options to forbid/allow questions, which is a general characteristic of forbid/allow questions. If sets of forbid/allow questions are analysed, it is predicted that a larger mean number of 'not forbid' answers will be obtained compared to the mean number of 'yes allow' answers, and that this is due to differences in the mapping stage of the question-answering process.

The next question is how the framework proposed in the previous sections can account for variations in asymmetries found, and whether the Yes/No[+] Theory can be generalized to wording effects other than those caused by the use of forbid/allow. Two issues need to be addressed in this respect: firstly, why attitude strength has a greater influence on the answers obtained to forbid/allow questions than linguistic characteristics (other than the use of forbid/allow) and secondly, why the asymmetry found varies over questions. The Yes/No[+] framework will be shown to account for both of these phenomena.

Analyses incorporating sets of forbid/allow questions demonstrated that the use of forbid/allow has a general effect on the answers. The Yes/No[+] Theory describes the mechanisms underlying this process. At the same time, analyses revealed again and again that the wording effect varies considerably over pairs of forbid/allow questions. Sometimes no wording effect is found and sometimes 'yes forbid' is answered with greater frequency than 'not allow', instead of the predicted asymmetry of more 'not forbid' than 'yes allow' answers. Meta-analytic techniques showed a relation between certain question, respondent or questionnaire characteristics and the size of the wording effect and demonstrated that the effects of those characteristics might be generalized beyond the level of specific questions and question content.

For the meta-analysis, the dependent variable was the asymmetry size obtained for each forbid/allow question. A larger asymmetry size (as an effect of oral administration modes, for example) was interpreted by comparing it to an equivalent forbid/allow question posed in a different administration method. This was a hypothetical comparison, however, because the equivalent question was never actually posed. Consequently, the meta-analyses could not provide conclusive evidence of whether a larger asymmetry size was due to a change in the answers to forbid questions (respondents mapping more of their answers onto 'not forbid' in oral administration modes than in written ones), or a change in the answers to allow questions (respondents mapping more of their answers onto 'not allow'), or a change in the answers to forbid questions as well as allow questions. In the interpretation of meta-analytic results, it was assumed that both answering scales had changed when a larger asymmetry occurred, based on the assumption that answering affirmatively to forbid/allow questions was difficult for respondents due to the extreme connotations of 'forbid' as well as 'allow'.

Analyses focusing on the differences in scales between forbid/allow questions showed that the assumption that 'no' to either question represents a repository of different meanings could not be confirmed. Yet the analyses did point out various differences between the answering options to forbid and allow questions, which provide grounds for a re-interpretation of the meta-analytic findings and an integration of these findings within the general framework of the Yes/No[+] Theory.

The meta-analyses showed a particular relation between smaller asymmetries and questions posed to respondents with a higher level of education, questions about non-complex issues, questions about abstract issues, questions that are relatively concrete (associated with punishment rather than moral judgment), and questions about issues that are not relevant to the respondents. Such a list of question or respondent characteristics is useful, for the characteristics can be related to cognitive characteristics of the respondents or cognitive consequences following from the task, such as time pressure (oral administration modes) or attitude strength (educational level, complexity, relevance). Moreover, they can be used as a point of departure for the formulation of new hypotheses. As a test of existing hypotheses concerning variations in the asymmetry size, the hypothesis formulated by Bishop et al. (1988) that oral administration modes lead to larger asymmetries holds[2], but the effect is so small as to be negligible. Another hypothesis predicted a larger effect relating to the moral nature of the prohibition or the issue (Waterplas et al., 1988), an aspect open to further investigation in future experimental research. However the most substantial causes of variation in asymmetry size according to the meta-analysis seem to be the variables related to

---

[2] Oral administration modes were shown to be related to a larger asymmetry size. This effect is in accordance with predictions by various survey researchers, who suggested that respondents have less time to think about the meaning of the question and the implications of their answers in oral administration modes, and are therefore more susceptible to response effects in general. Integration of this result within the Yes/No[+] Theory, would imply a question-answering process in which respondents, in any administration mode, retrieve or form an evaluation towards the issue in the question (for example 'abortion'). The next step is that respondents have to map their evaluation onto one of the response options. Due to the time pressure in oral administration modes, they do not have much time to think about the implications of their answer. The answering options to forbid questions are relatively well-defined, so time pressure does not seem very likely to influence the mapping of evaluations onto the forbid answering options. There might be a slight tendency to map the evaluation onto the moderate 'not forbid' due to time pressure, but it is more likely that respondents answering an allow question under time pressure are particularly likely to choose the 'not allow' option, as the answering options to allow questions are less well-defined.

attitude strength. Of the linguistic characteristics of the questions, only abstractness showed an effect. The content variables coded hardly showed any effect at all.

The complexity of the issue proved to be an important factor explaining variation in the asymmetry size. Analysed together with other variables such as relevance of the issue and abstractness, complexity displayed some sort of ceiling effect. If a question is about a complex issue, it no longer matters whether the issue is relevant to respondents or whether it is worded in abstract terms: questions about complex issues lead to larger asymmetries. The complexity of the issue is related to the attitude strength of the respondents, as complex issues are likely to be more difficult to evaluate, and to cause ambivalence and uncertainty about one's own evaluation. The effect of complexity could therefore be in accordance with predictions based on the attitude strength hypotheses. Integration of this finding within the Yes/No⁺ Theory suggests, however, that the effect of attitude strength is not caused by respondents who hold weak opinions mapping their evaluation onto 'not forbid' as well as 'not allow' because of the extreme connotations of both verbs. Instead, the suggested interpretation is that this effect of complexity is due to the well-defined meaning of 'yes forbid'. The answering option 'yes forbid' is extreme in its meaning and relatively well-defined in implying an opinion against the issue. As a complex issue probably causes ambivalence in many respondents, the answering option 'yes forbid' will not attract a large number of respondents. The answering option 'not allow' is less extreme and less well-defined, and it is therefore easier to map an ambivalent opinion onto this option than onto 'yes forbid'. This explains the consistent effect of issue complexity over questions on the asymmetry size obtained.

All this raises the question of why attitude strength seems to play such an important role as a cause of variations in the asymmetry size, whereas linguistic or content variables hardly do so. The Yes/No⁺ Theory suggests this is caused by the fact that respondents start the answering process by distilling from the question text the central issue on which they are supposed to hold an opinion or of which they are expected to form an evaluation.

This distilling process is deliberate and complex, and it means that the words used in the question are not processed more deeply than necessary to fulfil this task. The question text as a whole would seem to serve as an instruction to the reader. The first instruction is to retrieve or form an evaluation on an issue. Respondents construct a blueprint of the issue, without employing any unjustifiable effort in doing so. Many subtle wording or content characteristics may not have any impact on the representation of the issue. In the terms of Verhagen (1997), subtle linguistic or content characteristics do not easily reach the 'threshold value' necessary to affect the actual representation of the issue within the complex process of the purposeful distillation of the central issue. Accordingly, small wording or content characteristics can affect the representation of the issue, but each wording or content characteristic can also strengthen or weaken the effects of other words or linguistic characteristics.[3] From this it follows that linguistic variation does not necessarily affect early processes, such as interpretation or attitude retrieval.

Variation in linguistic characteristics of the question exert next to no influence on the effect of forbid/allow, whereas the use of forbid/allow (a linguistic characteristic in itself) has a major influence on the answers obtained. The Yes/No[+] Theory puts forward the explanation that respondents do not see the linguistic elements 'forbid' and 'allow' as parts of the issue to be evaluated, but as qualifying dimensions to be used during the mapping process. The qualifiers forbid/allow combined with yes/no indicate a positive or negative evaluation of the issue, varying in extremity and definition of meaning. In this mapping process, it is not odd that characteristics of attitude strength (which are related to extremity of the evaluation) play an important part, whereas linguistic or content variables are of minor importance.

Although the input from the question text comes early in the question-answering process, the effect of forbid/allow shows it can affect processes that occur later on, such as the mapping of the evaluation onto the answering options. The question-answering process for forbid/allow questions can therefore be modelled as a complex interaction between text and reader. Hence, question-answering is not necessarily as linear a process as perhaps implicitly suggested by Tourangeau and Rasinski's model.

The general conclusion should be that variation in the asymmetry size can be explained by the distribution of attitudes in the population, as well as by the strength of the attitudes held. If questions deal with issues on which the opinions are likely to be divided across the population of respondents, the asymmetry is likely to be large, since extreme opinions are less likely to occur than moderate opinions. If questions are posed about issues on which a certain consensus in public opinion exists either for or against, the asymmetry is less likely to occur.

---

[3] This is also why the context should be taken into account when coding linguistic characteristics. Nominalized phrases, for example, are supposed to increase the linguistic complexity of the text. The verbs 'forbid' and 'allow', however, are often accompanied by nominalized phrases as part of their construction. Nominalized phrases are therefore less likely to increase linguistic complexity in this specific context compared to a context in which nominalizations could easily be avoided.

8.4 GENERALIZATION OF THE YES/NO⁺ THEORY

The use of the verbs 'forbid' and 'allow' has an effect at the mapping stage of the question-answering process. This is due to the fact that the verbs are viewed as an evaluative dimension for judging the issue, and not as a part of the issue to be evaluated. The question text is seen as an instruction to form or retrieve an evaluation of an issue like 'smoking in public places', and to map the evaluation for or against onto one of the available answering options 'yes/no allow' or 'yes/ no forbid'. From this, it follows that a wording effect is likely to arise at the mapping stage for other questions in which words are used that form an evaluative dimension for judging the issue. This section first discusses the extent to which the Yes/No⁺ Theory, including the 'relative extremity explanation' and 'relatively well-defined meaning hypothesis', can be generalized to other contrastive questions. Accordingly, the Yes/No⁺ Theory will be extended to a theory about questions containing qualifying dimensions, instead of being limited to questions containing forbid/allow. Secondly, the Yes/No⁺ framework will be put forward as a basis for formulating testable hypotheses with respect to the question-answering process underlying other response effects.

A strong case can be made for generalizing the finding that the forbid/allow asymmetry should be attributed to the mapping stage in the question-answering process to all forbid/allow questions. Questions containing these verbs were shown to measure similar attitudes in both experiments reported in Chapter 4, in which analyses were conducted over sets of forbid/allow questions about a variety of issues, at two times of measurement. This result was confirmed in 10 experiments reported in Chapter 6, which also consisted of many forbid/allow questions. In these experiments, strong indication was found that forbid/allow questions measure similar attitudes when accompanied by two-point (yes/no) answering scales, as well as by seven-point (agree-disagree) scales, in addition to the finding of congenericity for four-point scales (yes!-no!) reported in Chapter 4. For all these types of forbid/allow questions, the wording effect was shown to arise during the mapping stage of the question-answering process, although the mapping mechanisms differed depending on the number of scale points offered. Accordingly, the conclusion of the current research is that a wording effect due to the use of forbid/allow in the question text will always be attributable to the mapping stage of the question-answering process and not to the attitude retrieval stage.

This finding for forbid/allow questions, implies a possibility of generalizing to at least one other type of wording effect: the use of different answering scales. The Yes/No⁺ Theory assumes that respondents begin by retrieving or forming an attitude towards the issue in the question, and then translating this evaluation into one of the answering options. Wording effects caused by variation in the question form (such as yes/no questions versus forced-choice questions) and wording effects due to differences in the number, order or labels of response options are also likely to arise at the mapping stage.

The next question is for which other contrastive questions patterns comparable to the forbid/allow asymmetry may be expected to arise. 'Forbid' and 'allow' are contradictories, which means that the words logically exclude each other's meaning: to 'not forbid' implies 'to allow', to 'not allow' implies 'to forbid'. For this very reason one would expect an equal number of 'yes forbid' responses and 'not allow' responses. However, a similar wording effect to the forbid/allow asymmetry depends on more than just the contradictory meanings of the verbs being used. It should also be the case that 'yes' to one question is more extreme than 'no' to the other. With this in mind, an asymmetry in the same direction could be expected for pairs like 'oblige/leave free', 'break off/continue' and 'abolish/maintain'. In each of those contradictory verb pairs, the first verb seems to have a relatively strong causal meaning and implies a strong antagonist, whereas the latter verb suggests a weaker force. The option 'not continue' seems less extreme than 'yes break off' and 'not break off' seems less extreme than 'yes continue'. This verb pair seems similar to forbid/allow, in that an antagonist who 'continues' is less strong than an antagonist who 'breaks off'. Furthermore, 'continue' can imply removing a barrier, albeit a temporary one, as well as not inserting a barrier. Accordingly, one would expect a similar pattern for continue/break off questions and for forbid/allow questions.[4]

For the contradictory verb pair prohibit/permit, 'not prohibit' seems less extreme than 'yes permit', and 'not permit' may be less extreme than 'yes prohibit'. An asymmetry similar to forbid/allow questions may therefore be expected. The mapping process within versions may differ, however, as the answering options to 'permit' are better defined in their meanings than the answering options to 'allow'. The option 'yes permit' may refer to removing a barrier, but not to not inserting a barrier: it carries more 'causing' and less 'letting' in its meaning and therefore implies a stronger antagonist. Permit questions can therefore be seen as more reliable measures of the underlying attitude than allow questions. Following this line of reasoning, predictions can also be made about the wording effects and mapping processes for other contradictory verb pairs. The Yes/No[+] Theory and Boxes 8.2 and 8.3 can be a useful tool for formulating expectations about wording effects for other contradictory verbs in attitude questions.

---

[4] Blankenship (1940) reported a wording effect of 5% in a different direction. It should be noted, however, that only one question was posed and the significance of the finding was not reported.

It may be possible to find similar contradictories in a category other than verbs: adverbs for example. It is difficult to think of cases that could be used in attitude questions, however. The word pair married/unmarried, for example, is contradictory but it is difficult to conceptualize its use as an evaluative qualifier in attitude questions.

A specific subclass of contradictory contrastive questions are questions containing a syntactic negation. Syntactic negations can either be used in the evaluative dimension of the question, or in the description of the issue for opinion retrieval. The use of an explicit negation in the qualifier, such as 'not' or 'no' (e.g. 'Do you think the government should not allow abortion? yes/no', or 'The government should not allow abortion. agree-disagree') may make the meaning of the answering options ambiguous. One respondent against abortion may map his answer onto 'no', whereas another may map a similar opinion onto 'yes'. In this case the response effect may be attributed to a whirling, an unstable, mapping process caused by large variances between respondents in the way they map similar opinions onto the answering options, creating a large overlap in the meanings of 'yes' and 'no' to questions containing explicit negations. This is basically a more technical explanation of why the use of syntactic negations is generally advised against.

Many verb pairs that seem contradictory at first sight are in fact contrary, as their opposition admits of degrees. In the opposition 'restrict/release', for example, at least the verb 'restrict' seems scalar. These verbs were used by Waterplas et al. (1988), in a question about residential rights for the families of immigrant workers. In another word pair used by Waterplas et al., 'regulate' versus 'leave free' (*reglementeren/vrijlaten*), it seems possible to regulate an issue to a limited extent, but less possible to leave an issue free to a limited extent, which makes these contradictories seem asymmetrically scalar. The scalarity of 'regulate' could make this verb relatively ill-defined and moderate compared to 'leave free', which could mean that the use of this verb pair causes a wording effect comparable in direction to the forbid/allow asymmetry.[5]

For contrastive questions containing verbs that are both scalar, such as 'increase/decrease', it is difficult to construct yes/no questions that are still comparable. The answer 'not increase' can imply 'decrease' as well as 'leave things as they are', which means that these verb pairs are not each other's logical opposites. It seems logical to expect a larger asymmetry for these questions, as 'no' to either question is chosen by respondents who feel things should be left as they are, as well as by respondents who think the practice at stake should not be decreased or not be increased.

---

[5] The fact that Waterplas et al. found a wording effect of more 'yes' to one question than 'no' to the other, is not conclusive on this respect, as it concerned only one question.

The same applies to contrastive questions containing contrary qualifiers, such as good-bad or sufficient-insufficient. For yes/no questions containing these words, an asymmetry in favour of 'no' is to be expected (as 'not good' is expected to be less extreme than 'bad', and 'not bad' is probably less extreme than 'good'), although the combination of yes/no questions and scalar contrastives is not very logical in any case. A wording effect is also to be expected when an answering scale offering a wider range of options is used for these contrary questions. This effect could also be attributed to mapping differences, as this result was obtained for seven-point-scale forbid/allow questions as well.

To sum up, the Yes/No[+] Theory can be extended to become a Yes/No[+] Qualifier Hypothesis. Answers to attitude questions in which a qualifying dimension is offered for judging an issue, are expressed in relation to this qualifying dimension. According to this theory, the use of forbid/allow, good-bad, or any other qualifying dimension in attitude questions does not affect the attitudes retrieved, but does affect the meanings of the answering options, thus causing differences at the mapping stage of the question-answering process (see Box 8.4).

Extension of the Yes/No[+] Theory

The answering options 'yes/no' or 'agree/disagree' are not perceived by respondents as a straightforward 'yes' or 'no', 'agree' or 'disagree', but are given meaning relative to the meaning and perceived extremity of the qualifying dimension used in the question. Attitude questions containing different qualifying dimensions for judging the issue in question will produce differences in the answers obtained. This will be caused by differences at the mapping stage of the question-answering process and not by differences during the stages of question interpretation or attitude retrieval.

***Box 8.4**: Generalization of the Yes/No[+] Theory*

In addition, an asymmetry comparable to the forbid/allow asymmetry is likely to occur for contradictories or asymmetric contradictories where the negative answering option to one of the two questions is more moderate than the affirmative answering option to the opposite question. Furthermore, if the answering options to one of the two questions are ill-defined, that question is expected to provide a less reliable measurement of the attitude.

In the light of the above, it seems prudent for survey practice to prefer the question wording that implies the most extreme position when agreed to in questions for which wording effects are expected. This was the case for forbid questions. 'Yes forbid' was the most extreme and well-defined option, conferring a moderate and consistent meaning on the negative answer by implication and making forbid questions a relatively reliable measure of the underlying attitude. Consequently, the - some might say bold - hypothesis resulting from this research, is that preference should be given to the extreme, and in most cases negative, question wording: 'forbid' should be preferred to 'allow', and 'bad' to 'good', although it should be noted that extremity is always dependent on context. Practical advice following from this study will be elaborated on in Section 8.5.

In addition to the generalization of the Yes/No[+] Theory to other contradictories or contraries, the extent to which the Yes/No[+] Theory can be generalized to other wording effects should also be discussed. Are all wording effects caused by differences arising at the mapping stage?

The most likely answer is no, probably not. For other wording effects, or response effects in general, the Yes/No[+] Theory can and should be used to formulate hypotheses to be tested in experimental research. The current research has shown that it is doubly important to make a rough distinction between the stage of question interpretation and attitude retrieval on the one hand, and the stage of mapping the evaluation onto the response options on the other. Not only does it provide theoretical assistance in unravelling the question-answering process underlying response effects, but it is also important for practical purposes. It enables the researcher to decide whether measurements differ in their validity or reliability and how the observed answers relate to the true attitudes of the respondents the researcher is seeking to uncover. Wording effects caused by substantially lengthening the question text in order to provide extra information, or by including counter-arguments, for example, could be expected to arise at the attitude retrieval stage of the question-answering process, whereas a phenomenon like socially desirable answering behaviour can be expected to arise at the mapping stage.

8.5 IMPLICATIONS FOR PRACTICE

Practical advice relating to the forbid/allow asymmetry is not only relevant because many public opinion surveys are concerned with the question whether actions should be forbidden or allowed, but also because explanations for the forbid/allow asymmetry can be extended to other questions in which the qualifier in the question is varied. This is often the case in questionnaires, since survey handbooks recommend using a variety of positively and negatively worded questions about the same issue, to avoid answering tendencies in one specific direction and to obtain balance.

Survey research can be divided into three basic stages: construction of the questionnaire, administration of the survey, and interpretation of the data. At the first stage, the starting point is a research goal, accompanied by some content theory concerning the phenomena to be measured. Using theoretical variables as a starting point, raw variables (operationalizations) are constructed and various survey questions are developed to serve as indicators for these raw variables (Emans, 1990). At the second stage, a sampling procedure is used and one or more times of measurement are selected for approaching the respondents who are supposed to answer the questions. At the final stage, the answers obtained are interpreted and related to the content theory and research goals which formed the starting point of the research process. Survey research (indeed all research) is therefore a cyclic process in which each stage is inextricably bound up with the other. A wrong choice at one stage inevitably leads to uninterpretable or incorrect results. From this, it follows that right and wrong are always relative concepts in survey research. A survey question can be phrased awkwardly in relation to one research question or goal but be perfectly adequate as an indicator for another research question. Also, a survey question can be properly phrased and elicit valid answers but if the interpretation of those answers is not valid, the validity of the research process as a whole will nevertheless be affected.

Below, the items of practical advice following from the Yes/No[+] Theory described in the previous sections will be discussed for each stage of survey research. Some practical implications can also be derived from other findings reported here, concerning issues such as the stability of attitudes or the use of two-point scales as opposed to multi-point scales. These will also be discussed.

For *the stage of questionnaire design,* several practical implications can be derived from the current research. The main finding is that forbid/allow questions measure similar attitudes but that the answers are expressed differently on the answering scales due to the use of forbid/allow. The observed scores (e.g. the percentages or means) obtained for an allow question differ from those obtained for a forbid question, in spite of the fact that respondents retrieve similar attitudes. This implies that forbid and allow questions are equally valid but that this does not necessarily guarantee the validity of the researcher's interpretation of the answers in terms of the attitude she intended to measure.

In principle, forbid/allow questions are equally valid and there is strong reason to believe that the same is true of other contrastive questions, as well as similarly worded questions accompanied by a different number of scale points: forbid questions followed by a yes/no scale can be assumed to be just as valid as forbid questions accompanied by a multiple-point scale. This is due to the fact that respondents answer survey questions by roughly interpreting the question and retrieving an evaluation of the central issue in the question. Their next step is to translate this evaluation (for or against the sale of magic mushrooms, for example) into the answering options. In doing this, they use the dimensions offered in the answering options, as well as the qualifier used in the question. In forbid/allow questions, this qualifier is the verb 'forbid' or 'allow'. In other questions it may be 'good' or 'bad', or 'break off' versus 'continue'. This means there is no reason for preferring one question wording to the other, or a larger number of scale points to a smaller number, at least in terms of the validity of the measure in relation to the content theory adopted.

The close relationship between the three stages of survey research forces the researcher to think about the way she will interpret the data from the stage when the questionnaire is constructed. The fact that respondents are shown to map their evaluation onto the answering options in relation to the qualifying dimension used in the question, means the researcher should take care not to venture beyond the scope of this qualifying dimension when interpreting the answers. When constructing the questionnaire, the researcher must clearly define the exact nature of the response she wishes to elicit from her respondents, and phrase the question in accordance with this research question as much as possible. If the researcher wants to know whether respondents think something is 'bad', she should not ask whether it should be 'forbidden' and vice versa. If she wants to find out whether respondents are generally for or against the sale of magic mushrooms, she should phrase the question in appropriately general terms and not ask respondents whether they think it should be forbidden.

The questionnaire designer should also consider whether her research goal is to distinguish between extreme groups of respondents, or whether she is interested in more subtle differences between respondents' opinions. If the latter is the case, she should use questions followed by multi-point answering scales instead of yes/no questions. If not, the most effective approach is to use yes/no questions containing a qualifying term that is extreme, thereby ensuring that its answering options are well-defined.

Answers to extreme questions reflect the underlying attitude more consistently than answers to questions that contain moderate qualifiers. What is more, the meanings of answering options to questions containing extreme qualifiers are easier to distinguish from each other. The 'no+' answers to extreme questions can be interpreted with relative accuracy as referring to a moderate 'true' opinion. Depending on the research goal, the 'yes+' answer to extreme questions can also be interpreted with reasonable accuracy, since only respondents holding extreme opinions may be expected to choose that option. Questions in corrective referendums in the Netherlands, for example, are phrased something like 'Do you think the decision of the city council to legalize the sale of magic mushrooms should be upheld?' or 'Do you think the decision of the city council to legalize the sale of magic mushrooms should be reversed?'[6]. The 'uphold' qualifier is rather moderate,

---

[6] The question texts for referenda are usually much more complicated. The Amsterdam corrective referendum held in 1995, contained the question: "Do you agree/disagree with the council decision to uphold the decision of 21 April 1993, no. 227 (City Council Gazette

which might create difficulties in distinguishing the meanings of the yes/no answers to this question from each other. Alternatively, the 'reverse' qualifier may be expected to be quite extreme, because stating that a decision about which the city council members have had endless meetings should be reversed can be assumed to be rather radical. Hence, a relatively small number of citizens may be expected to respond 'yes reverse', but those respondents may be assumed to feel strongly and genuinely that the decision should be reversed. Among the citizens answering 'not reverse' there may be many people very moderately against reversal. If a consultative referendum were to be held, with a question like 'Do you think the city council should decide to forbid the sale of magic mushrooms?', the answering option 'yes forbid' would be relatively extreme. This means it is likely that a relatively small number of respondents will choose that option, whereas a larger moderate group of respondents will be likely to answer 'not forbid'. This example also shows that the decision as to what constitutes an extreme qualifier calls for a semantic 'gut reaction', as well as a sensitivity to the specific context in which the qualifier is used. A rule of thumb is to compare the extremity of possible qualifiers, as well as the definition of the answering options which accompany the question. The qualifier 'allow', for example, causes the answering options to be less well-defined, as 'yes allow' can refer to 'not insert a barrier' as well as 'remove a barrier'. This causes allow questions to be less suitable for making clear distinctions between groups of respondents in terms of extreme opinions for or against an issue.

The fact that respondents have been shown to retrieve a general evaluation towards the issue and map their answer onto the answering options using the qualifying dimension in the question, has some additional implications. First of all, it implies that researchers should, whenever possible, avoid using only single questions to measure attitudes. In order to distill the 'true' evaluation of an issue the attitude should be measured by using various dimensions on which the evaluation can be expressed. However, it is advisable to avoid explicit negations in the qualifying terms, as this causes differences between respondents in the way they interpret the meanings of the answering options and thus creates difficulties for the researcher when it comes to interpreting the answers. The description of the issue in the question should also be varied, so that the full issue can be captured over a set of questions. The current research suggests that one question

---

dpt. 1, p. 1057) regarding the earmarking of land for the construction of a tram line through the *Vrije Geer* meadow in the direction of the *Middelveldsche Akerpolder*? Agree with this council decision/Disagree with this council decision". ["Bent u het eens/oneens met het raadsbesluit vast te houden aan zijn besluit van 21 April 1993, nr. 227 (Gemeente-blad afd. 1, blz. 1057), inzake het handhaven van de reservering voor een tramtracé recht door het weilandje de Vrije Geer in de richting van de Middelveldsche Akerpolder. Eens met dit raadsbesluit/Oneens met dit raadsbesluit"].

about a complex issue causes ambivalence and problems in mapping an evaluation onto the answering options. For many research questions a better grasp of respondents' attitudes will be obtained by breaking down the complex issue into smaller subissues. Furthermore, by using such a procedure in which a range of questions serves to indicate a single underlying construct, the measurement becomes less dependent on idiosyncratic variants or wording that is too specific.

In the current research, the sets of questions were not pretested as to the extent to which they reflected an underlying attitude. In practice, the ideal approach would be to conduct pilot studies in order to find the relevant dimensions of the attitude one wants to address, with a view to achieving greater homogeneity and better possibilities for distinguishing differences between respondents' attitudes. Generally speaking, the more questions that are used as indicators of an underlying construct the better. It is also important to pretest the questions on their comprehensibility, answerability and the extent to which they are interpreted as the researcher intended. Since it turns out that respondents retrieve fairly general evaluations towards the issue based on the question text, the researcher should make sure that this is indeed the issue she intended to measure. A rule of thumb is to remember that survey research is a form of standardized communication between researcher and respondents. The researcher should not only reason from her research goals and content theory, but should also continue to bear in mind how she restricts the communication situation for the respondents in expressing their opinions towards the issues she wants to assess.

As the current research focused on question wording, only a limited number of implications for *the stage of survey administration* can be drawn from it. This does not mean that the selection of respondents, the handling of non-response, the selection of interviewers and all types of other factors related to the administration stage are not important. However, other research is far better suited to providing more thorough advice on these aspects.

The most important recommendation on survey administration that follows from the current research is to choose the time of measurement carefully. In the current study, some experiments were conducted using attitudes towards issues that were highly topical at the time of measurement. Discussions on these issues were appearing in the newspapers on a daily basis. For these issues, it turned out that the attitudes measured changed rather drastically over a relatively short (four week) period. Although differently worded questions (forbid/allow questions) measure the same attitude at one time of measurement, questions worded similarly with a four week interval between times of measurement have been shown to measure different attitudes from the same respondents. This shows that relatively homogeneous measurements of a certain trait obtained at a given time of measurement does not imply the measurement of a stable trait over time. The attitudes (or opinions, for that matter) construed from the answers obtained at one time of measurement should be interpreted in light of the specific context of public discussion at that specific time of measurement, especially if the questions do not constitute a very homogeneous set of indicators of the underlying construct. This is especially relevant for public opinion polls conducted on very short notice, consisting of a small number of questions on highly topical issues. Based on the current study, it can be concluded that this type of research tends to give a fleeting impression of volatile opinions and should be interpreted as such. If the researcher is looking for traits that are more stable, multiple times of measurement are recommended, or failing that, at least a range of questions that homogeneously measure the same trait by addressing it in different ways.

As to *the interpretation stage* of survey research, various practical conclusions can be drawn from the current study. As the research process is cyclic, advice concerning the interpretation stage is of course related to the advice already given for the questionnaire construction stage. In general, the Yes/No[+] Theory implies that respondents retrieve similar attitudes when answering questions containing different qualifiers but map their evaluation differently onto the response options due to the use of a specific qualifier. This means that respondents' answers to single questions should always be interpreted in light of the qualifier that was used. 'Yes' and 'no' should not be viewed as nominal categories implying a straightforward for or against evaluation, but as the extremes of an interval scale that should be interpreted together with the qualifying term in the question: 'yes forbid [issue x]', or 'no, not allow [issue x]'. The same holds for agree-disagree scales: the answers given on these interval scales should be interpreted together with the qualifying term in the question ('I strongly disagree with forbidding [issue x]'). When interpreting or reporting the answers, researchers should be precise in reporting it along these lines. If a researcher is not in fact interested in the opinions for or against forbidding/allowing but wants to know the number of respondents who are generally in favour of or against the issue, she should word the question differently in order to better reflect the goal of the research.

When interpreting single questions, the answers to questions containing extreme qualifiers can be traced back to the true value with relative ease. It may be assumed that respondents answering 'yes forbid' are very much in favour of forbidding and that respondents answering 'not forbid' are homogeneously and moderately against forbidding the issue. If the researcher is interested in homogeneity, she should focus on the 'not forbid' answers in her report. If she is interested in extremity, she should focus on the group of respondents (likely to be smaller and more heterogeneous in their true opinions) who answered 'yes forbid'. Greater care should be taken in interpreting the answers to allow questions.

The answering options are less extreme in their meanings, causing less distinction between the differences in opinions of respondents. In addition, the answering option 'yes allow' is particularly ill-defined and should be interpreted as meaning 'remove a barrier' as well as 'not insert a barrier'. When interpreting the answers to many yes/no questions containing a qualifying dimension, a rule of thumb is to try and imagine the respondents mapping their evaluation onto the response options. If one of the options is clearly more extreme, the researcher could focus on the likeliness of a relatively small group choosing that option. If one option is not very well-defined, the other will not be very well-defined either, making it likely that moderate respondents will be represented in both options.

Questions accompanied by multiple-point scales provide increased opportunities for respondents to map their evaluations onto the scales. Moderate respondents can use more scale points to express their moderateness. Through the use of multiple-point scale questions subtle differences between respondents' attitudes can be better assessed and interpreted. In light of the fact that differences in the answers obtained reflect differences in mapping similar attitudes onto the answering scales, it is not advisable to 'summarize' answers obtained using a multiple-point scale on a scale containing less points. It is better to let respondents translate their evaluation onto the scale points the researcher wants to work with themselves, than for the researcher to perform a transformation of the answering scale after the answers have been obtained.

For the interpretation stage, the advice to use a range of questions to measure an underlying attitude (addressing the issue in different ways and using differing qualifying dimensions) means that analysing procedures should be used that somehow combine the different questions into one indicator for the underlying attitude. Homogeneity can be assessed using homogeneity measures such as Cronbach's Alpha, followed by a relatively straightforward method of computing a mean attitude score for a homogeneous set of questions. The interpretation of this score will be less dependent on the characteristics of single questions.

The practical advice provided here could lead cynics to think that surveys or at least surveys consisting of standardized closed questions should be forbidden. It is important to note that this is emphatically not the strategy propounded in the current research. Firstly, for many research goals and questions it is important to standardize and be able to make comparisons between respondents, companies, countries or any other unit of research. The use of standardized closed questionnaires provides a relatively easy way of doing this. Secondly, open standardized questions, or even open unstandardized questions, will lead to just as many mapping differences as closed questions with slight differences in wording. When answering closed questions the evaluations are expressed differently than a situation in which open questions are answered, but the latter is not necessarily better. Furthermore, in cases where comparisons between respondents or other units of research have to be based on the data obtained, the answers to open questions have to be 'translated' and coded by the researcher, whereas for closed questions this is done by the respondents themselves.

The general rule is to think of survey research as standardized communication between researcher and respondents. A researcher should reason from her research goals and questions but should also try and place himself/herself in the position of the respondents. She should try to imagine how the respondents will interpret the questions and what restrictions are placed on their possibilities for answering. The researcher should therefore try to strike a balance between the goal of answering the research question and the restrictions she is imposing on the respondents in communicating what they think or feel. The main ways to find a golden mean between the research goals and the communicative restrictions imposed are by using several questions as indicators of one construct and pretesting the questions on construct validity and answerability.

8.6 EPILOGUE

This study has provided a theory to explain the forbid/allow asymmetry, a theory which can serve as a basis for practical advice concerning both the use of these questions and the interpretation of the answers they elicit. Previous experiments have been summarized and integrated, existing hypotheses have been refined and tested, and new hypotheses have been formulated. The cognitive and communicative framework underlying all hypotheses and analyses has been shown to provide an integrative theory allowing the formulation of a monocausal explanation of the asymmetry, an explanation which is also able to account for the variation caused by complex interactions between text, context and reader.

Only one question concerning the forbid/allow asymmetry remains unanswered: what are the absolute meanings of the answering options to forbid/allow questions? This question could provide the focus for future forbid/allow research, as a follow-up to the analysis and comparison of the relative meanings of the answering options. It is to be expected that these variations in meaning can be explained by various background variables, such as attitude strength. The current research has been able to point out which background variables can be regarded as important and has modelled the variance in the meanings of the answering options. A suggestion for future research might be to measure the effects of these background variables on the variation in the meanings of the answering options experimentally, with a view to further explaining and reducing the bandwidth of these meanings.[7]

For future research on wording effects in general, the Yes/No[+] Theory provides a stimulating framework for formulating further hypotheses. The designs and methods proposed in the current study have proven useful in the testing of such aspects. The framework presented in the current study can also be used for other response effects. This study shows that hypotheses concerning individual response effects can be formulated more sharply by fitting them to general models of question answering and text interpretation. Eventually, this may lead to a new model of survey research in which a variety of response effects can be treated as data and not as features distorting an objective measurement.

In the remainder of this final section, some strengths of the current research will be discussed, as well as some points of attention for future research along similar lines.

8.6.1 Attitudes versus answers

The basic model describing the question-answering process for attitude questions consists of question interpretation, attitude retrieval or formation, rendering a judgment, and reporting the evaluation by mapping the judgement onto one of the precoded answering categories. For each of these stages in the question-answering process, theories concerning language interpretation, attitude structures and communication behaviour can be used to describe the subprocesses more precisely. However, these processes are widely regarded as complex, intertwined and partly subconscious. An important strength of the current research is that the model of the question-answering process is simplified into two distinguishable stages: question interpretation and attitude retrieval or formation on the one hand, and translating the judgment into the precoded answering options on the other. This distinction is especially relevant to survey practice, as it addresses the validity of survey questions by separating the question of whether the attitudes the researcher intended to measure are retrieved, from the extent to which the researcher's interpretation of the answers obtained can be viewed as a good 'translation' of the attitude that was retrieved.

---

[7] The interpretation of these meta-analytic effects was limited in this research however, because the dependent variable was the asymmetry size, instead of the percentage 'yes forbid' as well as the percentage 'not allow'. Since the variance in the effect of the use of forbid/allow turned out to be large, it was expected to be difficult to pinpoint unequivocal effects of background characteristics if two dependent variables were defined. However, a consequent restriction on the interpretation of the analyses was the impossibility of discovering in which direction the answers 'shifted' due to a background variable. Within an experimental approach, this could be modelled more easily.

In order to apply this basic cognitive framework of the question-answering processes to describing the mechanisms underlying the forbid/allow asymmetry, existing hypotheses, such as the connotations hypothesis, had to be reinterpreted. Research designs also had to be developed in order to test the resulting hypotheses: traditional split ballot designs are satisfactory as tests of the existence of a wording effect in a specific context but presuppose too many similarities between the psychometric properties of the questions to pinpoint the stage of the question-answering process at which the response effect arises. An important contribution of the current study is the integration of insights from cognitive and psychometric theory, resulting in an extension of traditional split ballots into correlational designs that closely match the research questions focusing on the cognitive mechanisms during question-answering.

The design and analysis principles proposed in this study can be used to obtain an understanding of the causes of many other response effects. As for the theoretical distinction between attitudes measured and answers obtained, it should be noted that the concept of 'attitudes' was simplified somewhat in the current research. Forbid/allow questions are attitude questions, as they ask for an evaluation and can therefore be distinguished from questions measuring factual or behavioural information, or knowledge. Attitudes were defined in this study as evaluative constructs that have to be retrieved from long-term memory or formed in order to answer the question. It was assumed that attitudes would manifest themselves in a commonality between questions, a fairly common assumption in psychological theory. At the same time, psychological theory generally assumes that attitudes are relatively 'deep' and stable traits, whereas the attitudes measured in the current study seemed to be more volatile.

In the current research and future research along similar lines, the concept of 'attitudes' can be used fairly loosely, as the focus is on differences between sets of questions worded differently; the commonality measured with a set of forbid questions (or a set of allow questions) is not the primary focus. Instead, the effect of question wording on the degree of commonality is what matters. In this light, the distinction between 'attitudes' and the mapping stage is convincing, for although the 'attitudes' were found to change over time, the question-answering mechanisms themselves were shown not to be dependent on the time of administration. At several times of measurement, forbid/allow answers were shown to differ due to the stage of mapping the answers and not to be caused by a difference in the commonality measured by a set of forbid or allow questions. This evaluative commonality for forbid/allow questions could well be an attitude.

8.6.2 Question-answering as a communication process

The current research demonstrates that explaining wording effects within a cognitive communicative framework has important implications for data collection and analysis, as well as for the status of the theories used. Research working within a communicative framework should take into account a complex interaction between text and reader characteristics: characteristics of the respondents (such as attitude strength) affect how they deal with the text and at the same time characteristics of the text and the context may interact with each other. The Yes/No$^+$ Theory was developed to describe the main mechanism underlying the forbid/allow asymmetry and other contrastive questions. In order to account for the many factors that cause the wording effect to vary, several general cognitive communicative theories were used as points of reference. The most important of these were Tourangeau and Rasinski's model of the question-answering process for attitude questions and Sperber and Wilson's relevance theory, which describes readers as not necessarily computing a deep representation of the utterance as a whole but inferring a semantic blueprint with enough contextual effects without unjustifiable effort. To describe and predict more concrete effects of text, readers or context, a large variety of more restricted theories were used. These were sometimes based on earlier response effects research, sometimes on earlier research into text interpretation and were sometimes derived from more general cognitive notions such as 'processing effort'. Describing a complex communication process such as the answering of attitude questions, means attempting to model a very complex process in which many aspects are deeply intertwined. The current research explicitly demonstrates that it is all but impossible to achieve a description of this kind by relying solely on powerful theory-driven strategies.

In order to compensate for this lack of powerful theories for each potentially relevant aspect of the question-answering process, the aim should be to identify general mechanisms underlying a wording effect and leave room for variation due to specific context or reader characteristics. The current study shows that this can be done by employing various techniques and designs. First of all, analysing over sets of questions is recommended instead of analysing on the basis of single questions, as are using sets of questions as indicators of one trait and replicating research at several times of measurement, as well as employing meta-analytic techniques. Secondly, research should not limit itself to the study of fixed effects (e.g. means), but should also take account of the variation around those means between questions or respondents. These variations are particularly important in giving an insight into the communication processes underlying the product (the answers) obtained. Thirdly, it is important to take effect sizes into account and to compare these for various effects: working within a communicative cognitive framework many variables may be expected to affect the process outcomes to a statistically significant extent. It is important to establish some additional insight into the importance of each effect, or at least their relative importance compared to the other effects, in order to have some touchstone for evaluating the substantiality of each affecting variable. The current research shows that by using these strategies general conclusions can be drawn about the occurrence as well as about the causes of a wording effect.

The cognitive and communicative framework used provides a starting point for integrating the more or less detached auxiliary hypotheses survey researchers implicitly use in designing their surveys and interpreting the data. This study therefore provides opportunities for integrating the theories and methods necessary to assess the validity of survey measures, and for ultimately arriving at a general model of survey research. On a more general level, the description this study provides of the processes underlying complex language use tasks (e.g. answering attitude questions) in real-life contexts shows that although language forms the early input of the process, it does not necessarily have a direct effect on the outcomes of the process. A straightforward analysis of the verbs 'forbid' and 'allow' proved insufficient. A process of reasoning about what readers do with the linguistic input showed that the explanation should revolve around the combination of the answering options and the use of 'forbid' and 'allow', instead of focusing solely on the use of forbid/allow. This suggests that language interpretation in complex tasks is not necessarily a process of linear, modular computation. In order to understand language interpretation in these contexts, it needs to be conceptualized as a complex instruction which the reader takes up in order to fulfil the specific task he is purposefully performing.

This study shows that it is possible to draw general conclusions about communicative and cognitive processes within a real-life language-use setting, as long as the hypotheses match the designs and methods chosen and as long as the researcher remains aware of variation between readers, texts and the interaction between them. The 'black box', symbolizing the processes within the minds of language users, will probably never be opened completely but much about these processes can be revealed by peeking through the keyhole.

REFERENCES

Anderson N.H. (1981), *Foundations of information integration*. New York: Academic Press

Andrews F.M. (1984), Construct validity and error components of survey measures: a structural modeling approach. In: *Public Opinion Quarterly 48*, 409-442

Angleitner A., John O.P., Löhr F.J. (1986), It's what you ask and how you ask it: an itemmetric analysis of personality questionnaires. In: Angleitner A. and Wiggins S. (eds.), *Personality assessment via questionnaires: current issues in theory and measurement*. Berlin: Springer Verlag, 61-107

Ayidiya S.A., McClendon M.J. (1990), Response effects in mail surveys. In: *Public Opinion Quarterly 54*, 229-247

Bartelds J.F., Jansen E.P.W.A., Joossens T.H. (1989), *Enquêteren [Survey research]*. Groningen: Wolters-Noordhoff

Bateson N. (1984), *Dataconstruction in social surveys*. Contemporary Social Research Series, London: Allen & Unwin

Belson W.A. (1981), *The design and understanding of survey questions*. Aldershot: Gower

Bem D.J. (1972), Self-perception theory. In: Berkowitz L. (ed.), *Advances in experimental social psychology 6*, New York: Academic Press, 1-62

Bergh H. van den, Eiting M., Otter M. (1988), Differentiële effecten van vraagvorm bij aardrijkskunde en natuurkunde examens [Differential effects of question form in nature and science exams]. In: *Tijdschrift voor Onderwijsonderzoek 13*, 270-284

Bergh H. van den, Eiting M. (1989), A method of estimating rater reliability. In: *Journal of Educational Measurement 26*, 29-40

Bergh H. van den (1990), On the construct validity of multiple-choice items for reading comprehension. In: *Applied Psychological Measurement 14*, 1-12

Billiet J., Loosveldt G., Waterplas L. (1984), *Het survey-interview onderzocht. Effecten van het ontwerp en gebruik van vragenlijsten op de kwaliteit van de antwoorden. [The survey interview investigated. Effects of the design and use of questionnaires on the quality of the answers]*. Sociologisch Onderzoeksinstituut Leuven

Billiet J. (1989), Wat te doen? beschouwingen over het nut van pasklare voorschriften voor het ontwerpen van survey-vragen [What to do? Reflections on the use of ready-made advice on the design of survey questions]. In: Zouwen J. van der, Dijkstra W. (eds.), *Sociaal wetenschappelijk onderzoek met vragenlijsten. Methoden, knelpunten, oplossingen*. Amsterdam: VU-Uitgeverij, 35-52

Bishop G.F., Oldendick R.W., Tuchfarber A.J. (1984), What must my interest in politics be if I just told you "I don't know"? In: *Public Opinion Quarterly 48*, 510-519

Bishop G.F. (1987), Experiments with the middle response alternative in survey questions. In: *Public Opinion Quarterly 51*, 220-232

Bishop G., Hippler H.-J., Schwarz N. and Strack F. (1988), A comparison of response effects in self-administred and telephone surveys. In: Groves R.M., Biemer P., Lyberg L., Massey J., Nicholls W. and Waksberg J. (eds.), *Telephone survey methodology*. New York: Wiley, 273-282

Blankenship A.B. (1940), The influence of question form upon the response in a public opinion poll. In: *Psychological Record 3*, 345-422

Bollen K.A. (1989), *Structural equations with latent variables*. New York: Wiley

Bruinsma C. (1987), *Systematic errors in survey interviews; a methodological study on the effect of significant others and other sources of bias on evaluations of job qualities and union actions*. Amsterdam: VU-Uitgeverij

Campbell D.T., Fiske D.W. (1959), Convergent and discriminant validation by the multitrait-multimethod matrix. In: *Psychological Bulletin 56*, 81-105

Cannell C.F., Miller P.V., Oksenberg L. (1981), Research on interviewing techniques. In: Leinhardt S. (ed.), *Sociological methodology 1981*. San Francisco: Jossey Bass

Cantril H. (1940), Experiments on the wording of questions. In: *Public Opinion Quarterly 4*, 330-332

Chaffin R., Herrmann D.J. (1984), The similarity and diversity of semantic relations. In: *Memory and Cognition 12*, 134-141

Chaffin R., Herrmann D.J. (1988), The nature of semantic relations: a comparison of two approaches. In: Evens M.W (ed.), *Relational models of the lexicon. Representing knowledge in semantic networks*. Cambridge University Press, 289-334

Chaiken S. (1980), Heuristic versus systematic information processing and the use of source versus message cues in persuasion. In: *Journal of Personality and Social Psychology 39*, 752-766

Cicourel A.V. (1982), Interviews, surveys and the problem of ecological validity. In: *The American Sociologist 17*, 11-20

Clark H. H. (1973), The Language-as-Fixed-Effect-Fallacy: a critique of language statistics in psychological research. In: *Journal of Verbal Learning and Verbal Behaviour 12*, 335-359

Clark H. H., Schober M.F. (1992), Asking questions and influencing answers, what is to be done? In: Tanur J.M. (ed.), *Questions about questions, inquiries into the cognitive bases of surveys*. Russel Sage Foundation, 15-48

Cohen J. (1977), *Statistical power analysis for the behavioral sciences* (revised ed.). New York: Academic Press

Converse P.E. (1970), Attitudes and non-attitudes: continuation of a dialogue. In: Tufte E.R. (ed.), *The quantitative analysis of social problems*. Reading: Addison-Wesley, 168-189

Converse J.M. (1976), Predicting no opinion in the polls. In: *Public Opinion Quarterly 40*, 515-53

Cook T.D., Cooper H., Cordray D.S., Hartmann H., Hedges L.V., Light R.J., Louis T.A., Mosteller F. (1992), *Meta-analysis for explanation. A casebook*. New York: Russell Sage Foundation

Cox III E.P. (1980), The optimal number of response altnernatives for a scale: a review. In: *Journal of Marketing Research 17*, 407-422

Cronbach L.J., Meehl P.E. (1955), Construct validity in psychological tests. In: *Psychological Bulletin 52*, 281-302

Dijkstra W., Zouwen J. van der (1977), Testing auxiliary hypotheses behind the interview. In: *Annals of Systems Research 6*, 49-63

Dijkstra W., Zouwen J. van der (eds.) (1982), *Response behaviour in the survey-interview*. London: Academic Press

Douma W.H. (1956), *De leesbaarheid van landbouwliteratuur [The readibility of literature on agricultural science]*. Landbouwhogeschool Wageningen

Eagly A.H., Chaiken S. (1993), *The psychology of attitudes*. Harcourt Brace Jovanovich College Publishers

Emans B. (1990), *Interviewen: theorie, techniek en training [Interviewing: theory, techniques and training]*. Groningen: Wolters Noordhoff

Falthzik A.M., Jolson M.A. (1974), Statement polarity in attitude studies. In: *Journal of Marketing Research 11*, 102-105

Fazio R.H., Sherman S.J., Herr P.M (1982), The feature-positive effect in the self-perception process: does not doing matter as much as doing? In: *Journal of Personality and Social Psychology 42 (3)*, 401-411

Fishbein M., Ajzen I. (1975). *Belief, attitude, intention and behaviour: an introduction to theory and research*. Reading: Addisson-Wesley

Fiske S.T., Pavelchak M.A. (1986), Category-based versus piecemeal-based affective responses: developments in schema-triggered affect. In: Sorrentino R.M., Higgins E.T. (eds.), *Handbook of motivation and cognition*. New York: Guilford Press, 167-203

Frazier L. (1985), Syntactic complexity. In: Dowty D., Karttunen L., Zwicky A. (eds.), *Natural language parsing*. Cambridge UK: Cambridge University Press

Gove W.R. (1982), Systematic response bias and characteristics of the respondent. In: Dijkstra W. and Zouwen J. van der (eds.), *Response behaviour in the survey-interview*. London: Academic Press, 167-187

Graesser A.C., Murachver T. (1985), Symbolic procedures of question answering. In: Graesser A.C., Black J.B. (eds.), *The psychology of questions*, Hillsdale Erlbaum, 15-87

Graesser A.C., Franklin S.P. (1990), Quest: a cognitive model of question answering. In: *Discourse Processes 13*, 279-303

Grice H.P. (1975), Logic and Conversation. In: Cole P. & Morgan J.L. (eds.), *Speech acts* (Syntax and Semantics 3), New York: Academic Press

Günther U., Groeben N. (1978), Abstraktheidssuffix-Verfahren: Vorschlag einer objektiven ökonomischen Messung der Abstraktheit/Konkretheit von Texten [Proposal for an objective economical measure of abstractness/concreteness]. In: *Zeitschrift für Experimentelle und Angewandte Psychologie 25*, 55-74

Hippler H.-J., Schwarz N. (1986), Not forbidding isn't allowing: the cognitive basis of the forbid/allow asymmetry. In: *Public Opinion Quarterly 50*, 87-96

Hippler H.J., Schwarz N., Sudman S. (1987), *Social information processing and survey methodology*. New York: Springer Verlag.

Hippler H.J., Schwarz N. (1987), Response effects in surveys. In: Hippler H.J, Schwarz N., Sudman S. (eds.), *Social information processing and survey methodology*. New York: Springer Verlag, 106-107

Holleman B.C. (1996), Wording effects in attitude questions. A structural modelling approach. Paper presented at the *Fourth International Conference on Social Science Methodology*, Colchester, July 3-5

Holleman B.C. (1997), Is verbieden niet toelaten? Een meta-analyse [Is forbidding not allowing? A meta-analysis]. In: Bergh H. van den, Bertens N., Damen M., Janssen D.J. (eds.), *Taalgebruik ontrafeld, verslag van het 7ᵉ Viot-congres*. Dordrecht: ICG-publicaties, 427-437

Holleman B.C. (1997), Asking survey questions: should it be forbidden or not be allowed? Paper presented at the *7th Meeting of the Society for Text and Discourse*, Utrecht July 10-12

Holleman B.C. (1999), Wording effects in survey research. Using meta-analysis to explain the forbid/allow asymmetry. In: *Journal of Quantitative Linguistics 6*, 29-40

Holleman B.C. (1999), The nature of the forbid/allow asymmetry. Two correlational studies. In: *Sociological Methods & Research 28/2*, 209-244

Holleman B.C. (1999), Is nee eigenlijk ja? Over de betekenis van antwoorden op vragenlijstvragen [Does no in fact mean yes? On the meaning of the answers to survey questions]. Paper presented at the *VIOT-congres 1999*, Delft, December 20-22

Houtkoop-Steenstra H. (1991), Hoe een gesloten vraag toch open kan zijn [How a closed question can be open]. In: *Tijdschrift voor Taalbeheersing 13*, 185-196

Houtkoop-Steenstra H. (1993), Voetangels en klemmen bij experimenteel onderzoek naar sturende vragen [Mantraps and pitfalls in experimental research on leading questions]. In: *Tijdschrift voor Taalbeheersing 15*, 109-123

Jobe J.B., Loftus E.F. (1991, eds.), Cognition and survey measurement [Special Issue]. *Applied Cognitive Psychology 5/1*

Jobe J.B., Mingay D.J. (1991), Cognition and survey measurement: history and overview. In: *Applied Cognitive Psychology 5/1*, 175-192

Jöreskog K.G. (1971), Statistical analysis of sets of congeneric tests. In: *Psychometrika 36*, 109-133

Jöreskog K.G., Sörbom D. (1986), *LISREL VI. Analysis of linear structural relationships by maximum likelihood, instrumental variables and least squares methods.* Uppsala: University of Uppsala

Kiesler S., Sproull L.S. (1986), Response effects in the electronic survey. In: *Public Opinion Quarterly 50* (3), 402-413

Krosnick J.A., Alwin D.F. (1987), An evaluation of a cognitive theory of response order effects in survey measurement. In: *Public Opinion Quarterly 51*, 201-219

Krosnick J.A., Schuman H. (1988), Attitude intensity, importance, and certainty and susceptibility to response effects. In: *Journal of Personality and Social Psychology 54 (6)*, 940-952

Krosnick J.A., Abelson R.P. (1992), The case for measuring attitude strength in surveys. In: Tanur J.M. (ed.), *Questions about questions, inquiries into the cognitive bases of surveys.* Russell Sage Foundation, 177-203

Krosnick J.A., Petty R.E (1995), Attitude strength: an overview. In: Petty R.E., Krosnick J.A. (eds.), *Attitude strength. Antecedents and consequences.* Lawrence Erlbaum, 1-24

Laurent A. (1972), Effects of question length on reporting behavior in the survey interview. In: *Journal of the American Statistical Association 67/338*, 298-305

Lord F.M., Novick M.R. (1968), *Statistical theories of mental test scores.* Reading: Addisson Wesley

Mellenbergh G.J. (1980), Theorie op verschillende niveaus [Theory at different levels]. In: *Nederlands Tijdschrift voor de Psychologie 35*, 275-288

Molenaar N.J. (1982), Response-effects of "formal" characteristics of questions. In: Dijkstra W., Zouwen J. van der (eds.), *Response behaviour in the survey-interview.* London: Academic Press, 49-89

Molenaar N.J. (1986), *Formuleringseffecten in survey-interviews, een non-experimenteel onderzoek [Wording effects in survey interviews, a non-experimental investigation]*. Amsterdam: VU-Uitgeverij

Molenaar N.J. (1991), Recent methodological studies on survey questioning. In: *Quality and Quantity 25*, 167-187

Nisbett R.E., Ross L. (1980), *Human inference: strategies and shortcomings of social judgment*. Englewood Cliffs: Prentice-Hall

Onrust M., Verhagen A., Doeve R. (1993), *Formuleren [Phrasing]*. Houten: Bohn Stafleu van Loghum

Petrič I. (1992), *Predicting listening performance for news texts*. Dissertation Utrecht University

Petty R.E., Cacioppo J.T. (1984), The effects of involvement on responses to argument quantity and quality: Central and peripheral routes to persuasion. In: *Journal of Personality and Social Psychology 46*, 69-81

Petty R.E., Rennier G.A., Cacioppio J.T. (1987), Assertion versus interrogation format in opinion surveys. Questions enhance thoughtful responding. In: *Public Opinion Quarterly 51*, 481-494

Pligt J. van der, Vries N. de (1995), *Opinies en attitudes. Meting, modellen, theorie [Opinions and attitudes. Measurement, models and theory]*. Amsterdam/Meppel: Boom

Reese S.D., Danielson W.A., Shoemaker P.J, Chan T.-K, Hsu H.-L (1986), Ethnicity-of-interviewer effects among Mexican-Americans and Anglos. In: *Public Opinion Quarterly 50*, 563-572

Rugg D. (1941), Experiments in wording questions II. In: *Public Opinion Quarterly 5*, 91-92

Sacks H. (1987), On the preferences for agreement and contiguity in sequences in conversation. In: Button G. & Lee J.R.E. (eds.), *Talk and social organisation*. Clevedon: Multilingual Matters, 54-69

Saris W.E. (1990), Design of the research project. In: Saris W.E., Meurs A. van (eds.), *Evaluation of measurement instruments by meta-analysis of multitrait-multimethod studies. KNAW-Verhandelingen 143*, 216-221

Schuman H., Presser S. (1981), *Questions and answers in attitude surveys. Experiments on question form, wording and context*. London: Academic Press

Schuman H. (1982), Artifacts are in the mind of the beholder. In: *The American Sociologist 17*, 21-28

Schwarz N., Sudman S. (eds.) (1992), *Context effects in social and psychological research.* New York: Springer Verlag

Schwarz N., Sudman S. (eds.) (1995), *Answering questions.* San Francisco: Jossey-Bass

Schwarz N., Hippler H.-J. (1987), What response scales may tell your respondents: Informative functions of response alternatives. In: Hippler H.-J., Schwarz N., Sudman S. (eds.), *Social information processing and survey methodology.* New York: Springer Verlag, 163-178

Schwarz N., Strack F., Hippler H.-J., Bishop G. (1991), The impact of administration mode on response effects in surveys. In: *Applied Cognitive Psychology 5 (3),* 193-212

Silver B.D., Anderson B.A., Abramson P.R. (1986), Who overreports voting? In: *American Political Science Review 80,* 613-624

Sperber D., Wilson D. (1986), *Relevance: Communication and cognition.* Oxford: Basil Blackwell

Strack F., Martin L.L, Schwarz N. (1987), The social determinants of information use in judgements of life-satisfaction. In: *European Journal of Social Psychology 18,* 429-442

Suchman L., Jordan B. (1990), Interactional troubles in face-to-face survey interviews. In: *Journal of the American Statistical Association 85/409,* 232-253

Suchman L., Jordan B. (1992), Validity and the collaborative construction of meaning in face-to-face surveys. In: Tanur J.M. (ed.), *Questions about questions: inquiries into the cognitive basis of surveys.* New York: Russell Sage, 241-267

Sudman S., Bradburn N.M. (1974), *Response effects in surveys: a review and synthesis.* Chicago: Aldine

Sudman S., Bradburn N.M. (1982), *Asking questions. A practical guide to questionnaire design.* San Francisco: Jossey-Bass Publishers

Sudman S., Bradburn N.M, Schwarz N. (1996). *Thinking about answers. The application of cognitive processes to survey methodology.* San Francisco: Jossey-Bass Publishers

Talmy L. (1988), Force Dynamics in language and cognition. In: *Cognitive Science 12,* 49-100

Tanur J.M. (1992), *Questions about questions: inquiries into the cognitive basis of surveys.* New York: Russell Sage

Tourangeau R. (1987) Attitude measurement: A cognitive perspective. In: H.J. Hippler, Schwarz N., Sudman S. (eds.), *Social information processing and survey methodology.* New York: Springer Verlag, 149-162

Tourangeau R., Rasinski K. (1988), Cognitive processes underlying context effects in attitude measurement. In: *Psychological Bulletin 103,* 299-314

Verhagen A. (1997), Context, meaning and interpretation, in a practical approach to linguistics. In: Lentz L. & Pander Maat H. (eds.), *Discourse analysis and evaluation: functional approaches*. Amsterdam/Atlanta: Rodopi, 7-39

Waterplas L., Billiet J., Loosveldt G. (1988), De verbieden versus niet toelaten asymmetry. Een stabiel formuleringseffect in survey-onderzoek? [The forbid/allow asymmetry. A stable wording effect in survey research?]. In: *Mens en Maatschappij 63*: 399-415

Wegener D.T., Downing J., Krosnick J.A., Petty R.E. (1995), Measures and manipulations of strength-related properties of attitudes: current practice and future directions. In: Petty R.E., Krosnick J.A. (eds.), *Attitude strength. Antecedents and consequences*. Lawrence Erlbaum, 455-487

Wentland E.J., Smith K.W. (1993), *Survey responses, an evaluation of their validity*. Academic Press

Wolf F.M. (1986), Meta-analysis, quantitative methods for research synthesis. *Sage University Paper series on quantitative applications in the social sciences, series no. 07-059*. Beverly Hills: Sage Publications

Wood W. (1982), Retrieval of attitude-relevant information from memory: effects on susceptibility to persuasion and on intrinsic motivation. In: *Journal of Personality and Social Psychology 42*, 798-810

Wijffels J., Bergh H. van den, Dillen S. van (1992), Het sturend effect van vragen met voorbeeldantwoorden [The leading effect of questions accompanied by example answers]. In: *Tijdschrift voor Taalbeheersing 14 (2)*, 136-148

Zouwen J. van der (1974), A conceptual model for the auxiliary hypotheses behind the interview. In: Rootselaar J. van (ed.), *Annals of systems research 4*, 21-37

Zouwen J. van der, Dijkstra W. (eds.) (1989), *Sociaal-wetenschappelijk onderzoek met vragenlijsten. Methoden, knelpunten, oplossingen [Social science research using questionnaires. Methods, bottlenecks, solutions]*. Amsterdam: VU-uitgeverij

AUTHOR INDEX

THE FORBID/ALLOW QUESTIONS
POSED IN TWO NEW EXPERIMENTS
(Chapters 3 and 4)

1. Vindt u dat de overheid stadsuitbreiding buiten de huidige stadsgrenzen moet verbieden/toelaten als dit ten koste gaat van weide- of natuurgebieden?
2. Vindt u dat de overheid militaire oefeningen in of vlakbij natuurgebieden moet verbieden/toelaten?
3. Vindt u dat de Tweede Kamer uitbreiding van Schiphol met een vijfde baan moet verbieden/toelaten?
4. Vindt u dat de overheid gaswinning in de Waddenzee moet verbieden/toelaten als natuurlijke kenmerken van het gebied daardoor worden aangetast?
5. Vindt u dat de Tweede Kamer de aanleg van wegen door natuurgebieden moet verbieden/toelaten?
6. Vindt u dat de overheid snelheden hoger dan 90 km/u op de snelwegen moet verbieden/toelaten?
7. Vindt u dat de overheid het verhogen van treintarieven door de NS moet verbieden/toelaten?
8. Vindt u dat de overheid autorijden op zondag moet verbieden/toelaten?
9. Vindt u dat de overheid het gebruik van wegwerpbatterijen moet verbieden/toelaten?
10. Sommige mensen verkopen hun huis niet aan allochtonen. Vindt u dat de overheid dit moet verbieden/toelaten?
11. Op sommige scholen zitten veel kinderen van allochtonen. Vindt u dat de overheid afzonderlijke klassen voor Nederlandse en allochtone kinderen op die scholen moet verbieden/toelaten?
12. Vindt u dat de overheid racistisch getinte toespraken in het openbaar moet verbieden/toelaten?
13. Vindt u dat de overheid uitsluiting van allochtonen voor bepaalde vacatures moet verbieden/toelaten?
14. In moslim-culturen vindt men het belangrijk zelf dieren te slachten, en dit niet door een slager te laten doen. Vindt u dat de overheid het thuis slachten van dieren moet verbieden/toelaten?
15. Vindt u dat de overheid besnijdenis van vrouwen moet toelaten?
16. Vindt u dat de overheid huwelijken met meerdere vrouwen voor mensen uit polygame culturen moet verbieden/toelaten?
17. Vindt u dat de overheid de nachtelijke oproep tot het gebed vanaf moskeeën moet verbieden/toelaten?

Results for questions not included in the analyses (Chapters 3/4)

18. Some local councils ask money per kilogram of domestic litter produced by private househoulds ("the polluter pays"). Do you think the government should forbid/allow these local taxes?
    T1: not forbid 56.9%, yes allow 47.8%; χ^2 1.6 (df=1), p=.21); T2: not forbid 67.4%, yes allow 60.6%; χ^2 .96, p=.33

19. Do you think the government should forbid/allow the canceling of railway lines by the NS [Netherlands Rail]?
    T1: not forbid 42.4%, yes allow 17.2%, χ^2 14.47, p<.001; T2: not forbid 47.9%, yes allow 20.2%, χ^2 16.72, p<.001

20. In view of the brooding of birds in fields it is an issue whether fields may be mowed during certain periods of the year. Do you think the government should forbid/allow the mowing of fields during the months of May and June?
    T1: not forbid 53.9%, yes allow 50.5%, χ^2 .21, p=.64; T2: not forbid 54.3%, yes allow 51%, χ^2 .2, p=.65

21. Do you think the government should forbid/allow the legalisation of economic refugees?
    T1: not forbid 57%, yes allow 36.4%, χ^2 8.2, p<.001; T2: not forbid 56.6%, yes allow 34.8%, χ^2 11.77, p<.001

22. In order to avoid 'white' and 'black' schools, some local councils use a spreading policy of ethnic pupils over public schools. Do you think the government should forbid/allow this spreading policy?
    T1: not forbid 92.4%, yes allow 89.2%, χ^2 .58, p=.48; T2: not forbid 90.9%, yes allow 90.6%, χ^2 .00, p=.95

23. Do you think the government should forbid/allow the legalisation of people asking asylum that are not willing to learn Dutch?
    T1: not forbid 24.7%, yes allow 22.2%, χ^2 .17, p=.68; T2: not forbid 31.3%, yes allow 22.8%, χ^2 1.7, p=.19

24. Do you think the government should forbid/allow commerce with countries in which human rights are possibly violated (like in Iraq, or like South Africa during the Apartheids-regime)?
    T1: not forbid 24.7%, yes allow 33.7%, χ^2 1.86, p=.17; T2: not forbid 30.3%, yes allow 20.4%, χ^2 2.46, p=.12

qst	characteristics from the experimental setting			linguistic/psychologogical characteristics					content-related characteristics					
	ed	sm	ad	va	sn	nom	rel	com	mo	wh	ac	pun	mor	stq
a	-	-	o	v	-	-	.79	.92	-	-	a	-	m	-
b	-	-	o	v	-	-	.79	.92	-	-	a	-	m	-
c	-	-	o	v	-	-	.79	.92	-	-	a	-	m	-
d	-	-	o	v	-	-	.79	.92	-	-	a	-	m	-
e	-	-	o	-	-	-	?	.77	-	-	a	-	m	-
f	-	-	o	-	-	n	.14	.25	-	-	a	p	m	-
g	-	-	o	-	-	-	.62	.23	-	-	a	-	-	-
h	-	-	o	-	-	n	.14	0	-	w	a	-	m	-
i	-	q	o	-	-	n	.46	.31	-	-	a	-	m	-
j	-	-	-	-	>	n	.43	0	m	-	-	-	-	-
k	s	-	o	-	-	n	.57	.23	-	-	-	-	-	-
l	s	-	-	-	-	n	.57	.23	-	-	-	-	-	-
m	s	-	o	-	-	n	.57	.23	-	-	-	-	-	-
n	s	-	-	-	-	n	.57	.23	-	-	-	-	-	-
o	-	-	o	-	-	n	.46	.31	-	-	a	-	m	-
p	-	-	o	v	-	-	.92	.15	-	-	a	-	m	-
q	-	-	o	-	>	-	1	.5	-	-	a	-	m	-
r	-	-	o	v	-	-	.79	.92	-	-	a	-	m	-

	ed	sm	ad	va	sn	nom	rel	com	mo	wh	ac	pun	mor	stq
1	s	-	-	v	-	-	.92	.85	m	w	a	-	-	-
2	s	-	-	-	-	-	.62	.15	-	-	a	-	-	-
3	s	-	-	-	-	n	.79	.54	-	-	a	-	-	-
4	s	-	-	v	-	-	.93	.54	m	-	a	-	-	-
5	s	-	-	v	-	n	.93	.62	-	-	a	-	-	-
6	s	-	-	-	-	-	.57	.25	-	-	a	p	-	-
7	s	-	-	-	-	n	.23	.33	-	-	a	-	-	-
8	s	-	-	-	-	-	.23	.46	-	-	a	-	-	-
9	s	-	-	-	-	n	.54	.31	-	-	a	-	-	-
10	s	- ,	-	-	>	-	.5	.38	-	w	a	p	m	f
11	s	-	-	-	>	-	1	.5	-	-	a	-	m	f
12	s	-	-	v	-	-	.86	.38	-	-	a	-	m	f
13	s	-	-	v	-	n	.93	.77	-	-	a	p	m	f
14	s	-	-	-	>	n	.23	.5	-	w	a	-	m	f
15	s	-	-	-	-	n	.57	.25	-	-	a	-	m	f
16	s	-	-	-	-	-	.23	.77	-	w	a	-	m	f
17	s	-	-	-	-	-	0	.69	-	-	a	-	m	f

qst= question number (a-r see Table 2.1, 1-17 see Table 3.1); *ed*= educational level: (-) heterogeneous sample or women in city area, (s) homogeneous sample of students; *sm*= sampling method: (-) random, (q) quota; *ad*= method of administration: (o) face-to-face, phone, or a mix of phone and face-to-face, (-) written;

va= (v) vague/abstract, (-) not vague; *sn*= number of sentences: (>) questions containing more sentences, (-) questions containing one sentence; *nom*= nominalisation+predicate: (n) questions containing a nom+pred, (-) questions not containing one; *rel*= mean relevance score per question; *com*= mean complexity score per question;

mo= argument pro forbidding in the question: (m) presence of an argument, (-) absence of an argument (absence of the argument was given code 1, presence was given code 0); *wh*= explicit reference to whom something is forbiddden/allowed: (w) explicit reference, (-) implicit; *ac*=whether or not an explicit actor: (a) government or related actor, (-) implicit actor; *pun*=prohibition beforehand, punishment afterwards?: (p) prohibition beforehand, (-) punishment afterwards; *mor*= moral versus judicial issues: (m) moral prohibition, (-) judicial prohibition; *stq*= status quo: (-) issue allowed at time of measurement, (f) issue forbidden at time of measurement.

DESCRIPTION OF THE TEN EXPERIMENTS
AND THEIR FORBID/ALLOW QUESTIONS
(Chapters 6 and 7)

• experiment 1
theme: youth culture
subjects and procedure: 100 secondary school pupils (Havo/VWO) in four different classes, written questionnaire administered during class.
questions (version 1):
1. Vind je dat de regering de verkoop van sofdrugs ook aan mensen jonger dan 18 jaar moet toelaten? *Do you think the government should allow the sale of soft drugs also to people under 18?*
2. Vind je dat de overheid de verkoop van ECO-drugs (bijvoorbeeld paddo's) moet verbieden? *Do you think the government should forbid the sale of ecological drugs (e.g. magic mushrooms)?*
3. Vind je dat het dragen van petjes in de klas moet worden toegelaten? *Do you think wearing baseball caps should be allowed in class?*
4. Vind je dat het op school dragen van bomberjacks met Nederlandse vlaggetjes moet worden verboden? *Do you think wearing bomberjackets with Dutch flags on them should be forbidden?*
5. Vind je dat het dragen van hoofddoekjes in de klas moet worden toegelaten? *Do you think wearing head scarves in class should be allowed?*
6. Vind je dat de regering het uitzenden van geweldsfilms op de televisie voor 20.00 moet verbieden? *Do you think the government should forbid the broadcasting of violent films before 8 p.m.?*
7. Vind je dat het verhuren van geweldsvideo's aan jongeren onder de 18 moet worden toegelaten? *Do you think renting violent videos to people under 18 should be allowed?*

• experiment 2
theme: medical choices
subjects and procedure: 100 university students in university canteens, written questionnaire
questions (version 1):
8. Vind je dat de overheid het klonen van dieren moet verbieden? *Do you think the government should forbid the cloning of animals?*
9. Vind je dat de overheid adoptie van kinderen door mannelijke homoparen moet toelaten? *Do you think the government should allow gay male couples to adopt children?*
10. Vind je dat de overheid kunstmatige inseminatie bij alleenstaande vrouwen moet verbieden? *Do you think the government should forbid artificial insemination for single women?*
11. Vind je dat de overheid dierproeven voor de ontwikkeling van cosmetische artikleen moet verbieden? *Do you think the government should forbid the testing of cosmetic products on animals?*

12. Vind je dat de overheid moet toelaten dat gynaecologen eicellen in de baarmoeder plaatsen om de kans op kinderen te vergroten? *Do you think the government should allow gynaecologists to implant female germ cells in order to increase the likelihood of pregnancy?*

13. Vind je dat de overheid plastische chirurgie, als dat vanwege schoonheidsredenen wordt gedaan, moet toelaten? *Do you think the government should allow plastic surgery if this is done for cosmetic reasons?*

• experiment 3

theme: hooligans

subjects and procedure: 100 secondary school pupils (4-HAVO/VWO) in four different classes, written questionnaire during classes

questions (version 1):

14. Vind je dat het verboden moet zijn voor een burgemeester om een risicowedstrijd af te gelasten? *Do you think council mayors should be forbidden to cancel high-risk soccer games?*

15. Vind je dat de overheid een nadrukkelijke aanwezigheid van de ME tijdens risciowedstrijden moet verbieden? *Do you think the government should forbid the visible presence of special police units during high-risk soccer games?*

16. Vind je dat het toegelaten moet zijn voor een scheidsrechter om de wedstrijd te staken wanneer er oerwoudgeluiden komen van de tribune? *Do you think the referee should be allowed to stop a soccer game when the audience is insulting players by making 'jungle noises' from the stands?*

17. Vind je dat de overheid bij risicowedstrijden supporters van de uitspelende club moet verbieden de wedstrijd bij de wonen? *Do you think the government should forbid supporters of the visiting club to watch the game from the stadium if it is a high-risk game?*

18. Stel dat de supporters van een club zich misdragen. Vind je dat het dan toegelaten moet zijn voor de Voetbalbond om die club te straffen voor het gedrag van haar supporters? *Suppose supporters of a club misbehave. Do you think the Soccer Union should be allowed to punish the club for the behaviour of its supporters?*

19. Vind je dat het toegelaten moet worden dat de politie supporters die bekend staan als voetbalvandalen uit voorzorg in de cel zet op de dag dat hun club een wedstrijd speelt? *Do you think the police should be allowed to detain supporters who are known hooligans on the days their club is playing as a precautionary measure?*

• experiment 4

theme: supermarket policies

subjects and procedure: 100 supermarket customers, oral questionnaire

questions (version 1):

20. Vindt u dat de overheid moet verbieden dat supermarkten 's avonds na 18.00 open zijn? *Do you think the government should forbid supermarkets to be open after 6 p.m.?*

21. Vind u dat de overheid moet verbieden dat supermarkten op zondag open zijn? *Do you think the government should forbid supermarkets to be open on Sundays?*

22. Vindt u dat de overheid de verkoop van vloeibare zuivelproducten, zoals melk, karnemelk en yoghurt, in niet-herbruikbare kartonnen verpakkingen, moet verbieden? *Do you think the government should forbid the sale of liquid dairy products (such as milk and yoghurt) in non-recyclable packaging?*

23. Vindt u dat de overheid het verstrekken van gratis plastic tasjes in supermarkten moet verbieden? *Do you think the government should forbid the handing out of free plastic bags in supermarkets?*

24. Vindt u dat de overheid de verkoop van wijn in flessen zonder statiegeld moet verbieden? *Do you think the government should forbid the sale of wine in non-returnable bottles?*

25. Vindt u dat de overheid de verkoop van rookwaren in supermarkten moet verbieden? *Do you think the government should forbid the sale of cigarettes in supermarkets?*

• experiment 5
theme: euthanasia and organ donation
subjects and procedure: 118 secondary school pupils (VWO), written questionnaire during classes
questions (version 1):

26. Een patiënt lijdt aan een ongeneeslijke ziekte en heeft veel pijn. De patiënt heeft zelf om voortijdige levensbeëindiging gevraagd. Vind je dat euthanasie in deze situatie toegelaten moet worden? *A patient is suffering from an incurable disease and is in a lot of pain. The patient himself has asked for his life to be terminated. Do you think euthanasia should be allowed in that situation?*

27. Een patiënt ligt langdurig in coma. Hij heeft een aantal jaren daarvoor aangegeven dat, wanneer hij ooit in een langdurige coma zou raken, zijn leven beëindigd mag worden. Vind je dat euthanasie in deze situatie toegelaten moet worden? *A patient is in a long-lasting coma. A number of years earlier he has stated that if he should ever be in a state of long-lasting coma, his life may be terminated. Do you think euthanasia should be allowed in that situation?*

28. Een zwaar depressieve vrouw ziet al jaren geen uitweg meer. Zij verzoekt haar arts om haar leven te beëindigen. Vind je dat euthanasie in deze situatie toegelaten moet worden? *A badly depressive woman has lived without hope for many years. She asks her family doctor to end her life. Do you think euthanasia should be allowed in that situation?*

29. Een patiënt ligt in coma. Zijn familie geeft toestemming om zijn leven te beëindigen. De patiënt heeft hierover zelf nooit een uitspraak gedaan. Vind je dat euthanasie in deze situatie toegelaten moet worden? *A patient is in a coma. His family give their consent to terminate his life. The patient himself has never expressed his opinion on this point. Do you think euthanasia should be allowed in that sitation?*

30. Een patiënt sterft. Het ziekenhuis wil zijn organen voor transplantatie gebruiken. De patiënt heeft hierover zelf nooit een uitspraak gedaan. Vind je dat donortransplantatie in deze situatie toegelaten moet worden? *A patient dies. The hospital wishes to use his organs for transplantation. The patient himself has never expressed his opinion on this point. Do you think donor transplantation should be allowed in that situation?*

31. Een patient sterft. Zijn longen zijn nog in goede staat. Een ander patient heeft om te blijven leven binnen zeer korte tijd een long nodig. Noch door de eerste patient, noch door zijn familie is toestemming gegeven voor donotransplantatie. Vind je dat donortransplantatie in deze situatie toegelaten moet worden? *A patient dies. His lungs are still in good condition. Another patient urgently needs a lung in order to stay alive. Neither the first patient nor his family have given permission for donor transplantation. Do you think that donor transplantation should be allowed in that situation?*

• experiment 6
theme: safety in traffic
subjects and procedure: 100 subjects in the central hall of a railway station, written questionnaire
questions (version 1):
32. Vindt u dat de overheid telefoneren tijdens het autorijden moet verbieden? *Do you think the government should forbid the use of mobile phones while driving?*
33. Vindt u dat de overheid reclame langs de snelweg moet toelaten? *Do you think the government should allow billboards alongside motor ways?*
34. Vindt u dat de overheid onbeveiligde spoorwegovergangen (spoorwegovergangen zonder spoorbomen) moet toelaten? *Do you think the government should allow unprotected level crossings (without barriers)?*
35. Vindt u dat de overheid het inhalen door vrachtwagens op snelwegen moet verbieden? *Do you think the government should forbid trucks to pass cars on motor ways?*
36. Vindt u dat de overheid het rijden zonder helm op een snorfiets moet toelaten? *Do you think the government should allow riding a motorised bicycle without safety helmet?*
37. Vindt u dat de overheid skeeleren in voetgangersgebieden moet verbieden? *Do you think the government should forbid skeelering in pedestrian areas?*

• experiment 7
theme: young people and television
subjects and procedure: 100 workers in a hospital, written questionnaire administered in canteens during lunch break
questions (version 1):
38. Vindt u dat de overheid moet verbieden dat jongeren roken in Nederlandse televisieprogramma's en films? *Do you think the government should forbid youngsters to smoke in Dutch television programs and films?*
39. Vindt u dat de overheid moet toelaten dat jongeren alcohol drinken in Nederlandse televisieprogramma's en films? *Do you think the government should allow youngsters to drink alcohol in Dutch television programs and films?*
40. Vindt u dat de overheid moet verbieden dat er gevloekt wordt in Nederlandse televisieseries? *Do you think the government should forbid swearing in Dutch television series?*
41. Vindt u dat de overheid moet toelaten dat speelfilms op televisie uitgezonden worden zonder vermelding van een minimumleeftijd? *Do you think the government should allow the broadcast of feature films on television without stating the minimum age?*

42. Vindt u dat de overheid moet toelaten dat gewelddadige speelfilms voor 22.00 uur op televisie uitgezonden worden? *Do you think the government should allow the broadcasting of violent movies on television before 10 p.m.?*
43. Vindt u dat de overheid moet verbieden dat schokkende beelden getoond worden in de vroege journaals? *Do you think the government should forbid showing shocking items during early editions of the news on television?*

• **experiment 8**
theme: commercials
subjects and procedure:100 students and teachers of university, written questionnaire in canteens
questions (version 1):
44. Vindt u dat de overheid ethisch-geladen reclames, zoals de Benetton-reclames, moet verbieden? *Do you think the government should forbid ethically loaded commercials and advertisements, such as the Benetton advertisements?*
45. Vindt u dat de overheid reclame voor alcohol moet toelaten? *Do you think the government should allow commercials for alcholic drinks?*
46. Vindt u dat de overheid sluikreclame in televisieprogramma's moet verbieden? *Do you think the government should forbid plugged (hidden) advertising in television programs?*
47. Vindt u dat de overheid reclame voor 06-sexlijnen op de televisie moet toelaten? *Do you think the government should allow advertisements for telephone sex on television?*
48. Vindt u dat de overheid het verspreiden van reclamefolders op straat moet verbieden? *Do you think the government should forbid the distribution of commercial flyers to people in the street?*
49. Vindt u dat de overheid reclame door middel van vliegtuigen moet toelaten? *Do you think the government should allow advertising by means of airplanes?*

• **experiment 9**
theme: fixed quota [numberus fixus] and restricted number quota [plaatsingsfixus] for university studies
subjects and procedure: 118 pupils in the fifth and sixth grade of secondary school (VWO), written questionnaire during classes
questions (version 1):
50. Vind je dat de overheid scholieren die geen toegespitst vakkenpakket hebben moet verbieden mee te loten voor een studie met numberus fixus? *Do you think the government should forbid pupils without the required combination of school-leaving certificate subjects to draw lots for fixed-quota disciplines?*
51. Vind je dat de overheid universiteiten moet toelaten om eigen lotingscreiteria te formuleren voor numerus fixus studies (bijvoorbeeld door mensen met een bepaald cijfergemiddelde direct in te loten)? *Do you think the government should allow universities to formulate their own lottery criteria for fixed-quota disciplines (e.g. by allowing people with a set grade average in outright?*
52. Vind je dat de overheid scholieren moet verbieden mee te loten voor meerder numerus fixus studies? *Do you think the government should forbid pupils to draw lots for more than one fixed-quota discipline?*

53. Vind je dat de overheid universiteiten moet toelaten om toelatingsexamens voor numerus fixus studies te hanteren? *Do you think the government should allow universities to set entrance examinations for fixed-quota disciplines?*
54. Vind je dat de overheid scholieren moet verbieden om mee te loten voor meerdere studies met een plaatsingsfixus? *Do you think the government should forbid pupils to draw lots for more than one restricted-number course?*
55. Vind je dat de overheid unversiteiten moet verbieden eigen lotingscriteria te formuleren ten aanzien van de plaatsingsfixus? *Do you think the government should forbid universities to formulate their own lottery criteria for restricted-number courses?*

• experiment 10
theme: right-wing political parties
subjects and procedure: 118 pupils from five secondary school classes, written questionnaire administered during classes
questions (version 1):

56. Vind je dat de overheid uitzendingen op de televisie voor extreem-rechtse partijen moet verbieden? *Do you think the government should forbid broadcasts for extreme right-wing political parties?*
57. Vind je dat de overheid demonstraties van extreem rechts moet verbieden? *Do you think the government should forbid demonstrations by the extreme right?*
58. Vind je dat de overheid bijeenkomsten van extreem-rechts moet verbieden? *Do you think the government should forbid meetings of the extreme right?*
59. Vind je dat de overheid openbare toespraken van extreem-rechtse partijen moet verbieden? *Do you think the government should forbid public speeches of extreme right-wing parties?*
60. Vind je dat de overheid berichten in de media over extreem-rechtse partijen moet verbieden? *Do you think the government should forbid media coverage of extreme right-wing parties?*
61. Vind je dat de overheid extreem-rechtse partijen moet verbieden? *Do you think the government should forbid extreme right-wing political parties?*